EUROPEAN HANDB

AUSTR...

RAILWAYS

LOCOMOTIVES, MULTIPLE UNITS & TRAMS

FOURTH EDITION

The complete guide to all Locomotives and Multiple Units of the Railways of Austria also Tramway and Metro vehicles

Brian Garvin & Peter Fox

Published by Platform 5 Publishing Ltd., Wyvern House, Sark Road, Sheffield S2 4HG, England.
Printed in England by Wyndeham-Hubbard, Dronfield, Sheffield.
ISBN 1 902336 49 6

0-6-4T 598.02 owned by Club 598 at Waidhofen a.d. Ybbs crosses the River Ybbs with a Ybbstalbahn charter train near Furth-Prolting on 20 October 2004. **Rail Photoprints**

CONTENTS

INTRODUCTION

Welcome to this new edition of Austrian railways. The previous edition was published in 1995 and since that time many changes have taken place making it difficult to say which has had the biggest effect.

In recent years there has been the enlargement of the European Union which now includes the many countries that border Austria that were once communist states and others that are aspiring to become members of the EU. The EU features in the open access regulations which have been slow to take effect in Austria but the private sector is now starting to make its presence felt.

ÖBB has reorganised itself into several business units which are now companies with a view to possible privatisation. Some lines have lost their passenger services whilst others now lack through services where provincial boundaries are crossed (e.g. St. Valentin–Krems). ÖBB is nearing the end of a period of renewing its locomotive fleet and readers will find many classes of locomotives are now missing from the current fleet but in some cases survive in the nostalgia collection.

The private railways have remained rather static but some have invested in new stock and passenger traffic continues to grow in most cases. In the case of the Zillertalbahn even freight traffic is at a high level.

Austria remains a fine country for the railway enthusiast: frequent, comfortable trains over scenic routes and lovely branch lines. On the private lines there are many splendid journeys to be had and travellers are advised not to miss the delights of the Stern & Hafferl routes!

It is to be hoped that the appearance of this new edition will be of help when travelling around Austria.

Brian Garvin, Peter Fox

A BRIEF HISTORY OF AUSTRIA

Österreich, the German name for Austria, has its origins in the territory known as the Ostmark (Eastern March), established by Charlemagne in the Donau (Danube) valley in 803 AD. When Charlemagne died the Magyars overran the Ostmark. In 955 the Hungarians were defeated by Otto I and the Ostmark re-established. From 996 the Ostmark was referred to as *Ostarrichi* which eventually evolved into the name *Österreich*.

For several centuries from the Middle Ages until 1918, Austria was ruled by the Hapsburg Empire (also known as the Austro-Hungarian Empire as it also included Hungary until the declaration of Hungarian independence in 1848).

1918 saw the end of World War I and of the Hapsburg Empire, and the following year the treaty of St. Germain defined Austria's borders. In 1920 a new constitution was drawn up which established the Republic of Austria. After an attempted Nazi coup in 1934, 1938 saw the *Anschluss* (annexation) of the country and incorporation into Germany by Hitler. Austria then once again came to be known as the Ostmark.

After World War II Austria regained its former borders and was occupied by Soviet, British, French and American forces. All four of these signed the Austrian State Treaty in 1955 which established Austria as an independent and neutral country. Since 1995 Austria has been a member of the EU and is also a signatory to the Schengen Agreement, meaning an end to border controls for travellers between Austria and Germany or Italy.

ACKNOWLEDGEMENTS

For this edition we would like to thank Karl Zochmeister and Franz Gemeinböck in Austria, the staff at the ÖBB workshops at Linz, St. Pölten and Knittelfeld and the many LCGB members who send in their visit reports to the author.

The following references were consulted during its preparation:

Eisenbahnführer Österreich, Eisenbahn. Eisenbahn Kurier. Continental Railway Journal, LCGB Bulletin, LOK Report, Schienenverkehr Aktuell, Today's Railways, ÖBB Handbook, BBÖ Lokomotiv-Chronik 1923-1938 (Slezak).

THE RAILWAYS OF AUSTRIA

Austria is a very mountainous country, and this is reflected in the fact that many of its main lines are curvy and hence severely speed-restricted, since they have to go up, down, around and through mountains. Because of this, journey times between centres can be long for the distances involved, but the scenic views are magnificent. There are some higher-speed routes, however, particularly in the plain around Wien (Vienna).

As well as the Austrian State Railways (the Österreichische Bundesbahnen - ÖBB), there are also a number of independent railways owned either by the province, as in the case of the Steiermarkische Landesbahnen, the local authority as in the case of the Salzburger Lokalbahn or privately. There are also tramway systems in Wien (a tram-lovers paradise with over 1600 trams!), Graz, Innsbruck, Linz and Gmunden and a Metro in Wien.

The state has had an involvement in the railways from quite early days, but there were many private companies whose initials crop up from time to time. Austria itsself has had a chequered history which has had an effect on its railways. Over the years the state system has had various changes of title viz.

01/07/1884	kkStB	kaiserliche-königliche österreichische Staatsbahnen
12/11/1918	DÖStB	Deutschösterreichische Staatsbahnen
21/10/1919	ÖStB	Österreichische Staatsbahnen
01/04/1921	BBÖ	Bundesbahnen Österreich
18/03/1938	DRB	Deutsche Reichsbahn
27/04/1945	ÖStB	Österreichische Staatseisenbahn
05/08/1947	ÖBB	Österreichische Bundesbahnen

Some details of the old companies follow:

KEB Kaiserin Elizabeth Bahn ('Westbahn').
KFJB Kaiser Franz-Josefs Bahn
KFNB Kaiser Ferdinands Nordbahn.
KRB Kronprinz Rudolf Bahn (St. Valentin/Amstetten–Selzthal–St. Michael–Villach–Tarvisio).
NÖLB Niederösterreichische Landesbahnen (Korneuburg–Mistelbach–Hohenau, Tammersdorf–Dobermannsdorf and others).
NÖSWB. Niederösterreichische Südwestbahn (Leobersdorf–Hainfeld-St. Pölten, Pöchlarn–Kienberg Gaming and others).
ÖNWB Österreichische Nordwestbahn (Wien–Retz–Praha).
SB Südbahngesellschaft (Wien–Bruck a. d. Mur–Ljubljana–Trieste).
StEG Österreichische-Ungarische Staatseisenbahngesellschaft ('Ostbahn').

ABBREVIATIONS USED

The following abbreviations are used in this book:

AOMC Aigle–Ollon–Monthey–Champéry (Swiss Private Railway)
ATM Auto und Technik Museum
Bh Bauhof
Bhf Bahnhof
Bm. Bahnmeister
BBÖ Bundesbahnen Österreich (pre war).
BDZ Bulgarski Durzhavni Zheleznitsi
CD Ceské Dráhy (Czech Railways)
CFF Caile Ferrate Forestiere (Romanian Forestry Railways)
CFI Caile Ferrate Industrie (Romanian Industrial Railways)
CFR Caile Ferrate Romane (Romanian State Railways).
CSD Ceskoslovenské Státní Dráhy (Czechoslavakian State Railways).
DB Deutsche Bundesbahn (German Federal Railway).
DR Deutsche Reichsbahn
DRB Deutsche Reichsbahn
EAB Elektro Anlagen Bau
EBS Elektro Betriebs Stelle
EC Eisenbahn Club or Eurocity (type of train service)
EFZ Eisenbahnfreunde Zollernbahn (Germany)
EM Eisenbahn Museum

6

FS	Ferrovie dello Stato (Italian State Railways)
GKB	Graz Köflacher Bahn
GySEV	Györ–Sopron–Ebenfurthi Vasút
HE	Historische Eisenbahn
HW	Hauptwerkstätte
JZ	Jugoslovenske Zeleznice (Yugoslavian State Railways).
KFN	Kaiser Ferdinands Nordbahn
kkStB	Kaiserlische-Königlische Österreichische Staatsbahnen
KMB	Kärtner Museums Bahnen
LBPH	Lokalbahn Payerbach–Hirschwang
MÁV	Magyar Államvasutak (Hungarian State Railways).
NWP	Neumarkt–Waizenkirchen–Peuerbach (Now part of Linzer Lokalbahn)
OBL	Ober Bau Lager (Track department store)
ODK	Österreichische Drau Kraftwerk
ÖBB	Österreichische Bundesbahnen
ÖCD	Österreichische Club für Diesellokgeschichte
ÖGEG	Österreichische Gesellschaft für Eisenbahn Geschichte
ÖGLB	Österreichische Gesellschaft für Lokalbahnen
PKP	Polskie Koleje Panstwowe (Polish State Railways)
R	Reserve
RB	Rittner Bahn
RL	Regional Leitung
SB	Südbahn
SBB	Schweizerische Bundesbahn
SKGLB	Salzkammergut Lokalbahn
Sm	Signalmeister
SOB	Südostbahn
SS	Südliche Staatsbahn
StLB	Steiermärkische Landesbahnen
STB	Stubaitalbahn
Sudb	Südbahn
Sulm	Sulmtalbahn
SUZ	Schnell Umbau Zug
SVB	Salzburger Verkehrsbetrieb
SZ	Slovenske Zeleznice (Slovenian Railways)
SZU	Sihltal–Zürich–Uetliberg–Bahn (Switzerland)
TS	Technische Services
TM	Technical Museum
VBW	Vereinigte Bern Worb Bahnen (Switzerland)
VSM	Veluwsche Stoomtrein Maatschappij, Beekbergen, Netherlands
WSB	Wynetal und Suhrentalbahn, Switzerland
WSV	Waldviertler Schmalspur Verein
Z	Stored
ZSSK	Zeleznicná Spolocnost Slovensko, a.s. (Slovak Railways)

Front cover: Although all of ÖBB's main routes are electrified, there is still a large network of non-electrified lines for which a new fleet of diesel locomotives and DMU's have been purchased. A mixed freight, triple-headed by diesels 2016 087-6 and 2016 086-7 in multiple plus 2068 022-9 with a seperate driver, leaves Gleisdorf in the direction of Graz on the evening of 21 July 2005.

Back cover top: The Graz-Köflacher Bahn operates the world's oldest operational steam locomotive in the form of 0-6-0 No. 671. This locomotive which has never been withdrawn from traffic was built in 1875. It is seen on an IGE-Bahntouristik charter on 8 February 2005.

Back cover bottom: Stern und Hafferl operate a mixed bag of lines in the Oberösterreich province of which two are metre-gauge. 23 112 stands in the station a.k.a. the shed yard at Vorchdorf with the 13.15 Traunseebahn working to Gmunden on 3 June 2005. **Peter Fox (3)**

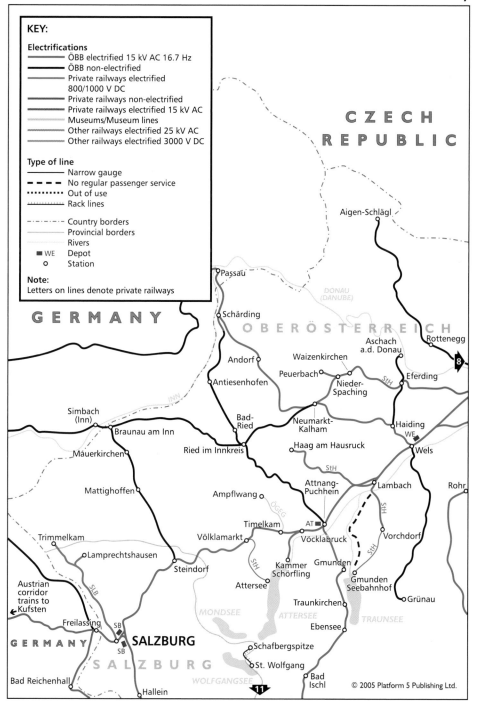

KEY:

Electrifications
━━━ ÖBB electrified 15 kV AC 16.7 Hz
━━━ ÖBB non-electrified
━━━ Private railways electrified
      800/1000 V DC
━━━ Private railways non-electrified
━━━ Private railways electrified 15 kV AC
━━━ Museums/Museum lines
━━━ Other railways electrified 25 kV AC
━━━ Other railways electrified 3000 V DC

Type of line
──── Narrow gauge
━ ━ ━ No regular passenger service
·········· Out of use
⊹⊹⊹⊹⊹ Rack lines

─·─·─· Country borders
──── Provincial borders
──── Rivers
■ WE Depot
○   Station

Note:
Letters on lines denote private railways

GERMANY

CZECH REPUBLIC

Aigen-Schlägl

Passau

DONAU (DANUBE)

Schärding

OBERÖSTERREICH

Aschach a.d. Donau
Rottenegg
8

Andorf
Waizenkirchen
Peuerbach
Eferding
Antiesenhofen
Nieder-Spaching
StH

Simbach (Inn)
Bad-Ried
Neumarkt-Kalham
Haiding
WE
Braunau am Inn
Mäuerkirchen
Ried im Innkreis
Haag am Hausruck
Wels
INN

Mattighoffen
StH
Attnang-Puchhein
Lambach
Rohr
Ampflwang
ÖGEG
StH

Trimmelkam
Timelkam
AT
Vöcklabruck
Vorchdorf
Lamprechtshausen
Völklamarkt
StH
Steindorf
Kammer Schörfling
Gmunden
Attersee
Gmunden Seebahnhof
Grünau
Austrian corridor trains to
←Kufstein
SLB
Traunkirchen
MONDSEE
ATTERSEE
TRAUNSEE

Freilassing
SB
Ebensee
GERMANY
SB
SALZBURG
Schafbergspitze
SALZBURG
St. Wolfgang
Bad Reichenhall
WOLFGANGSEE
11
Bad Ischl
© 2005 Platform 5 Publishing Ltd.
Hallein

CZECH REPUBLIC

Litschau
Waldkirchen a.d. Thaya
České Budějovice
Drosendorf
Heidenreichstein
Raabs
WSV
Alt Nagelberg
Waidhof
GM
Schwarzenau
České Velenice
Gmünd
Göpfritz
Sigmundsherberg
Weitra
NIEDERÖSTERREICH
Zwettl
Horni Dvořiště
Gross
Gerungs
Summerau
Hadersdorf
Krems
KR
OBERÖSTERREICH
Spitz
7
Martinsberg-
Gutenbrunn
9
Herzogenburg
Urfahr
Emmersdorf
St. Nikola
Struden
Melk
St. Pölten
StH
Hbf
SP
LZ
Pöchlarn
LINZ
Ober Grafendorf
Traun
DONAU
(DANUBE)
St. Valentin
Weiselburg
Mank
Amstetten
Rabenstein
Steyr
LB
Purgstall
Kirchberg
Steyr
Scheibbs
ÖGEG
Laubenbach-
Mühle
Gresten
Grünberg
WH
Türnitz
Waidhofen a.d. Ybbs
Ybbsitz
Kienberg-
Gstadt
ÖGLB
Gaming
Markt St. Aegyd
Kogelsbach
Lunz am See
Kastenreith
Kleinreifling
Grosshollenstein
Mariazell
Neuberg Ort
STEIERMARK
12
© 2005 Platform 5 Publishing Ltd.
Hieflau

CZECH REPUBLIC

Břeclav

Laa a.d. Thaya

Poysdorf

Zellerndorf

Obermannsdorf

Hohenau

Drösing

Mistelbach

Zistersdorf

SLOVAKIA

Hollabrunn

Ernstbrunn

Gaweinstahl

Sulz

Gross Schweinbarth

NIEDERÖSTERREICH

Stockerau

Oberdsorf

Gänserndorf

Absdorf-Hippersdorf

Korneuburg

Tulln

Marchegg

FD

Floridsdorf

Siebenbrunn

WIEN (VIENNA)

Stadlau

8

Tullnerbach

WW

1 FJB
2 West
3 Mitte
4 Oper
5 Süd
6 Meidling
7 Flughafen Wien

WS WO

DONAU (DANUBE)

WLB

Baden

Bruck a.d. Leitha

Neusiedl

Mannersdorf

Weissenbach

Leobersdorf

Wampersdorf

Gutenstein

Sollenau

Ebenfürth

GySEV

BURGENLAND

NEUSIEDLER SEE

Puchberg

Wiener Neustadt

Wulkprodersdorf

NS

Hochschneeberg

Hirschwang

Payerbach

Sopron

Deutschkreutz

GySEV

Fertöszent-Miklós

Semmering Pass

MZ

Mürzzuschlag

© 2005 Platform 5 Publishing Ltd.

Aspang

13

HUNGARY

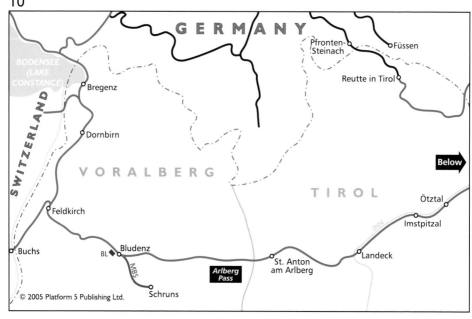

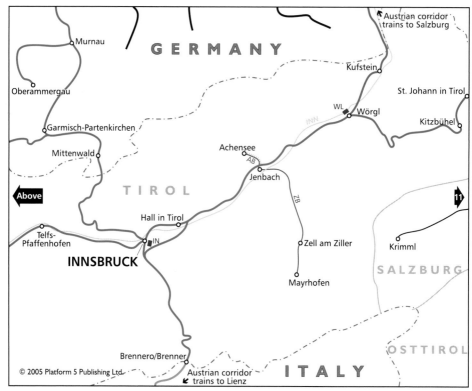

© 2005 Platform 5 Publishing Ltd.

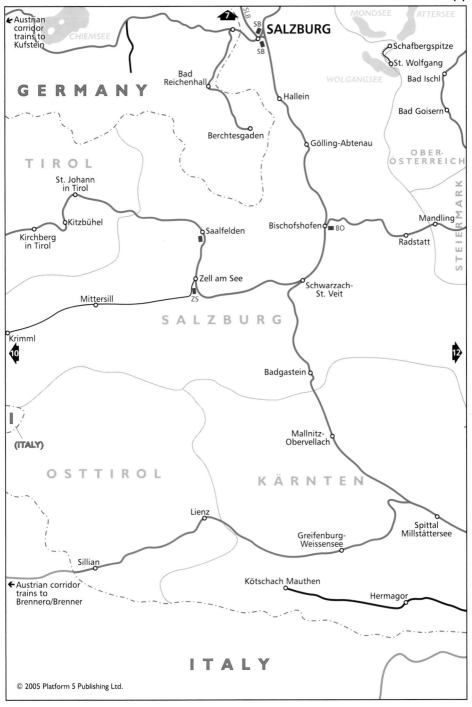

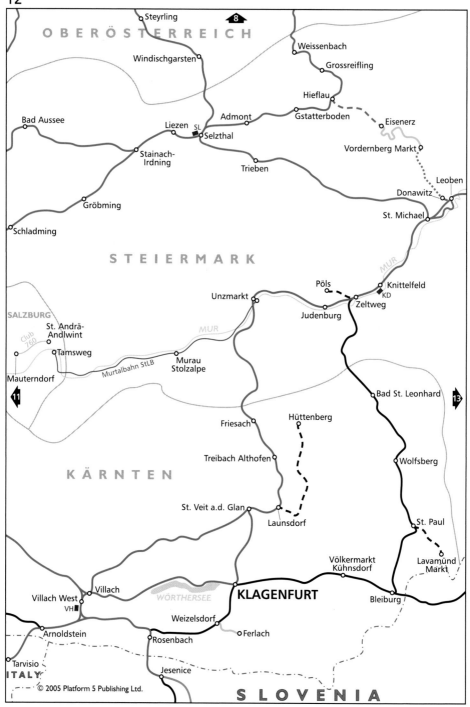

O B E R Ö S T E R R E I C H

Steyrling

Windischgarsten

Weissenbach

Grossreifling

Hieflau

Bad Aussee

Admont

Gstatterboden

Eisenerz

Liezen SL

Selzthal

Vordernberg Markt

Stainach-Irdning

Trieben

Leoben

Donawitz

St. Michael

Gröbming

Schladming

S T E I E R M A R K

MUR

Pöls

Knittelfeld
KD

Unzmarkt

Zeltweg

Judenburg

SALZBURG

St. Andrä-Andlwint

MUR

Club 760

Tamsweg

Murtalbahn StLB

Murau Stolzalpe

Mauterndorf

11

Bad St. Leonhard

13

Friesach

Hüttenberg

K Ä R N T E N

Treibach Althofen

Wolfsberg

St. Veit a.d. Glan

Launsdorf

St. Paul

Völkermarkt Kühnsdorf

Lavamünd Markt

Villach West
VH

Villach

WÖRTHERSEE

KLAGENFURT

Bleiburg

Weizelsdorf

Ferlach

Arnoldstein

Rosenbach

Tarvisio

ITALY

Jesenice

S L O V E N I A

© 2005 Platform 5 Publishing Ltd.

© 2005 Platform 5 Publishing Ltd.

▲ Class 1014 dual voltage electric 1014 013-5 at Sopron with a Deutschkreutz–Wien Süd service on 21 June 2005.   **Brian Denton**

▼ One of three Class 1014s painted in the special City Airport Train livery, 1014 007-7 at WienSüd on 1 June 2004.   **Ian Futers**

▲ Class 1016 is the ÖBB's single-voltage variant of the Siemens Taurus electric loco. 1016 046-3 is seen at St. Johann-in-Tirol on 3 August 2004. **Ian Futers**

▼ The dual-voltage variant of the Taurus is the 1116. 1116 063-7, leased to the GySEV and 1116 146-0 are seen stabled with a freight train at Villach Westbf. on 3 July 2005. **Brian Garvin**

▲ The 1042s were ÖBB's first class of "modern" electric locos and were built between 1963 and 1977. Class 1142 is a variant rebuilt with push-pull equipment. 1142 605-3 heads a Linz–Kleinreifling service at Enns on 20 July 2004.

▼ The 1042s were superceded on InterCity trains by the 1044s which had thyristor control and were built between 1974 and 1995. 1044 044-4 is seen at Villach Hbf with IC534, 08.22 Villach Hbf–Wien Süd at Gloggnitz on 23 July 2004.   **Brian Denton (2)**

1. ÖSTERREICHISCHE BUNDESBAHNEN (ÖBB) (AUSTRIAN FEDERAL RAILWAYS)
ORGANISATION
2004 Reorganisation

ÖBB has had yet another reorganisation which in effect has prepared the way for any eventual privatisation. The parts of the organisation that mostly affect traction etc. are shown below with other departments/organisations omitted.

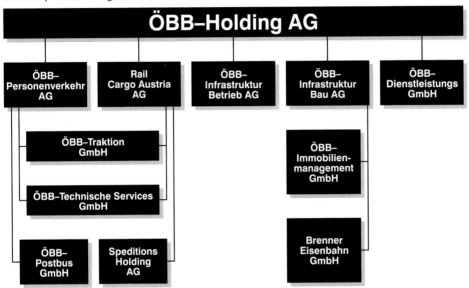

ÖBB Traktion GmbH

It is Traktion's job to supply the passenger and freight businesses with locomotives and drivers etc for their trains. Traktion also includes shunting staff as they couple locomotives to trains, detach vehicles etc. Where radio controlled locomotives are concerned shunters are in effect often the drivers. Most traction "depots" are at the same locations as Techische Services but there are additional locations where drivers are based which can be counted as sub-sheds and locomotives and units are likely to stable there. Traktion is divided up into three main areas (Bereich) as follows:

Bereich Nord – Floridsdorf.
Floridsdorf, Stadlau, Gmünd, Gross Schweinbarth, Hohenau, Krems, Mistelbach, Retz, Sigmundsherberg, Schwarzenau, Wien FJB.

Bereich Süd 1 – Wien Süd
Bruck an der Leitha, Oberwart, Wien Süd, Wien Zvbf, Wiener Neustadt.

Bereich Süd 2 – Graz
Bad Aussee, Bruck a.d. Mur, Fehring, Friedberg, Graz, Hieflau, Knittelfeld, Leoben, Mürzzuschlag, Selzthal.

Bereich Süd 3 – Villach
Klagenfurt, Lienz, St. Veit an der Glan, Spittal-Millstättersee, Villach, Wolfsberg.

Bereich West 1 – Linz
Amstetten, Kirchdorf, Kleinreifling, Linz, Linz Urfahr, St. Pölten, St. Valentin, Summerau, Wels, Wien West.

Bereich West 2 – Salzburg
Attnang-Puchheim, Bischofshofen, Braunau, Ebensee, Saalfelden, Schärding, Salzburg.

Bereich West 3 – Innsbruck
Bludenz, Innsbruck, Landeck, Wolfurt, Wörgl.

ÖBB Technische Services GmbH.

This is the maintenance arm and covers not only the main workshops but also what are the repair and maintenance facilities at depots and wagon shops. The main workshops are now referred to as Werke and the depots as Servicestellen.

Workshops

Werke	Function
Floridsdorf	EMUs.
Jedlersdorf	Wagons.
Knittelfeld	Snowploughs, OBW, MTW, special vehicles, wheelsets.
Linz	Electric locomotives plus Class 2016 diesels.
St. Pölten	Diesel locomotives (except Class 2016), DMUs and carriages.
Simmering	Carriages
Wörth	MBW, internal fitting and components

Depots

A list of depots and codes is given in Appendix 4 on page 128.

ÖBB TRAIN SERVICES

In recent years ÖBB has introduced some new categories for its trains. Current classifications are as follows:

IC	Inter City.
ÖBB IC	ÖBB Inter City train. An IC but with better quality stock and services.
EC	Euro City. International quality express train.
ÖBB EC	ÖBB Euro City train. An EC but with better quality stock and services.
EN	Euro Night. International sleeping car train.
ICE	Inter City Express (DB ICE in Austria).
CAT	City Airport Train.
D	Fast train.
ER	Euregio. New trains to adjacent countries (Czech Republic, Slovakia and Hungary).
E	Eilzug – semi-fast train.
S	Schnellbahn – fast suburban train.

LOCO & RAILCAR NUMBERING SYSTEM

The present ÖBB numbering scheme dates from 1953 when the former DRB system was replaced. ÖBB locomotives and units had, until recently, a two-part number. The first part was of four digits and referred to the class of vehicle. It was separated by a full-stop from the second part which was the serial number within the particular type. Variations within a type were often given running numbers in a separate hundred. eg: 1042.01, 1042.501.

Early in 1985 the scheme was amended for use with computers. The running number part is now always 3 digits and there is an additional check digit suffix, e.g. 1016 026-5. The class number and serial number are separated by a space.
The class coding system refers to the type of vehicle & its use as follows:

1st digit – Traction Code

0	Steam.
1	Electric Locomotives
2	Diesel Locomotives
3	Steam Railcars

4	Electric Multiple Units
5	Diesel Multiple Units
6	Driving Trailers (6000-6499 for EMUs, 6500-6999 for diesel railcars)
7	Intermediate Trailer
8	(Not used)
9	Tenders

2nd digit – Origin Code

0–5	Austrian or German standard types. (0 was not carried on steam locomotives).
6–8	Pre-DRG types
9	Various Foreign types

This system was later amended for electric traction:

0–7	AC Electrics
8	AC/DC Electrics
9	DC Electrics

The second digit is also increased by 1 to represent developments of types. Thus class 1116 is a development of class 1016. 1216 is a further development of the same.

3rd & 4th digits – Utilisation Code

Steam Locomotives

01–39	Passenger Tender
40–59	Freight Tender
60–79	Passenger Tank
80–96	Freight Tank
97	Rack Fitted
98–99	Narrow Gauge

Electric Locomotives

01–19	Express
20–39	Heavy Freight
40–59	Mixed Traffic
60–69	Shunter
70–89	Spare, but used for old types
90–99	Narrow Gauge

Railcars

01–19	Express
20–59	Local
60–79	Baggage
80–89	Light Railbus
90–99	Narrow Gauge

Diesel Locomotives

01–19	Express Passenger Locomotive over 2000 h.p.
20–39	Heavy Freight Locomotive over 2000 h.p.
40–59	Mixed Traffic Locomotive 1000-2000 h.p.
60–64	"B" wheel arrangement locomotive under 1000 h.p.
65–69	"C" wheel arrangement locomotive under 1000 h.p.
70–79	"D" wheel arrangement locomotive under 1000 h.p.
80–89	Free (was rack fitted locomotive) now used for self-propelled snowplough.
90–99	Narrow Gauge Locomotives

After the running number there is a computer check digit which double checks that all the preceding digits are correct. It is arrived at by multiplying the class and running number digits alternatively by 2 and 1. The resulting digits are added together and the sum deducted from the next whole ten gives the check number.

Example 1016 026-5

		1	0	1	6	0	2	6
	x	2	1	2	1	2	1	2
		2+	0+	2+	6+	0+	2+	1+2 = 15

20 – 5 = 5

As these check numbers are actually carried on the locomotives and units they are included in this book.

So taking the example 1016 026-5. This is a mixed traffic electric locomotive. 1116 026-4 is a dual-voltage development of Class 1016 and 1216 026-3 is a further development for three system operation. Class 1144 locos of Class 1044 fitted for push-pull working. Other examples are: 2067 072-5 is a six-wheeled diesel shunter, 4010 028-1 is an express EMU.

This system has served ÖBB well but a complication has now arisen with the new articulated EMUs and DMUs. The first sets to be delivered were the 4023s – a 3 section EMU. ÖBB numbered them in the traditional way making them classes 4023/7023/6023 but this was wrong as the there are two power cars. After much deliberation the units are now referred to just as a set e.g. 4023 001 but it is understood that for defect reporting etc the vehicles carry the 7023 etc descriptions inside. Similarly the 4024 sets have internal numbers 4024/7024/7124/ 6024! Also Class 1216 should really be Class 1816, being AC/DC!

1.1. ELECTRIC LOCOMOTIVES

CLASS 1012 Bo-Bo

This class was to be the ÖBB high Speed locomotive for the 21st Century. However the cost of the three prototypes was nearly twice that of a 1044! Moreover, the performance was poor and these two factors led to the abandonment of the plan to build large numbers of 1012s in favour of the Siemens Taurus class. All the 1012s have been out of service for some time with 001 dumped at Innsbruck West and the other two at Wörgl. They might be sold to a private operator. (Sweden has been rumoured as a likely destination). 1012 002/3 have now arrived at Linz Works prior to sale.

Built: 1995.
Builder – Mech. Parts: SGP.
Builder – Elec. Parts: Siemens (001), ABB (002), Elin (003).
One Hour Rating: 6400 kW.   **Weight:** 82.6 tonnes.
Maximum Tractive Effort: 240 kN.   **Length over Buffers:** 19.3 m.
Wheel Diameter: 1150 mm.   **Maximum Speed:** 200 km/h.
Systems: 15 kV 16.7 Hz/3000 V d.c.

Non-standard livery: White and red.

1012 001-2 **N** IN(Z)	1012 002-0 **N** IN(Z)	1012 003-8 **N** IN(Z)

CLASS 1014 Bo-Bo

A dual-voltage locomotive for working around Wien into the Czech Republic, Slovakia and Hungary at Breclav, Bratislava and Hegyeshalom/Sopron respectively where there is 25 kV electrification. Many are now employed on push-pull trains to Sopron. Three locomotives are painted in the special CAT livery (City Airport Train) for the fast trains from Wien to Wien Flughafen.

Built: 1993–1994.
Builder – Mech. Parts: SGP.
Builder – Elec. Parts: Elin.
One Hour Rating: 4300 kW.   **Weight:** 64 tonnes.
Maximum Tractive Effort: 190 kN.   **Length over Buffers:** 17.50 m.
Wheel Diameter: 1150 mm.   **Maximum Speed:** 170 km/h.
Systems: 15 kV 16.7 Hz/25 kV 50 Hz.

Non-standard liveries:

A Rail Cargo Austria.
C City Airport Train (green, white and grey).
N Cream and red sides, colours reversed in cab.

1014 001-0 **N**	WS	1014 008-5 **N**	WS	1014 014-3 **N**	WS
1014 002-8 **N**	WS	1014 009-3 **N**	WS	1014 015-0 **N**	WS
1014 003-6 **N**	WS	1014 010-1 **C**	WS	1014 016-8 **N**	WS
1014 004-4 **N**	WS	1014 011-9 **A**	WS	1014 017-6 **N**	WS
1014 005-1 **C**	WS	1014 012-7 **N**	WS	1014 018-4 **N**	WS
1014 007-7 **C**	WS	1014 013-5 **N**	WS		

CLASS 1016 TAURUS Bo-Bo

Disappointed with the 1012s, ÖBB shopped around and eventually turned to Siemens for a new main line locomotive type to be known as Taurus. The design chosen was the Siemens Eurosprinter which was proving popular at the time with exports to Spain and Portugal and on the DB where Class 152 is based on this series. In Septmber 1999 ÖBB ordered 50 Class 1016 and 25 Class 1116 the latter to be dual-voltage. The first three 1016s were built in München by Siemens Krauss Maffei but part of the deal with ÖBB was for a certain amount of local input. For the remainder the bodywork was fabricated in München and then taken to the ÖBB works in Linz where the locomotives were actually erected with cabs coming from the ÖBB works in Knittelfeld and bogies from the Siemens plant in Graz (the former SGP works). Most electrical equipment came from the Siemens plant in Erlangen, Germany. After a while ÖBB decided that the 1116 version met their need very well so no more 1016s were ordered. Besides working all over Austria the 1016s also get to München and Stuttgart in Germany.

Built: 2000–2001.
Builder – Mech. Parts: Siemens-Krauss-Maffei, ÖBB TS Linz, ÖBB TS Knittelfeld.

Builder – Elec. Parts: Siemens.
One Hour Rating: 6400 kW.
Maximum Tractive Effort: 300 kN.
Wheel Diameter: 1150 mm.
Non-standard livery:

Weight: 85 tonnes.
Length over Buffers: 19.28 m.
Maximum Speed: 230 km/h.

N 1016 023-2 is in blue livery "KYOTO EXPRESS ÖSTERREICHS GRÜNE SCHIENE".

1016 001-8	SB	1016 018-2	SB	1016 035-6	WW
1016 002-6	SB	1016 019-0	SB	1016 036-4	WW
1016 003-4	SB	1016 020-8	SB	1016 037-2	WW
1016 004-2	SB	1016 021-6	SB	1016 038-0	WW
1016 005-9	SB	1016 022-4	SB	1016 039-8	WW
1016 006-7	SB	1016 023-2 **N**	SB	1016 040-6	WW
1016 007-5	SB	1016 024-0	SB	1016 041-4	WW
1016 008-3	SB	1016 025-7	WW	1016 042-2	WW
1016 009-1	SB	1016 026-5	WW	1016 043-0	WW
1016 010-9	SB	1016 027-3	WW	1016 044-8	WW
1016 011-7	SB	1016 028-1	WW	1016 045-5	WW
1016 012-5	SB	1016 029-9	WW	1016 046-3	WW
1016 013-3	SB	1016 030-7	WW	1016 047-1	WW
1016 014-1	SB	1016 031-5	WW	1016 048-9	WW
1016 015-8	SB	1016 032-3	WW	1016 049-7	WW
1016 016-6	SB	1016 033-1	WW	1016 050-5	WW
1016 017-4	SB	1016 034-9	WW		

CLASS 1116   TAURUS   Bo-Bo

This is the dual-voltage 1016 with the first locomotive built in München and all others at Linz in a similar way to the 1016s. ÖBB ordered a large fleet of Taurus locos (400 altogether) and preferred the dual-voltage version as there was hardly any price difference to the single voltage locos. However certain plans have not come to pass and as locos were also needed for working into Italy and Slovenia where there is 3000 V DC electrification ÖBB cancelled the last 68 1116s and replaced the order with 50 class 1216 – the version with 3000 V DC equipment. The 1116s are real multi-purpose locomotives which now work deep into Germany territory getting as far north as Hamburg and Dortmund on express freight and EuroCity train duties respectively. The 1116s also work into Hungary and are understood to have a diagram that gets one to Szolnok! Both the MAV and GySEV have small batches of 1116s as Class 1047 and these locos work deep into Austria with the MAV locos getting to Linz whilst the GySEV locos get down to Villach on Inter City and freight trains. The nickname of Taurus reflects the strength of the locomotive but they could also be called Doh-Ray-Mee-Fahs due to the electrical noises when starting up! 1161 061–065 are now leased to GySEV for 20 years.

Built: 2000–(2005).
Builder – Mech. Parts: Siemens-Krauss-Maffei, ÖBB TS Linz, ÖBB TS Knittelfeld.
Builder – Elec. Parts: Siemens.
One Hour Rating: 6400 kW.
Maximum Tractive Effort: 300 kN.
Wheel Diameter: 1150 mm.
Systems: 15 kV 16.7 Hz/25 kV 50 Hz.

Weight: 85 tonnes.
Length over Buffers: 19.28 m.
Maximum Speed: 230 km/h.

Non-standard liveries:

N 1116 200-5 is "SEMMERING 150".
N 1116 246-8 is "50 JAHRE BUNDESHEER".

1116 001-7	WW	1116 012-4	WW	1116 023-1	WW
1116 002-5	WW	1116 013-2	WW	1116 024-9	WW
1116 003-3	WW	1116 014-0	WW	1116 025-6	WW
1116 004-1	WW	1116 015-7	WW	1116 026-4	SB
1116 005-8	WW	1116 016-5	WW	1116 027-2	SB
1116 006-6	WW	1116 017-3	WW	1116 028-0	SB
1116 007-4	WW	1116 018-1	WW	1116 029-8	SB
1116 008-2	WW	1116 019-9	WW	1116 030-6	SB
1116 009-0	WW	1116 020-7	WW	1116 031-4	SB
1116 010-8	WW	1116 021-5	WW	1116 032-2	SB
1116 011-6	WW	1116 022-3	WW	1116 033-0	SB

1116 034-8	SB	1116 098-3	IN	1116 162-7	VH
1116 035-5	SB	1116 099-1	IN	1116 163-5	VH
1116 036-3	SB	1116 100-7	IN	1116 164-3	VH
1116 037-1	SB	1116 101-5	IN	1116 165-0	VH
1116 038-9	SB	1116 102-3	IN	1116 166-8	VH
1116 039-7	SB	1116 103-1	IN	1116 167-6	VH
1116 040-5	WS	1116 104-9	IN	1116 168-4	VH
1116 041-3	WS	1116 105-6	IN	1116 169-2	VH
1116 042-1	WS	1116 106-4	IN	1116 170-0	VH
1116 043-9	WS	1116 107-2	IN	1116 171-8	VH
1116 044-7	WS	1116 108-0	IN	1116 172-6	VH
1116 045-4	WS	1116 109-8	IN	1116 173-4	VH
1116 046-2	WS	1116 110-6	IN	1116 174-2	VH
1116 047-0	WS	1116 111-4	SB	1116 175-9	VH
1116 048-8	WS	1116 112-2	SB	1116 176-7	IN
1116 049-6	WS	1116 113-0	SB	1116 177-5	IN
1116 050-4	WS	1116 114-8	SB	1116 178-3	IN
1116 051-2	WS	1116 115-5	SB	1116 179-1	IN
1116 052-0	WS	1116 116-3	SB	1116 180-9	IN
1116 053-8	WS	1116 117-1	SB	1116 181-7	IN
1116 054-6	WS	1116 118-9	SB	1116 182-5	IN
1116 055-3	WS	1116 119-7	SB	1116 185-8	IN
1116 056-1	WS	1116 120-5	SB	1116 186-6	WW
1116 057-9	WS	1116 121-3	SB	1116 187-4	WW
1116 058-7	WS	1116 122-1	SB	1116 188-2	WW
1116 059-5	WS	1116 123-9	SB	1116 189-0	WW
1116 060-3	WS	1116 124-7	SB	1116 190-8	WW
1116 061-1	GY	1116 125-4	SB	1116 191-6	WW
1116 062-9	GY	1116 126-2	SB	1116 192-4	WW
1116 063-7	GY	1116 127-0	SB	1116 193-2	WW
1116 064-5	GY	1116 128-8	SB	1116 194-0	WW
1116 065-2	GY	1116 129-6	SB	1116 195-7	WW
1116 066-0	VH	1116 130-4	SB	1116 196-5	WW
1116 067-8	VH	1116 131-2	SB	1116 197-3	WW
1116 068-6	VH	1116 132-0	SB	1116 198-1	WW
1116 069-4	VH	1116 133-8	SB	1116 199-9	WW
1116 070-2	VH	1116 134-6	SB	1116 200-5 **N**	WW
1116 071-0	VH	1116 135-3	SB	1116 201-3	VH
1116 072-8	VH	1116 136-1	WS	1116 202-1	VH
1116 073-6	VH	1116 137-9	WS	1116 203-9	VH
1116 074-4	VH	1116 138-7	WS	1116 204-7	VH
1116 075-1	VH	1116 139-5	WS	1116 205-4	VH
1116 076-9	VH	1116 140-3	WS	1116 206-2	VH
1116 077-7	VH	1116 141-1	WS	1116 207-0	VH
1116 078-5	VH	1116 142-9	WS	1116 208-8	VH
1116 079-3	VH	1116 143-7	WS	1116 209-6	VH
1116 080-1	VH	1116 144-5	WS	1116 210-4	VH
1116 081-9	VH	1116 145-2	WS	1116 211-2	VH
1116 082-7	VH	1116 146-0	WS	1116 212-0	VH
1116 083-5	VH	1116 147-8	WS	1116 213-8	VH
1116 084-3	VH	1116 148-6	WS	1116 214-6	VH
1116 085-0	VH	1116 149-4	WS	1116 215-3	VH
1116 086-8	IN	1116 150-2	WS	1116 216-1	VH
1116 087-6	IN	1116 151-0	VH	1116 217-9	VH
1116 088-4	IN	1116 152-8	VH	1116 218-7	VH
1116 089-2	IN	1116 153-6	VH	1116 219-5	VH
1116 090-0	IN	1116 154-4	VH	1116 220-3	VH
1116 091-8	IN	1116 155-1	VH	1116 221-1	SB
1116 092-6	IN	1116 156-9	VH	1116 222-9	SB
1116 093-4	IN	1116 157-7	VH	1116 223-7	SB
1116 094-2	IN	1116 158-5	VH	1116 224-5	SB
1116 095-9	IN	1116 159-3	VH	1116 225-2	SB
1116 096-7	IN	1116 160-1	VH	1116 226-0	SB
1116 097-5	IN	1116 161-9	VH	1116 227-8	SB

1116 228-6 SB	1116 247-6	1116 265-8
1116 229-4 SB	1116 248-4	1116 266-6
1116 230-2 SB	1116 249-2	1116 267-4
1116 231-0 SB	1116 250-0	1116 268-2
1116 232-8 SB	1116 251-8	1116 269-0
1116 233-6 SB	1116 252-6	1116 270-8
1116 234-4 SB	1116 253-4	1116 271-6
1116 235-1 SB	1116 254-2	1116 272-4
1116 236-9 SB	1116 255-9	1116 273-2
1116 237-7 SB	1116 256-7	1116 274-0
1116 238-5 SB	1116 257-5	1116 275-7
1116 239-3 SB	1116 258-3	1116 276-5
1116 240-1 SB	1116 259-1	1116 277-3
1116 241-9 SB	1116 260-9	1116 278-1
1116 242-7 SB	1116 261-7	1116 279-9
1116 243-5 SB	1116 262-5	1116 280-7
1116 244-3 SB	1116 263-3	1116 281-5
1116 245-0 SB	1116 264-1	1116 282-3
1116 246-8 **N** SB		

CLASS 1216   TAURUS   Bo-Bo

Siemens has classified these locomotives as ES64U4 although this ÖBB version will only have three voltages with the additional voltage being 3000 V DC for working into surrounding countries. The 50 locomotives ordered by ÖBB will be in three different versions. Version A will comprise 25 locos to work on ÖBB, DB, FS and SZ; Version B will be 10 locomotives for ÖBB, DB and SZ whilst Version C will be for 15 locomotives for ÖBB, DB, CD and ZSSK. It must be remembered that not only does an international locomotive need to have the capacity to operate off different voltages but it must also be fitted with the various safety systems used in the respective countries. The 1216 has had a slight redesign with the top headlight going above the cab once again and each cab will have two doors rather than a central door in the bodyside giving access to the cab via the equipment room.

Built: 2005–(2006).
Builder – Mech. Parts: Siemens-Krauss-Maffei, ÖBB TS Linz, ÖBB TS Knittelfeld.
Builder – Elec. Parts: Siemens.
One Hour Rating: 6400 kW.   **Weight:** 87 tonnes.
Maximum Tractive Effort: 300 kN.   **Length over Buffers:** 19.28 m.
Wheel Diameter: 1150 mm.   **Maximum Speed:** 230 km/h.
Systems: 15 kV 16.7 Hz/25 kV 50 Hz/3000 V d.c.

1216 001-6	1216 018-0	1216 035-4
1216 002-4	1216 019-8	1216 036-2
1216 003-2	1216 020-6	1216 037-0
1216 004-0	1216 021-4	1216 038-8
1216 005-7	1216 022-2	1216 039-6
1216 006-5	1216 023-0	1216 040-4
1216 007-3	1216 024-8	1216 041-2
1216 008-1	1216 025-5	1216 042-0
1216 009-9	1216 026-3	1216 043-8
1216 010-7	1216 027-1	1216 044-6
1216 011-5	1216 028-9	1216 045-3
1216 012-3	1216 029-7	1216 046-1
1216 013-1	1216 030-5	1216 047-9
1216 014-9	1216 031-3	1216 048-7
1216 015-6	1216 032-1	1216 049-5
1216 016-4	1216 033-9	1216 050-3
1216 017-2	1216 034-7	

CLASS 1042   Bo-Bo

These are the standard mixed traffic locos dating from the 1960s and starting off with the 1042.0 series then evolving into the 1042.5. The 1042.0 and the first batch of 1042.5 are now surplus and have no booked diagrams and will be withdrawn as they become due for works or need repairs thanks to the influx of 1116s. Some are now in reserve stock (R).

Built: 1963–77.
Builder – Mech. Parts: Simmering-Graz-Pauker.
Builder – Elec. Parts: Elin/Siemens/Brown-Boveri.
One Hour Rating: 3560 or 4000 kW.   **Weight:** 83.8 tonnes.
Maximum Tractive Effort: 255 kN.   **Length over Buffers:** 16.22 m.
Wheel Diameter: 1250 mm.   **Maximum Speed:** 130 or 150 km/h.
Electric Brake: Rheostatic (Class 1042.5 only).
Non-standard livery: 1042 018-0 and 1042 036-2 have a white stripe.

Class 1042.0. 3560 kW. 130 km/h.

1042 001-6	**0**	WW	1042 021-4	**0**	WW(R)	1042 046-1		WW(R)
1042 002-4	**0**	WW	1042 023-0	**0**	WW	1042 048-7	**0**	WW(R)
1042 005-7	**0**	WW	1042 029-7	**0**	WW	1042 049-5	**0**	WW(R)
1042 007-3		WW	1042 030-5	**0**	WW	1042 050-3	**0**	WW(R)
1042 012-3	**0**	WW	1042 032-1	**0**	WW	1042 052-9	**0**	WW
1042 013-1	**0**	WW	1042 033-9	**0**	WW	1042 054-5	**0**	WW
1042 014-9	**0**	WW	1042 034-7	**0**	WW	1042 055-2	**0**	WW
1042 015-6	**0**	WW	1042 035-4	**0**	WW	1042 056-0	**0**	WW
1042 017-2	**0**	WW(R)	1042 036-2	**N**	WW	1042 057-8	**0**	WW
1042 018-0	**N**	WW	1042 041-2	**0**	WW	1042 059-4	**0**	WW
1042 019-8	**0**	WW(R)	1042 043-8	**0**	WW(R)	1042 060-2	**0**	WW
1042 020-6	**0**	WW	1042 045-3	**0**	WW(R)			

Class 1042.5. 4000 kW. 150 km/h. Fitted with rheostatic braking.

1042 501-5	**0**	WW	1042 509-8	**0**	WW	1042 514-8	**0**	WW
1042 502-3	**0**	WW	1042 510-6	**0**	WW	1042 518-9	**0**	WW
1042 503-1	**0**	WW	1042 512-2	**0**	WW	1042 519-7	**0**	WW
1042 504-9		WW	1042 513-0	**0**	WW	1042 520-5	**0**	WW
1042 505-6	**0**	WW						

CLASS 1142   Bo-Bo

These locos are Class 1042.5 locos fitted for push-pull working. They were converted from 1042s in the 1995–2004 period as ÖBB changed many regional train services to push-pull operation. Today the 1142s are concentrated in the east and south of the country but they still turn up at Innsbruck on local trains that work through from Salzburg. Some are now in reserve stock (R).

1142 531-1		GZ(R)	1142 576-6	**0**	GZ(R)	1142 618-6		LZ
1142 533-7	**0**	GZ	1142 578-2		GZ	1142 619-4		GZ
1142 534-5	**0**	GZ	1142 579-0		LZ	1142 620-2		GZ
1142 535-2	**0**	GZ	1142 582-4	**0**	LZ	1142 621-0		GZ
1142 536-0	**0**	GZ	1142 586-5		LZ	1142 622-8		GZ
1142 538-6	**0**	GZ	1142 587-3		LZ	1142 623-6	**0**	GZ
1142 541-0	**0**	GZ	1142 588-1		LZ	1142 624-4		GZ
1142 542-8	**0**	GZ	1142 589-9		LZ	1142 625-1		GZ(R)
1142 546-9	**0**	GZ(R)	1142 590-7		GZ	1142 626-9		GZ
1142 549-3		GZ	1142 593-1		GZ	1142 627-7		GZ
1142 550-1		GZ	1142 595-6		LZ	1142 628-5		GZ
1142 551-9	**0**	GZ	1142 596-4		GZ	1142 629-3		GZ
1142 552-7		GZ	1142 598-0		GZ	1142 630-1		GZ
1142 553-5		GZ	1142 600-4		GZ	1142 631-9		GZ
1142 554-3		GZ	1142 601-2		GZ	1142 632-7		GZ
1142 555-0		GZ	1142 605-3		GZ	1142 633-5		LZ
1142 557-6	**0**	GZ	1142 606-1		GZ	1142 634-3		LZ
1142 558-4	**0**	GZ(R)	1142 607-9		GZ	1142 635-0		LZ
1142 562-6	**0**	GZ	1142 608-7		GZ	1142 636-8		LZ
1142 563-4	**0**	GZ	1142 609-5		LZ	1142 637-6		SL
1142 564-2	**0**	GZ	1142 610-3		LZ	1142 638-4		SL
1142 565-9	**0**	GZ(R)	1142 611-1		LZ	1142 639-2		SL
1142 566-7	**0**	GZ(R)	1142 612-9		LZ	1142 640-0		SL
1142 567-5	**0**	GZ	1142 613-7		LZ	1142 642-6		SL
1142 571-7	**0**	GZ(R)	1142 614-5		LZ	1142 643-4		SL
1142 572-5	**0**	GZ	1142 615-2		LZ	1142 644-2		SL
1142 574-1	**0**	GZ	1142 616-0		LZ	1142 645-9		SL
1142 575-8	**0**	GZ	1142 617-8		LZ	1142 646-7		SL

1142 647-5	SL	1142 669-9	WS	1142 688-9	WS
1142 648-3	SL	1142 670-7 **0**	WS	1142 689-7	WS
1142 649-1	SL	1142 671-5	WS	1142 690-5 **0**	WS
1142 650-9	SL	1142 672-3	WS	1142 691-3	WS
1142 651-7	SL	1142 673-1	WS	1142 692-1 **0**	WS
1142 653-3	SL	1142 674-9 **0**	WS	1142 693-9	WS
1142 654-1	SL	1142 675-6 **0**	WS	1142 694-7	WS
1142 655-8	SL	1142 676-4 **0**	WS	1142 696-2	WS
1142 656-6	SL	1142 677-2 **0**	WS	1142 697-0 **0**	WS
1142 657-4	SL	1142 678-0 **0**	WS	1142 698-8 **0**	WS
1142 658-2	SL	1142 679-8 **0**	WS	1142 699-6 **0**	WS
1142 659-0	SL	1142 680-6	WS	1142 700-2	WS
1142 660-8	SL	1142 681-4 **0**	WS	1142 701-0 **0**	WS
1142 661-6	SL	1142 682-2 **0**	WS	1142 702-8 **0**	WS
1142 662-4	SL	1142 683-0	WS	1142 703-6 **0**	WS
1142 663-2	SL	1142 684-8	WS	1142 704-4	WS
1142 664-0	WS	1142 685-5 **0**	WS	1142 705-1	WS
1142 665-7	WS	1142 686-3 **0**	WS	1142 706-9 **0**	WS
1142 667-3	WS	1142 687-1 **0**	WS	1142 707-7	WS
1142 668-1	WS				

CLASS 1044   Bo-Bo

These thyristor locos are a development of Class 1043 which was in effect the Swedish Rc2 type. The 1044s are the standard locomotives of the 1970/80s (1044.0) and 1980/90s (1044.2). They are mixed traffic locomotives and can be found working all sorts of trains all over Austria but are gradually losing ground on the express passenger trains to 1116s. The locomotives get to München, Ingolstadt and even Nürnberg working freights into Germany.

Built: 1974–1995.
Builder – Mech. Parts: Simmering-Graz-Pauker.
Builder – Elec. Parts: Brown-Boveri/Elin/Siemens.
One Hour Rating: 5300 kW.   **Weight:** 83 tonnes.
Maximum Tractive Effort: 314 kN.   **Length over Buffers:** 16.00 m.
Wheel Diameter: 1300 mm.   **Maximum Speed:** 160 km/h.

Non-standard livery: N As "**0**" but with colours reversed on front.

1044 003-0	LZ	1044 032-9	SB	1044 063-4	VH
1044 004-8	LZ	1044 033-7	SB	1044 064-2	VH
1044 005-5	LZ	1044 034-5	SB	1044 065-9	VH
1044 006-3	LZ	1044 035-2	SB	1044 066-7	VH
1044 007-1	LZ	1044 036-0	SB	1044 067-5	VH
1044 008-9	LZ	1044 037-8	SB	1044 068-3	VH
1044 009-7	LZ	1044 039-4	SB	1044 069-1	VH
1044 010-5	LZ	1044 040-2 **0**	VH	1044 070-9	VH
1044 011-3	LZ	1044 041-0	VH	1044 071-7	VH
1044 012-1	LZ	1044 042-8	VH	1044 072-5	VH
1044 013-9	LZ	1044 043-6	VH	1044 073-3	VH
1044 014-7	LZ	1044 044-4	VH	1044 074-1	VH
1044 015-4	LZ	1044 045-1	VH	1044 075-8	VH
1044 016-2	LZ	1044 046-9	VH	1044 077-4	VH
1044 017-0	LZ	1044 048-5	VH	1044 078-2	VH
1044 018-8	LZ	1044 049-3	VH	1044 079-0	VH
1044 019-6	LZ	1044 050-1	VH	1044 080-8	VH
1044 020-4	LZ	1044 052-7	VH	1044 081-6	VH
1044 021-2	LZ	1044 053-5	VH	1044 082-4	VH
1044 023-8	LZ	1044 054-3	VH	1044 083-2	VH
1044 024-6	SB	1044 055-0	VH	1044 084-0	VH
1044 025-3	SB	1044 056-8	VH	1044 085-7	VH
1044 026-1	SB	1044 057-6	VH	1044 086-5	VH
1044 027-9	SB	1044 058-4	VH	1044 087-3	VH
1044 028-7	SB	1044 059-2	VH	1044 088-1 **0**	VH
1044 029-5	SB	1044 060-0	VH	1044 089-9	VH
1044 030-3	SB	1044 061-8	VH	1044 090-7	VH
1044 031-1	SB	1044 062-6	VH	1044 091-5 **0**	VH

1044 092-3	N	VH	1044 107-9		BL	1044 122-8	VH
1044 093-1	0	BL	1044 108-7		BL	1044 123-6 0	VH
1044 094-9	0	BL	1044 109-5		BL	1044 124-4	VH
1044 095-6	0	BL	1044 110-3		BL	1044 125-1	VH
1044 096-4		BL	1044 111-1		BL	1044 126-9 0	VH
1044 097-2	0	BL	1044 112-9		BL	1044 259-8	WW
1044 098-0	0	BL	1044 113-7		BL	1044 260-6	WW
1044 099-8		BL	1044 114-5		BL	1044 261-4	WW
1044 100-4	0	BL	1044 115-2		BL	1044 262-2	WW
1044 101-2	0	BL	1044 116-0		BL	1044 263-0	WW
1044 102-0	0	BL	1044 117-8	N	BL	1044 264-8	WW
1044 103-8		BL	1044 118-6		BL	1044 266-3	WW
1044 104-6	0	BL	1044 119-4	0	BL	1044 267-1	WW
1044 105-3		BL	1044 120-2	0	BL	1044 268-9	WW
1044 106-1		BL	1044 121-0		BL	1044 269-7	WW

CLASS 1144 — Bo-Bo

Class 1044 locos fitted for push-pull working. 1144 200–219 are additionally fitted with remote radio control for banking duties on the Brenner line and possibly elsewhere. The rebuilt locomotives can also work in multiple with 1142, 1016/1116, 1014, 2016, DB 182 and can be controlled from ÖBB driving trailers of Classes 8033 and 8073.

Non-standard livery: N Rail Cargo Austria.

1144 200-1	IN	1144 227-4	IN	1144 253-0	IN
1144 201-9	IN	1144 228-2	BL	1144 254-8	IN
1144 202-7	IN	1144 229-0	IN	1144 255-5	IN
1144 203-5	IN	1144 230-8	IN	1144 256-3	IN
1144 204-3	IN	1144 231-6	BL	1144 257-1	IN
1144 205-0	IN	1144 232-4	IN	1144 258-9	IN
1144 206-8	IN	1144 233-2	BL	1144 265-4	WW
1144 207-6	IN	1144 234-0	IN	1144 270-4	WW
1144 208-4 N	IN	1144 235-7	BL	1144 271-2	WW
1144 209-2	IN	1144 236-5	BL	1144 272-0	IN
1144 210-0	IN	1144 237-3	BL	1144 273-8	IN
1144 211-8	IN	1144 238-1	IN	1144 276-1	IN
1144 212-6	IN	1144 239-9	IN	1144 277-9	IN
1144 213-4	IN	1144 240-7	IN	1144 278-7	IN
1144 214-2	IN	1144 241-5	IN	1144 278-7	IN
1144 215-9	IN	1144 242-3	IN	1144 280-3	WW
1144 216-7	IN	1144 243-1	IN	1144 281-1	IN
1144 217-5	IN	1144 244-9	IN	1144 282-9	IN
1144 218-3	IN	1144 245-6	IN	1144 283-7	WW
1144 219-1	IN	1144 246-4	IN	1144 284-5	WW
1144 220-9	BL	1144 247-2	IN	1144 285-2	WW
1144 221-7	BL	1144 248-0	IN	1144 286-0	WW
1144 222-5	IN	1144 249-8	IN	1144 287-8	WW
1144 223-3	BL	1144 250-6	IN	1144 288-6	WW
1144 224-1	BL	1144 251-4	IN	1144 289-4	WW
1144 225-8	BL	1144 252-2	IN	1144 290-2	WW
1144 226-6	BL				

CLASS 1063 — Bo-Bo

This class of three-phase motored centre-cab shunting locomotives helped to replace many older classes including 1040, 1245, 1061, 1161, 1062 and 1067. The first 37 locomotives are dualvoltage. Selzthal depot has been declared "a centre of excellence" for this type and thus received the locomotives previously allocated to Graz and Linz but duties remained unaltered. Salzburg once had an allocation but then it received a batch of 1163s and the 1063s went elsewhere. The locos are used as yard and station pilots and trip locos all over Austria.

Built: 1982–1991.
Builder – Mech. Parts: Simmering-Graz-Pauker.
Builder – Elec. Parts: Brown Boveri/Siemens/Elin.
Continuous Rating: 2000 kW.   **Weight:** 75.5 tonnes.

Maximum Tractive Effort: 260 kN
Wheel Diameter: 1145 mm.
Systems: 15 kV 16.7 Hz/25 kV 50 Hz.
Length over Buffers: 15.56 m.
Maximum Speed: 100 km/h.

1063 001-0		SL	1063 019-2	**0**	SL	1063 035-8	**0**	WS
1063 002-8		SL	1063 020-0	**0**	SL	1063 036-6	**0**	IN
1063 003-6		SL	1063 021-8	**0**	SL	1063 037-4	**0**	IN
1063 004-4		SL	1063 022-6	**0**	SL	1063 038-2		IN
1063 005-1		SL	1063 023-4	**0**	SL	1063 039-0		IN
1063 007-7	**0**	SL	1063 024-2	**0**	SL	1063 040-8		IN
1063 008-5	**0**	SL	1063 025-9	**0**	SL	1063 041-6		IN
1063 009-3	**0**	SL	1063 026-7	**0**	WS	1063 042-4		IN
1063 010-1	**0**	SL	1063 027-5	**0**	WS	1063 043-2		IN
1063 011-9		SL	1063 028-3	**0**	WS	1063 044-0		IN
1063 012-7	**0**	SL	1063 029-1	**0**	WS	1063 045-7		IN
1063 013-5		SL	1063 030-9	**0**	WS	1063 046-5		IN
1063 014-3	**0**	SL	1063 031-7	**0**	WS	1063 047-3		BL
1063 015-0		SL	1063 032-5	**0**	WS	1063 048-1		BL
1063 016-8	**0**	SL	1063 033-3		WS	1063 049-9		BL
1063 017-6		SL	1063 034-1	**0**	WS	1063 050-7		BL
1063 018-4	**0**	SL						

CLASS 1163 — Bo-Bo

This is an updated and restyled version of 1063 but only single voltage. The locomotives shunt and trip in their respective areas.

Built: 1994–1995.
Builder – Mech. Parts: Simmering-Graz-Pauker.
Builder – Elec. Parts: Brown Boveri/Siemens/Elin.
Continuous Rating: 2000 kW.
Maximum Tractive Effort: 260 kN
Wheel Diameter: 1145 mm.
Weight: 80.0 tonnes.
Length over Buffers: 15.56 m.
Maximum Speed: 100 km/h.

Non-standard livery: N White & red.

1163 001-9	**N**	SB	1163 008-4	**N**	SB	1163 015-9	**N**	VH
1163 002-7	**N**	SB	1163 009-2	**N**	SB	1163 016-7	**N**	VH
1163 003-5	**N**	SB	1163 010-0	**N**	SB	1163 017-5	**N**	VH
1163 004-3	**N**	SB	1163 011-8	**N**	SB	1163 018-3	**N**	VH
1163 005-0	**N**	SB	1163 012-6	**N**	SB	1163 019-1	**N**	VH
1163 006-8	**N**	SB	1163 013-4	**N**	SB	1163 020-9	**N**	VH
1163 007-6	**N**	SB	1163 014-2	**N**	VH			

CLASS 1064 — Co-Co

For the major new marshalling yards at Wien (Kledering) and Villach Süd (Fürnitz) a new heavy duty hump shunter was needed and these yards are where this class can be found.

Built: 1984–85.
Builder – Mech. Parts: Simmering-Graz-Pauker.
Builder – Elec. Parts: Elin/Siemens.
One Hour Rating: 2340 kW.
Maximum Tractive Effort: 370 kN.
Wheel Diameter: 1145 mm.
Weight: 112.2 tonnes
Length over Buffers: 18.50 m.
Maximum Speed: 80 km/h.

1064 001-9		WS	1064 005-0		WS	1064 008-4	**0**	VH
1064 002-7	**0**	VH	1064 006-8		WS	1064 009-2		WS
1064 003-5		WS	1064 007-6	**0**	VH	1064 010-0		WS
1064 004-3		VH						

CLASS 1822 — Bo-Bo

These dual-voltage locomotives were intended to be the first of 50-75 locos for through workings into Italy. However like the 1012s there have been many problems with the class and series production was abandoned. The five locos are all based in Innsbruck for workings through Italy to Lienz. However there is usually only about one locomotive in traffic! They will be replaced by the new 1216s and most likely to be sold on to a private operator in Poland. 1822 005-3 has now been sold to Poland.

Built: 1991–1992.
Builder – Mech. Parts: SGP.
Builder – Elec. Parts: ABB (001/3/5), Siemens (002/4).
One Hour Rating: 4300 kW.　　　　　**Weight:** 84 tonnes.
Maximum Tractive Effort: 280 kN.　　**Length over Buffers:** 19.30 m.
Wheel Diameter: 1100 mm.　　　　　**Maximum Speed:** 140 km/h.
Systems: 15 kV 16.7 Hz/3000 V d.c.

1822 001-2	IN		1822 003-8	IN		1822 004-6	IN
1822 002-0	IN						

CLASS 1099 C-C

These old locomotives are still struggling on not helped by the poor availability of the two new EMU sets of Class 4090. Some services on the Mariazellerbahn are now worked by DMUs! In early 2005 1099 004-2 was having a general overhaul at Linz works (it was still there in July) whilst the small workshop at St. Pölten Alpenbahnhof was overhauling 1099 016-6 but five others are dumped. It is highly likely that the valley section of the Mariazellerbahn will be made standard gauge. Go now while the old locos are still in use!

Built: 1909–14.
Builder – Mech.Parts: Krauss, Linz.
Builder – Elec.Parts: Siemens Wien.
Gauge: 760 mm.　　　　　　　　　　**System:** 6.6 kV a.c. 25 Hz.
One Hour Rating: 420 kW.　　　　　**Weight:** 49.8 tonnes.
Maximum Tractive Effort: 102 kN.　　**Length over Buffers:** 11.020 m.
Wheel Diameter: 800 mm.　　　　　　**Maximum Speed:** 50 km/h.

1099 001-8	M	SP	Landeshauptstadt St. Pölten	1099 009-1	M	SP(Z)	Rabenstein a/d Piel
1099 002-6	M	SP	GÖSING	1099 010-9	M	SP	HOFSTETTEN/GRÜNAU
1099 003-4	M	SP(Z)	Weinberg	1099 011-7	M	SP	PUCHENSTUBEN
1099 004-2	M	SP	Frankelfels	1099 012-5	M	SP(Z)	
1099 005-9	M	SP(Z)	Schwarzenbach/Pielach	1099 013-3	M	SP	Annaberg
1099 006-7	M	SP(Z)	Kirchberg/Piel	1099 014-1	M	SP	
1099 007-5	M	SP	MARIAZELL	1099 015-8	M	SP	
1099 008-3	M	SP	Loich	1099 016-6	M	SP	Ober Grafendorf

1.2. DIESEL LOCOMOTIVES

CLASS 2016   HERCULES   Bo-Bo

These locomotives are the quietest diesel locomotives ever encountered by your author. They are in effect a diesel version of the Taurus with which there are some common parts. All were built at the Siemens–Krauss Maffei works in München but as with the 1116s there is some Austrian input. (Bogies from Siemens SGP, Graz) The locomotives feature three-phase motors and can work in multiple with 1016, 1116, 1014, 1142, 1144 and be controlled from driving trailers. The class is replacing 2043s and 2143s but at the end of 2004 with 98 locomotives delivered ÖBB had yet to withdraw many of the older locomotives. The NS locomotives work all over the north east of Austria and down to Graz via the Wechsel route; WE locomotives are used on the lines radiating from Ried im Innkreis; VH locomotives work Knittelfeld– Klagenfurt–Villach– Kötschach-Mauthen; GZ locomotives work to Wiener Neustadt and Szombathely in Hungary.

Built: 2002–2004.
Builder – Mech Parts: Siemens-Krauss-Maffei.
Builder – Elec Parts: Siemens Erlangen.
Engine: MTU 16V4000 R41 of 2000kW.
Weight: 80 tonnes.

Transmission: Electric.	**Maximum Tractive Effort:** 235 kN.
Wheel Diameter: 1100 mm.	**Length over Buffers:** 19.275 m.
Train Heating: Electric.	**Maximum Speed:** 140 km/h.

Multiple Working: Up to six members of this class can work in multiple.

2016 001-6	NS	2016 037-0	NS	2016 069-3	WE
2016 002-4	NS	2016 038-8	NS	2016 070-1	WE
2016 003-2	NS	2016 039-6	NS	2016 071-9	WE
2016 004-0	NS	2016 040-4	NS	2016 072-7	WE
2016 005-7	NS	2016 041-2	VH	2016 073-5	WE
2016 006-5	NS	2016 042-0	VH	2016 074-3	GZ
2016 007-3	NS	2016 043-8	VH	2016 075-0	GZ
2016 008-1	NS	2016 044-6	VH	2016 076-8	GZ
2016 009-9	NS	2016 045-3	VH	2016 077-6	GZ
2016 010-7	NS	2016 046-1	VH	2016 078-4	GZ
2016 011-5	NS	2016 047-9	VH	2016 079-2	GZ
2016 012-3	NS	2016 048-7	VH	2016 080-0	GZ
2016 013-1	NS	2016 049-5	VH	2016 081-8	GZ
2016 014-9	NS	2016 050-3	VH	2016 082-6	GZ
2016 015-6	NS	2016 051-1	VH	2016 083-4	GZ
2016 016-4	NS	2016 052-9	VH	2016 084-2	GZ
2016 017-2	NS	2016 053-7	VH	2016 085-9	GZ
2016 018-0	NS	2016 054-5	VH	2016 086-7	GZ
2016 019-8	NS	2016 055-2	VH	2016 087-5	GZ
2016 020-6	NS	2016 056-0	VH	2016 088-3	GZ
2016 021-4	NS	2016 057-8	VH	2016 089-1	VH
2016 022-2	NS	2016 058-6	VH	2016 090-9	NS
2016 023-0	NS	2016 059-4	VH	2016 091-7	NS
2016 025-5	NS	2016 060-2	VH	2016 092-5	NS
2016 026-3	NS	2016 061-0	NS	2016 093-3	NS
2016 027-1	NS	2016 062-8	WE	2016 094-1	NS
2016 028-9	NS	2016 063-6	WE	2016 095-8	NS
2016 029-7	NS	2016 064-4	WE	2016 096-6	NS
2016 030-5	NS	2016 065-1	WE	2016 097-4	NS
2016 032-1	NS	2016 066-9	WE	2016 098-2	NS
2016 034-7	NS	2016 067-7	WE	2016 099-0	NS
2016 035-4	NS	2016 068-5	WE	2016 100-6	NS

CLASS 2043   B-B

This class is on the way out with most duties already taken over by the new 2016 and 2070 classes or even new DMUs. ÖBB is hoping to sell those locomotives still in good condition to private operators or track contractors. 2043 555-8 is still fitted with additional braking going back to the time when it worked iron ore trains on the Eisenerz–Vordernberg route.

Built: 1964–74.
Builder – Mech Parts: Jenbach.
Engine: Jenbach LM1500 of 1100 kW (1475 h.p.) plus 224 kW (300 h.p.) for train heating.
Transmission: Hydraulic. Voith L830 rU2.
Maximum Tractive Effort: 196 kN.   **Weight:** 68 tonnes.
Wheel Diameter: 950 mm.   **Length over Buffers:** 14.76 m.
Train Heating: Electric.   **Maximum Speed:** 110 km/h.

Note: 2043 062-5 has a Caterpillar engine of type 3516 STD for traction and a type 3408 DI-TR engine for heating.

2043 005-4	IN	2043 034-4	LZ	2043 057-5	KR
2043 006-2	VH	2043 035-1	KR	2043 058-3	KD
2043 008-8	VH	2043 037-7	WE	2043 059-1	IN
2043 009-6	KD (Z)	2043 038-5	VH	2043 060-9	WE
2043 010-4	IN	2043 039-3	KR	2043 061-7	KR (Z)
2043 011-2	KD (Z)	2043 040-1	IN	2043 062-5	KD
2043 012-0	WE	2043 041-9	WE	2043 063-3	LZ
2043 013-8	IN (Z)	2043 042-7	WE	2043 064-1	VH
2043 014-6	GM (Z)	2043 043-5	KD (Z)	2043 066-6	IN (Z)
2043 016-1	LZ	2043 044-3	LZ	2043 067-4	LZ (Z)
2043 017-9	GM (Z)	2043 045-0	LZ	2043 068-2	WE
2043 020-3	WE	2043 046-8	LZ (Z)	2043 069-0	VH (Z)
2043 021-1	WE	2043 047-6	LZ	2043 070-8	VH
2043 022-9	WE	2043 048-4	LZ	2043 071-6	GM (Z)
2043 023-7	IN	2043 049-2	IN	2043 073-2	IN
2043 025-2	WE	2043 050-0	KR	2043 074-0	VH (Z)
2043 026-0	WE (Z)	2043 051-8	LZ (Z)	2043 075-7	VH
2043 028-6	IN	2043 052-6	IN	2043 076-5	IN
2043 029-4	WE	2043 053-4	VH	2043 077-3	KR (Z)
2043 030-2	WE (Z)	2043 054-2	WE (Z)	2043 555-8	KD
2043 032-8	WE	2043 056-7	IN		

CLASS 2143 B-B

As with Class 2043 this class is also being phased out. Several locomotives have already been withdrawn or sold and more are to follow.

Built: 1965–77.
Builder – Mech Parts: SGP.
Engine: SGP T12c of 1100 kW (1475 h.p.) plus 224 kW (300 h.p.) for train heating.
Transmission: Hydraulic. Voith L830 rU2.
Maximum Tractive Effort: 197 kN.   **Weight:** 67 tonnes.
Wheel Diameter: 950 mm.   **Length over Buffers:** 15.76 m.
Train Heating: Electric.   **Maximum Speed:** 100 km/h.

m Fitted for multiple working.

Note: 2143 035-0 and 2143 040-0 have been restored to blood orange and green liveries respectively as "nostalgic" locos.

2143 004-6	NS	2143 028-5	KR	2143 045-9	m GZ
2143 009-5	NS	2143 029-3	GM	2143 046-7	m KR
2143 010-3	NS (Z)	2143 030-1	WO	2143 047-5	m GM
2143 011-1	WO	2143 031-9	GM (Z)	2143 048-3	m GM
2143 012-9	WO (Z)	2143 033-5	GM	2143 049-1	m WO
2143 013-7	NS	2143 034-3	m GM	2143 050-9	m KR
2143 014-5	WO	2143 035-0 **0**	m WO	2143 051-7	m WO
2143 015-2	NS (Z)	2143 036-8	m WO (Z)	2143 052-5	m WO
2143 016-0	WO	2143 037-6	m WO	2143 053-3	m WO
2143 018-6	NS	2143 038-4	m WO	2143 054-1	m KR
2143 021-0	WO	2143 039-2	m GM	2143 055-8	m KR
2143 022-8	WO	2143 040-0 **G**	m NS	2143 056-6	m WO
2143 023-6	KR (Z)	2143 041-8	m GM	2143 057-4	m WO (Z)
2143 024-4	GZ (Z)	2143 042-6	m GM	2143 058-2	m KR
2143 026-9	KR (Z)	2143 043-4	m KR	2143 059-0	m GZ
2143 027-7	KR	2143 044-2	m GZ	2143 060-8	m NS

2143 061-6	m	GZ	2143 067-3	m	WO	2143 073-1	m	WO
2143 062-4	m	WO	2143 068-1	m	KR	2143 074-9	m	WO (Z)
2143 063-2	m	KR	2143 069-9	m	WO	2143 075-6	m	KR
2143 064-0	m	WO	2143 070-7	m	WO	2143 076-4	m	NS
2143 065-7	m	GZ (Z)	2143 071-5	m	WO	2143 077-2	m	KR
2143 066-5	m	NS	2143 072-3	m	KR			

CLASS 2067   C

Whilst most of Class 2060 and 2062 have been withdrawn or transferred into departmental use the arrival of the 100 2016s and 90 2070s has only slightly affected the 2067s. However some locomotives are already in store and others no doubt will follow once Austria takes stock after the winter of 2004/5. The locomotives still have odd shunting duties and are often first call for light ballast trains.

Built: 1959–77.
Builder – Mech Parts: SGP.
Engine: SGP S12a (Caterpillar*) of 450 kW (603 h.p.).
Transmission: Hydraulic. Voith L28.
Maximum Tractive Effort: 147 kN.   **Weight:** 48.3 tonnes.
Wheel Diameter: 1140 mm.   **Length over Buffers:** 10.34 m.
Maximum Speed: 65 km/h.

m Fitted for multiple working.

2050 005-4		WO (Z)	2067 042-8	m	KD	2067 079-0		GZ
2050 008-8		WO (Z)	2067 043-6	m	GZ	2067 080-8		KD
2050 011-2		WO (Z)	2067 044-4	m	GZ	2067 081-6		WO
2050 012-0		WO (Z)	2067 045-1	m	KD	2067 082-4		IN (Z)
2050 015-3		WO (Z)	2067 046-9	m	KD	2067 083-2		IN
2050 016-1	m	WO (Z)	2067 047-7	*m	WE	2067 084-0		IN
2050 017-9	m	WO (Z)	2067 048-5	m	KD	2067 085-7		KD
2050 018-7	m	WO (Z)	2067 050-1		LZ	2067 086-5		GM
2067 001-4		VH	2067 051-9		LZ	2067 087-3		GM
2067 003-0		VH	2067 052-7		LZ	2067 088-1		LZ
2067 004-8		VH	2067 054-3		LZ	2067 089-9		WO
2067 006-3		VH	2067 055-0		LZ	2067 090-7		WO
2067 008-9		VH	2067 056-8	*	WE	2067 091-5		IN
2067 009-7		VH	2067 057-6		BL	2067 092-3		GZ
2067 010-5		VH	2067 058-4		BL	2067 094-9		WO
2067 011-3		GZ	2067 059-2		BL	2067 095-6		SB
2067 012-1		GZ	2067 060-0		BL	2067 096-4		WO
2067 013-9		VH	2067 061-8		IN	2067 097-2		SP
2067 014-7		SL	2067 062-6		IN	2067 098-0		WO
2067 017-0	*	SL	2067 063-4		IN	2067 099-8		IN
2067 018-8		GZ	2067 064-2		IN	2067 100-4		NS
2067 023-8	*	WE	2067 065-9		IN	2067 101-2	m	WO
2067 024-6		SB	2067 066-7		BL	2067 102-0	m	WO
2067 026-1		SB	2067 067-5		SP	2067 103-8	m	WO
2067 027-9		SB	2067 068-3		IN	2067 104-6	m	SB
2067 028-7		WE	2067 070-9		SB	2067 105-3	m	WO
2067 030-3		SP	2067 071-7		GM	2067 106-1	m	SP
2067 032-9		WE	2067 072-5		NS	2067 107-9	m	SP
2067 033-7	*	WE	2067 073-3		NS	2067 108-7	m	WO
2067 037-8		WE	2067 074-1		WO	2067 109-5	m	KD
2067 038-6		LZ	2067 075-8		NS	2067 110-3	m	WO
2067 039-4		WE	2067 077-4		BL	2067 111-1	m	WO
2067 041-0		KD	2067 078-2		NS			

CLASS 2167   C

As Class 2067 but fitted with radio remote control.

2167 093-0		KD	

CLASS 2068 B-B

These shunting locomotives are gradually being concentrated in the western part of Austria now that the 2070s have settled in. It is expected that the remaining locomotives at Wien and Wiener Neustadt will move west in 2005.

Built: 1989.
Builder – Mech. Parts: Jenbacher Werke.
Engine: JW 608DS (480 D*) of 820 kW (1100 h.p.) at 1500 rpm.
Transmission: Hydraulic. Voith L4r4zsU2.
Maximum Tractive Effort: 176 (147*) kN.   **Weight:** 75.5 tonnes.
Wheel Diameter: 950 mm.   **Length over Buffers:** 13.30 m.
Maximum Speed: 100 km/h.
Multiple Working: With one other member of the same class.

2068 001-3	* WO	2068 021-1	NS	2068 041-9	SB
2068 002-1	* BL	2068 022-9	KD	2068 042-7	KD
2068 003-9	* BL	2068 023-7	VH	2068 043-5	IN
2068 004-7	* WO	2068 024-5	KD	2068 044-3	GZ
2068 005-4	* WO	2068 025-2	GZ	2068 045-0	VH
2068 006-2	NS	2068 026-0	BL	2068 046-8	IN
2068 007-0	BL	2068 027-8	IN	2068 047-6	VH
2068 008-8	BL	2068 028-6	SB	2068 048-4	VH
2068 009-6	GZ	2068 029-4	GZ	2068 049-2	VH
2068 010-4	KD	2068 030-2	GZ	2068 050-0	GZ
2068 011-2	IN	2068 031-0	KD	2068 051-8	VH
2068 012-0	IN	2068 032-8	SB	2068 052-6	KD
2068 013-8	KD	2068 033-6	KD	2068 053-4	GZ
2068 014-6	VH	2068 034-4	IN	2068 054-2	NS
2068 015-3	VH	2068 035-1	GZ	2068 055-9	KD
2068 016-1	VH	2068 036-9	SB	2068 056-7	NS
2068 017-9	VH	2068 037-7	SB	2068 057-5	IN
2068 018-7	VH	2068 038-5	SB	2068 058-3	BL
2068 019-5	IN	2068 039-3	GZ	2068 059-1	GZ
2068 020-3	NS	2068 040-1	SB	2068 060-9	BL

CLASS 2070   HECTOR   B-B

This is a standard Vossloh/MaK single cab locomotive adapted to ÖBB requirements and nicknamed "HECTOR". Extras include remote radio control and automatic shunting couplers. An auxiliary engine of 21kW powers pre-heating equipment and cab air conditioning. The arrival of these new shunting and trip locomotives has allowed all class 2048 to be withdrawn and classes 2060 and 2062 to be withdrawn or cascaded into departmental use. This class is intended to be used in eastern Austria with the 2068s moving on to western Austria.

Built: 2001–2004.
Builder – Mech Parts: VSFT Kiel.
Engine: Caterpillar 3412E01-TTA JW 12 cyl of 738 kN.
Weight: 72 tonnes.
Transmission: Hydraulic. Voith L3t4zseU2.
Maximum Tractive Effort: 151/233 kN at 100/45 km/h.
Wheel Diameter: 1000 mm.   **Length over Buffers:** 14.13 m.
Train Heating: None.   **Maximum Speed:** 100 km/h.

2070 001-9	WE	2070 013-4	WO	2070 025-8	WO
2070 002-7	WE	2070 014-2	WO	2070 026-6	WE
2070 003-5	WE	2070 015-9	WO	2070 027-4	WE
2070 004-3	WE	2070 016-7	WO	2070 028-2	WE
2070 005-0	WE	2070 017-5	WO	2070 029-0	WE
2070 006-8	WE	2070 018-3	WO	2070 030-8	WE
2070 007-6	WE	2070 019-1	WO	2070 031-6	WE
2070 008-4	WE	2070 020-9	WO	2070 032-4	WE
2070 009-2	WE	2070 021-7	WO	2070 033-2	WE
2070 010-0	WE	2070 022-5	WO	2070 034-0	WE
2070 011-8	WO	2070 023-3	WO	2070 035-7	WE
2070 012-6	WO	2070 024-1	WO	2070 036-5	WE

2070 037-3	SP	2070 055-5	WO	2070 073-8	WE
2070 038-1	SP	2070 056-3	WO	2070 074-6	WE
2070 039-9	SP	2070 057-1	WO	2070 075-3	WE
2070 040-7	SP	2070 058-9	WO	2070 076-1	WE
2070 041-5	SP	2070 059-7	WO	2070 077-9	WE
2070 042-3	SP	2070 060-5	WO	2070 078-7	WE
2070 043-1	SP	2070 061-3	WO	2070 079-5	WE
2070 044-9	SP	2070 062-1	WO	2070 080-3	WE
2070 045-6	SP	2070 063-9	WO	2070 081-1	WE
2070 046-4	SP	2070 064-7	WO	2070 082-9	WE
2070 047-2	SP	2070 065-4	WO	2070 083-7	WE
2070 048-0	SP	2070 066-2	WO	2070 084-5	WE
2070 049-8	SP	2070 067-0	WO	2070 085-2	WE
2070 050-6	SP	2070 068-8	WO	2070 086-0	WO
2070 051-4	SP	2070 069-6	WO	2070 087-8	WO
2070 052-2	WO	2070 070-4	WO	2070 088-6	WO
2070 053-0	WO	2070 071-2	WE	2070 089-4	WO
2070 054-8	WO	2070 072-0	WE	2070 090-2	WO

CLASS 2080   B

This is a self-propelled snow-clearing machine.

Built: 1975.
Builder: Beilhack.
Engine: Deutz BF 12L413 of 260 kW (350 h.p.).
Transmission: Hydraulic.
Snowplough Power: 2 x 310 kW.   **Weight:** 42 tonnes.
Wheel Diameter: 1000 mm.   **Length over Buffers:** 12.35 m.
Maximum Speed: 80 km/h.

2080 001-7   IN |

CLASS 2180   B

Another self-propelled snow-clearing machine.

Built: 1982.
Builder – Mech Parts: Beilhack.
Engine: 370 kW (496 h.p.).
Transmission: Hydraulic.
Snowplough Power: 2 x 370 kW.   **Weight:** 43 tonnes.
Wheel Diameter: 1000 mm.   **Length over Buffers:** 12.35 m.
Maximum Speed: 80 km/h.

2180 001-6   VH |

CLASS 2092   C

This loco is used on pilot duties at Zell am See. It is in fact Wehrmacht type HF 130 C locomotive rebuilt with a larger cabs and other detail alterations.

Built: 1943–44.
Builder: Gmeinder.
Gauge: 760 mm.
Engine: Deutz 6 M517 of 100 kW (134 h.p.).   **Transmission:** Hydraulic.
Maximum Tractive Effort: 49 kN.   **Weight:** 16.5 tonnes.
Driving Wheel Dia.: 700 mm.   **Length over Buffers:** 5.325 m.
Max. Speed: 25 km/h.

2092 002-1   ZS |

CLASS 2095 B-B

The standard ÖBB locomotive for the narrow gauge which is found on all existing lines.

Built: 1958–62.
Builders: SGP Floridsdorf.
Gauge: 760 mm.
Engine: SGP 12a of 440 kW (590 h.p.). **Transmission:** Hydraulic.
Maximum Tractive Effort: 98 kN. **Weight:** 30 tonnes.
Driving Wheel Dia.: 900 mm. **Length over Buffers:** 10.40 m.
Maximum Speed: 60 km/h.

Non-standard liveries:

N 2095 001-0 is original red and cream.
N 2095 002-8 is all over red

2095 001-0 **N**	ZS (Z)		2095 009-3	WH	Hollenstein an der Ybbs
2095 002-8 **N**	ZS (Z)		2095 010-1	WH	
2095 003-6	ZS		2095 011-9	SP	
2095 004-4	SP	Bischofstetten	2095 012-7	GM	
2095 005-1	WH		2095 013-5	SP	Reprechtshofen
2095 006-9	SP		2095 014-3	GM	
2095 007-7	WH		2095 015-0	SP	Mank
2095 008-5	WH	LUNZ AM SEE			

1.3. ELECTRIC MULTIPLE UNITS

CLASS 4010　　　　　　　　　　6-CAR INTER-CITY UNITS

These EMUs were built for the "Transalpin" service and they were then easily the most comfortable trains in Austria. However on refurbishment some years ago the second class compartment stock was modified with standard seating, with the first class compartments in the composites (Class 7010.2) converted to second class. Their days are now numbered as the oldest vehicles are 40 years old. They will be replaced by new loco-hauled stock, but meanwhile the Graz units continue to work IC services to Innsbruck, Linz and Wien whilst the Wien FJB units work local services towards Gmünd. The units have been reformed and all except two restaurant cars have been withdrawn, being replaced by second class cars from withdrawn units. As built the compartment stock had seperate washrooms as well as toilets, but these have now been replaced with electrical equipment cabinets. Reliability is poor and it is not uncommon for a locomotive to be used to haul a 4010 set!

Sets 4010 022–025 were built with full air conditioning and the trailers weigh 45 tonnes.
D4hET + B4hTl + B4hTl + B4hTl + B4hTl (BR4hTL*) + AD4hES
(DMLV–TSO–TSK–TSK–TSK [TSO†, TSRB*]–DTBFO).

Built: 1965–78.
Builder-Mech Parts: SGP.
Builder-Elec. Parts: BBC/Siemens/Elin.
Traction Motors: 4 x 620 kW.
Accommodation: 0 + –/60 2T 2W + –/66 2T + –/60 2T + –/66 2T (§†–/60 2T, *–/9 34 unclassified) + 42/– 1T 1W.
Wheel Arrangement: Bo-Bo + 2-2 + 2-2 + 2-2 + 2-2 + 2-2.
Weight: 70.8 + 40 + 42 + 42 + 42 + 41 tonnes.
Length over Buffers: 16.82 + 26.4 + 26.4 + 26.4 + 26.4 + 26.7 m.
Maximum Speed: 150 km/h.

4010 001-8	7010 101-9	7110 101-8	7110 201-6	7010 122-5	6010 001-3	I	†	GZ
4010 004-2	7010 104-3	7110 104-2	7110 204-0	7110 222-2	6010 004-7	I	§	GZ
4010 006-7	7010 106-8	7110 106-7	7110 206-5	7110 114-1	6010 006-2	I		GZ
4010 007-5	7010 107-6	7110 107-5	7110 207-3	7110 214-9	6010 007-0	I	§	GZ
4010 008-3	7010 108-4	7110 108-3	7110 208-1	7310 003-4	6010 008-8	I	*	WF
4010 009-1	7010 109-2	7110 109-1	7110 209-9	7310 004-2	6010 009-6	I	*	WF
4010 010-9	7010 112-6	7110 112-5	7110 212-3	7110 215-6	6010 012-0	I	§	WF
4010 011-7	7010 111-8	7110 111-7	7110 211-5	7110 125-7	6010 015-3	I		GZ
4010 013-3	7010 113-4	7110 113-3	7110 213-1	7110 217-2	6010 013-8	I	§	GZ
4010 016-6	7010 102-7	7110 102-6	7110 202-4	7110 122-4	6010 022-9	I		GZ
4010 018-2	7010 118-3	7110 118-2	7110 218-0	7110 223-0	6010 018-7	I	§	GZ
4010 019-0	7010 105-0	7110 105-9	7110 205-7	7110 123-2	6010 005-4	I		GZ
4010 020-8	7010 120-9	7110 120-8	7110 220-6	7010 124-1	6010 020-3	I	†	GZ
4010 021-6	7010 121-7	7110 121-6	7110 221-4	7110 124-0	6010 023-7	I		GZ
4010 022-4					6010 002-1	I		FD
4010 024-0	7010 119-1	7110 119-0	7110 219-8	7110 224-8	6010 024-5	I	§	GZ
4010 025-7	7010 126-6	7110 126-5	7110 226-3	7010 110-0	6010 025-2	I	†	GZ
4010 028-1	7010 127-4	7110 127-3	7110 227-1	7010 125-8	6010 027-8	I	†	GZ
4010 029-9	7010 129-0	7110 129-9	7110 229-7	7110 225-5	6010 029-4	I	§	GZ

CLASS 4020　　　　　　　　　　　　　　3-CAR UNITS

This suburban EMU covers most of the Wien area with just a few units working around the Bludenz–Bregenz area. The sets are now being fitted with an emergency alarm brake override so that the driver can avoid the train stopping in tunnels etc when an emergency arises; 200 is added to the running number when this modification has been done. The units are now losing their traditional blue and cream S-Bahn livery for the new red, grey and white.

B4hET + B4hTl + B4hES (DMSO–TSO–DTSO).

Built: 1978–87.
Builder-Mech Parts: SGP.
Builders-Elec. Parts: BBC/Elin/Siemens.

Traction Motors: 4 x 300 kW.
Accommodation: –/56 + –/64 2T + –/64.
Wheel Arrangement: Bo-Bo + 2-2 + 2-2.
Length over Buffers: 23.30 + 22.8 + 23.3 m.
Maximum Speed: 120 km/h.

Class 4020.0. As built:

4020 012-3	7020 012-6	6020 012-8	S	FD	4020 073-5	7020 073-8	6020 073-0	S	FD
4020 013-1	7020 013-4	6020 013-6	S	FD	4020 074-3	7020 074-6	6020 074-8	S	FD
4020 024-8	7020 024-1	6020 024-3	S	FD	4020 078-4	7020 078-7	6020 078-9	S	FD
4020 025-5	7020 025-8	6020 025-0	S	FD	4020 082-6	7020 082-9	6020 082-1	S	FD
4020 028-9	7020 028-2	6020 028-4	S	FD	4020 083-4	7020 083-7	6020 083-9	S	FD
4020 029-7	7020 029-0	6020 029-2	S	FD	4020 098-2	7020 098-5	6020 098-7	S	WF
4020 036-2	7020 036-5	6020 036-7	S	FD	4020 104-8	7020 104-1	6020 104-3	S	FD
4020 037-0	7020 037-3	6020 037-5	S	FD	4020 112-1	7020 112-4	6020 112-6	S	BL
4020 041-2	7020 041-5	6020 041-7	S	FD	4020 113-9	7020 113-2	6020 113-4	S	BL
4020 052-9	7020 052-2	6020 052-4	S	FD	4020 114-7	7020 114-0	6020 114-2	S	BL
4020 053-7	7020 053-0	6020 053-2	S	FD	4020 115-4	7020 115-7	6020 115-9	S	BL
4020 055-2	7020 055-5	6020 055-7	S	FD	4020 116-2	7020 116-5	6020 116-7	S	BL
4020 056-0	7020 056-3	6020 056-5	S	FD	4020 117-0	7020 117-3	6020 117-5	S	BL
4020 058-6	7020 058-9	6020 058-1	S	FD	4020 118-8	7020 118-1	6020 118-3	S	BL
4020 066-9	7020 066-2	6020 066-4	S	FD	4020 119-6	7020 119-9	6020 119-1	S	BL
4020 068-5	7020 068-8	6020 068-0	S	FD	4020 120-4	7020 120-7	6020 120-9	S	FD

Class 4020.2. Fitted with emergency alarm system. Note: Units with no allocation are not yet converted.

4020 201-2	7020 201-5	6020 201-7	S	FD	4020 239-2	7020 239-5	6020 239-7	R	FD
4020 202-0	7020 202-3	6020 202-5	S	FD	4020 240-0	7020 240-3	6020 240-5	R	FD
4020 203-8	7020 203-1	6020 203-3	S	FD	4020 241-8	7020 241-1	6020 241-3	R	
4020 204-6	7020 204-9	6020 204-1	S	FD	4020 242-6	7020 242-9	6020 242-1	S	FD
4020 205-3	7020 205-6	6020 205-8	S	FD	4020 243-4	7020 243-7	6020 243-9	S	FD
4020 206-1	7020 206-4	6020 206-6	S	FD	4020 244-2	7020 244-5	6020 244-7	S	FD
4020 207-9	7020 207-2	6020 207-4	S	FD	4020 245-9	7020 245-2	6020 245-4	S	FD
4020 208-7	7020 208-0	6020 208-2	S	FD	4020 246-7	7020 246-0	6020 246-2	S	FD
4020 209-5	7020 209-8	6020 209-0	S	FD	4020 247-5	7020 247-8	6020 247-0	S	FD
4020 210-3	7020 210-6	6020 210-8	S	FD	4020 248-3	7020 248-6	6020 248-8	S	FD
4020 211-1	7020 211-4	6020 211-6	R	FD	4020 249-1	7020 249-4	6020 249-6	S	FD
4020 212-9	7020 212-2	6020 212-4	R		4020 250-9	7020 250-2	6020 250-4	S	FD
4020 213-7	7020 213-0	6020 213-2	R		4020 251-7	7020 251-0	6020 251-2	S	FD
4020 214-5	7020 214-8	6020 214-0	S	FD	4020 252-5	7020 252-8	6020 252-0	R	
4020 215-2	7020 215-5	6020 215-7	S	FD	4020 253-3	7020 253-6	6020 253-8	R	
4020 216-0	7020 216-3	6020 216-5	S	FD	4020 254-1	7020 254-4	6020 254-6	S	FD
4020 217-8	7020 217-1	6020 217-3	S	FD	4020 255-8	7020 255-1	6020 255-3	R	
4020 218-6	7020 218-9	6020 218-1	S	FD	4020 256-6	7020 256-9	6020 256-1	R	
4020 219-4	7020 219-7	6020 219-9	S	FD	4020 257-4	7020 257-7	6020 257-9	S	FD
4020 220-2	7020 220-5	6020 220-7	S	FD	4020 258-2	7020 258-5	6020 258-7	R	
4020 221-0	7020 221-3	6020 221-5	R	FD	4020 259-0	7020 259-3	6020 259-5	S	FD
4020 222-8	7020 222-1	6020 222-3	S	FD	4020 260-8	7020 260-1	6020 260-3	S	FD
4020 223-6	7020 223-9	6020 223-1	S	FD	4020 261-6	7020 261-9	6020 261-1	S	FD
4020 224-4	7020 224-7	6020 224-9	R		4020 262-4	7020 262-7	6020 262-9	S	FD
4020 225-1	7020 225-4	6020 225-6	R		4020 263-2	7020 263-5	6020 263-7	S	FD
4020 226-9	7020 226-2	6020 226-4	S	FD	4020 264-0	7020 264-3	6020 264-5	S	FD
4020 227-7	7020 227-0	6020 227-2	S	FD	4020 266-5	7020 266-8	6020 266-0	R	FD
4020 228-5	7020 228-8	6020 228-0	R		4020 267-3	7020 267-6	6020 267-8	S	FD
4020 229-3	7020 229-6	6020 229-8	R		4020 268-1	7020 268-4	6020 268-6	R	
4020 230-1	7020 230-4	6020 230-6	S	FD	4020 269-9	7020 269-2	6020 269-4	S	FD
4020 231-9	7020 231-2	6020 231-4	R	FD	4020 270-7	7020 270-0	6020 270-2	S	FD
4020 232-7	7020 232-0	6020 232-2	R	FD	4020 271-5	7020 271-8	6020 271-0	S	FD
4020 233-5	7020 233-8	6020 233-0	R	FD	4020 272-3	7020 272-6	6020 272-8	S	FD
4020 234-3	7020 234-6	6020 234-8	S	FD	4020 273-1	7020 273-4	6020 273-6	R	
4020 235-0	7020 235-3	6020 235-5	R	FD	4020 274-9	7020 274-2	6020 274-4	R	
4020 236-8	7020 236-1	6020 236-3	R		4020 275-6	7020 275-9	6020 275-1	S	FD
4020 237-6	7020 237-9	6020 237-1	R		4020 276-4	7020 276-7	6020 276-9	S	FD
4020 238-4	7020 238-7	6020 238-9	R	FD	4020 277-2	7020 277-5	6020 277-7	S	FD

4020	7020	6020		
4020 278-0	7020 278-3	6020 278-5	R	
4020 279-8	7020 279-1	6020 279-3	S	FD
4020 280-6	7020 280-9	6020 280-1	R	FD
4020 281-4	7020 281-7	6020 281-9	R	WF
4020 282-2	7020 282-5	6020 282-7	R	
4020 283-0	7020 283-3	6020 283-5	R	
4020 284-8	7020 284-1	6020 284-3	S	FD
4020 285-5	7020 285-8	6020 285-0	S	FD
4020 286-3	7020 286-6	6020 286-8	S	FD
4020 287-1	7020 287-4	6020 287-6	S	FD
4020 288-9	7020 288-2	6020 288-4	S	FD
4020 289-7	7020 289-0	6020 289-2	S	FD
4020 290-5	7020 290-8	6020 290-0	S	BL
4020 291-3	7020 291-6	6020 291-8	S	WF
4020 292-1	7020 292-4	6020 292-6	S	WF
4020 293-9	7020 293-2	6020 293-4	S	FD
4020 294-7	7020 294-0	6020 294-2	R	FD
4020 295-4	7020 295-7	6020 295-9	S	WF
4020 296-2	7020 296-5	6020 296-7	R	WF
4020 297-0	7020 297-3	6020 297-5	R	WF
4020 298-8	7020 298-1	6020 298-3	R	
4020 299-6	7020 299-9	6020 299-1	R	WF
4020 300-2	7020 300-5	6020 300-7	R	WF
4020 301-0	7020 301-3	6020 301-5	S	FD
4020 302-8	7020 302-1	6020 302-3	S	FD
4020 303-6	7020 303-9	6020 303-1	S	BL
4020 304-4	7020 304-7	6020 304-9	R	
4020 305-1	7020 305-4	6020 305-6	S	FD
4020 306-9	7020 306-2	6020 306-4	S	FD
4020 307-7	7020 307-0	6020 307-2	S	FD
4020 308-5	7020 308-8	6020 308-0	R	WF
4020 309-3	7020 309-6	6020 309-8	S	BL
4020 310-1	7020 310-4	6020 310-6	R	WF
4020 311-9	7020 311-2	6020 311-4	R	WF
4020 312-7	7020 312-0	6020 312-2	R	
4020 313-5	7020 313-8	6020 313-0	R	
4020 314-3	7020 314-6	6020 314-8	R	
4020 315-0	7020 315-3	6020 315-5	R	
4020 316-8	7020 316-1	6020 316-3	R	
4020 317-6	7020 317-9	6020 317-1	R	
4020 318-4	7020 318-7	6020 318-9	R	
4020 319-2	7020 319-5	6020 319-7	R	
4020 320-0	7020 320-3	6020 320-5	R	

CLASS 4023   TALENT   3-SECTION UNITS

These new articulated EMUs are electric versions of the Bombardier (Talbot) Talent DMUs. They have been obtained to modernise the local services around Salzburg which are now classed as S-Bahn services. When first delivered the three sections were numbered as 4023/7023/6023 just as a classic three-car set but those involved in this did not take into account that both driving cars are power cars. ÖBB have now changed their minds and the whole set is referred to as 4023 001 etc. (Presumably with some internal number or letter to denote in which actual part of a set a defect is located!). Besides covering the S-Bahn services some trains actually work through to such places as Schwarzach St. Veit and even Saalfelden. Intended for 140 km/h the licensing authorities in Austria are not happy with the braking power and have insisted upon magnetic brakes being fitted and until this is done the units are restricted to 120 km/h. In 2005/6 the units are expected to start working to Freilassing and Berchtesgaden in Germany.

BDhET (DMSO–TSO–DMSO).

Built: 1960.
Builder – Mech Parts: Bombardier.
Builder – Elec. Parts: Elin.
Traction Motors: 4 x 250 kW.
Accommodation: –/38 (16) + –/48 + –/40 (9) 1W 1TD.
Wheel Arrangement: Bo-2-2-Bo.
Length over Couplers: 52.12 m.
Maximum Speed: 140 km/h.

4023 001-3	R	SB	
4023 002-1	R	SB	
4023 003-9	R	SB	
4023 004-7	R	SB	
4023 005-4	R	SB	
4023 006-2	R	SB	Stadt Salzburg
4023 007-0	R	SB	Stadt Seekirchen a.W.
4023 008-8	R	SB	
4023 009-6	R	SB	
4023 010-4	R	SB	Golling an der Salzach
4023 011-2	R	SB	Stadt Neumarkt

CLASS 4024   TALENT   4-SECTION UNITS

This new EMU is a four car version of 4023 from the same manufacturer. These units are intended for suburban duties around Wien and other areas. Like the 4023s the units have been found lacking in braking power and the speed reduced until modified. From the winter 2004/5 timetable the units started working on route S7 Wien–Wolfsthal and S45 Hütteldorf–Handelskai. Early in 2005 some 25 sets had been delivered and low numbered sets were seen on driver training duties at Bruck an der Mur, Graz, Knittelfeld and Selzthal so obviously some sets will be located in this area. Like the 4023s each set just has one number. It is reported that a batch of these units is likely to be allocated to Innbruck and will take over from 1144s and DB 111s on local services to Rosenheim etc. Bludenz is also to receive 11 sets.

BDhET (DMSO–TSO–TSO–DMSO).

Built: 1960.
Builder – Mech Parts: Bombardier, Aachen.
Builder – Elec. Parts: Elin.
Traction Motors: 4 x 250 kW.
Accommodation: –/38 (16) + –/48 –/48 + –/40 (9) 1W 1TD.
Wheel Arrangement: Bo-2-2-2-Bo.
Weight: 93.5 tonnes.
Length over Couplers: 52.12 m.
Maximum Speed: 140 km/h.

4024 001-2	**R**	GZ	4024 047-5	**R**	4024 092-1	**R**
4024 002-0	**R**	GZ	4024 048-3	**R**	4024 093-9	**R**
4024 003-8	**R**	GZ	4024 049-1	**R**	4024 094-7	**R**
4024 004-6	**R**	GZ	4024 050-9	**R**	4024 095-4	**R**
4024 005-3	**R**	GZ	4024 051-7	**R**	4024 096-2	**R**
4024 006-1	**R**	GZ	4024 052-5	**R**	4024 097-0	**R**
4024 007-9	**R**	FD	4024 053-3	**R**	4024 098-8	**R**
4024 008-7	**R**	WW	4024 054-1	**R**	4024 099-6	**R**
4024 009-5	**R**	WW	4024 055-8	**R**	4024 100-2	**R**
4024 010-3	**R**	WW	4024 056-6	**R**	4024 101-0	**R**
4024 011-1	**R**	WW	4024 057-4	**R**	4024 102-8	**R**
4024 012-9	**R**	WW	4024 058-2	**R**	4024 103-6	**R**
4024 013-7	**R**	WW	4024 059-0	**R**	4024 104-4	**R**
4024 014-5	**R**	WW	4024 060-8	**R**	4024 105-1	**R**
4024 015-2	**R**	FD	4024 061-6	**R**	4024 106-9	**R**
4024 016-0	**R**	WW	4024 062-4	**R**	4024 107-7	**R**
4024 017-8	**R**	WW	4024 063-2	**R**	4024 108-5	**R**
4024 018-6	**R**	FD	4024 064-0	**R**	4024 109-3	**R**
4024 019-4	**R**	SB	4024 065-7	**R**	4024 110-1	**R**
4024 020-2	**R**	SB	4024 066-5	**R**	4024 111-9	**R**
4024 021-0	**R**	FD	4024 067-3	**R**	4024 112-7	**R**
4024 022-8	**R**	FD	4024 068-1	**R**	4024 113-5	**R**
4024 023-6	**R**	FD	4024 069-9	**R**	4024 114-3	**R**
4024 024-4	**R**	FD	4024 070-7	**R**	4024 115-0	**R**
4024 025-1	**R**	FD	4024 071-5	**R**	4024 116-8	**R**
4024 026-9	**R**	FD	4024 072-3	**R**	4024 117-6	**R**
4024 027-7	**R**	FD	4024 073-1	**R**	4024 118-4	**R**
4024 028-5	**R**	FD	4024 074-9	**R**	4024 119-2	**R**
4024 029-3	**R**	SB	4024 075-6	**R**	4024 120-0	**R**
4024 030-1	**R**	FD	4024 076-4	**R**	4024 121-8	**R**
4024 031-9	**R**	FD	4024 077-2	**R**	4024 122-6	**R**
4024 032-7	**R**	FD	4024 078-0	**R**	4024 123-4	**R**
4024 033-5	**R**	FD	4024 079-8	**R**	4024 124-2	**R**
4024 034-3	**R**	FD	4024 080-6	**R**	4024 125-9	**R**
4024 035-0	**R**	BL	4024 081-4	**R**	4024 126-7	**R**
4024 036-8	**R**	BL	4024 082-2	**R**	4024 127-5	**R**
4024 037-6	**R**	FD	4024 083-0	**R**	4024 128-3	**R**
4024 038-4	**R**	FD	4024 084-8	**R**	4024 129-1	**R**
4024 039-2	**R**	FD	4024 085-5	**R**	4024 130-9	**R**
4024 040-0	**R**	FD	4024 086-3	**R**	4024 131-7	**R**
4024 041-8	**R**		4024 087-1	**R**	4024 132-5	**R**
4024 042-6	**R**		4024 088-9	**R**	4024 133-3	**R**
4024 043-4	**R**		4024 089-7	**R**	4024 134-1	**R**
4024 044-2	**R**		4024 090-5	**R**	4024 135-8	**R**
4024 045-9	**R**		4024 091-3	**R**	4024 136-6	**R**
4024 046-7	**R**					

CLASS 4124　　　TALENT　　　4-SECTION UNITS

These are to be dual-voltage 4024s to be used in the Wien area on services that run over the frontier into the Czech Republic, Hungary and Slovakia where the lines are electrified at 25 kV AC. Full details not yet available.

4124 001-1 **R**	4124 009-4 **R**	4124 017-7 **R**
4124 002-9 **R**	4124 010-2 **R**	4124 018-5 **R**
4124 003-7 **R**	4124 011-0 **R**	4124 019-3 **R**
4124 004-5 **R**	4124 012-8 **R**	4124 020-1 **R**
4124 005-2 **R**	4124 013-6 **R**	4124 021-9 **R**
4124 006-0 **R**	4124 014-4 **R**	4124 022-7 **R**
4124 007-8 **R**	4124 015-1 **R**	4124 023-5 **R**
4124 008-6 **R**	4124 016-9 **R**	4124 024-3 **R**

CLASS 4090　　　MARIAZELLERBAHN 3/4-CAR UNITS

Two new units were built in 1994 for this 760 mm narrow gauge line.

4090 001: B4hET + B4hTl + B4hTl + B4hET (DMBSO–TSO–TSO–DMBSO).
4090 003: B4hET + B4hTl + B4hES (DMBSO–TSO–DTSO).

Built: 1994.
Builder – Mech Parts: SGP.
Builder – Elec. Parts: Elin.
Traction Motors: 4 x 330 kW three phase.
Accommodation: –/40 1T + –/56 (+–/56) + –/40 1T.
Wheel Arrangement: Bo-Bo + 2-2 (+ 2-2) + 2-2.
Weight: 36 + 28 (+28) + 36 or 23 tonnes.
Length over Couplers: 17.30 + 16.30 (+ 16.30) + 17.30 m.
Maximum Speed: 70 km/h.

Non-Standard Livery: N White with red bands at solebar and cantrail level.

4090 001-1	7090 001-4	7090 002-2	4090 002-9	**N**	SP
4090 003-7	7090 003-0		6090 001-6	**N**	SP

1.4. DIESEL RAILCARS

CLASS 5022 DESIRO 2-SECTION ARTICULATED DMUS

Whilst Bombardier has supplied new EMUs it is the Siemens "Desiro" DMU that has been purchased for non-electrified lines. 20 sets are on order which are likely to be allocated to Linz (4 sets for the Urfahr services) and Graz (16 sets for Graz–Fehring–Wiener Neustadt route).

BDVT (DMBSO).

Built: 2004 onwards.
Builder: Siemens, Krefeld.
Wheel Arrangement: B-(2)-B.
Engine: Two MTU engines of 315 kW.
Transmission: Hydrodynamic.

Weight: 70.7 tonnes.
Length over Couplers: 20.850 + 20.850 m.
Floor height: 575/1250 mm.
Maximum Speed: 120 km/h.
Accommodation: –/41 (10) 1W 1TD + –/66.

5022 001-1	**R**	GZ	5022 021-9 **R**	5022 041-7	**R**
5022 002-9	**R**	GZ	5022 022-7 **R**	5022 042-5	**R**
5022 003-7	**R**	GZ	5022 023-5 **R**	5022 043-3	**R**
5022 004-5	**R**	GZ	5022 024-3 **R**	5022 044-1	**R**
5022 005-2	**R**	LZ	5022 025-0 **R**	5022 045-8	**R**
5022 006-0	**R**	GZ	5022 026-8 **R**	5022 046-6	**R**
5022 007-8	**R**	GZ	5022 027-6 **R**	5022 047-4	**R**
5022 008-6	**R**	GZ	5022 028-4 **R**	5022 048-2	**R**
5022 009-4	**R**	GZ	5022 029-2 **R**	5022 049-0	**R**
5022 010-2	**R**	GZ	5022 030-0 **R**	5022 050-8	**R**
5022 011-0	**R**	LZ	5022 031-8 **R**	5022 051-6	**R**
5022 012-8	**R**	GZ	5022 032-6 **R**	5022 052-4	**R**
5022 013-6	**R**	GZ	5022 033-4 **R**	5022 053-2	**R**
5022 014-4	**R**	GZ	5022 034-2 **R**	5022 054-0	**R**
5022 015-1	**R**	GZ	5022 035-9 **R**	5022 055-7	**R**
5022 016-9	**R**	LZ	5022 036-7 **R**	5022 056-5	**R**
5022 017-7	**R**	GZ	5022 037-5 **R**	5022 057-3	**R**
5022 018-5	**R**	LZ	5022 038-3 **R**	5022 058-1	**R**
5022 019-3	**R**	GZ	5022 039-1 **R**	5022 059-9	**R**
5022 020-1	**R**	GZ	5022 040-9 **R**	5022 060-7	**R**

CLASS 5047 SINGLE UNITS

Branch line closures and service adjustments have seen these single unit DMUs redistributed in recent years. The workings now covered are as follows:

KR: Krems–Sigmundsherberg, Schwarzenau area, St. Pölten area etc.
VH: Villach–Rosenbach–Klagenfurt; Villach–Kötschach Mauthen.
NS: The various branches around Wiener Neustadt.
GZ: Spielfeld Strass–Bad Radkersburg.
WO: Branches to north and east of Wien
WE: Branches around Ried im Innkreis; Wels–Grunau; Linz Urfahr–Aigen Schlägl, St. Valentin–Nikola Struden.

BD4VT (DMBSO).

Built: 1987–95.
Builder: JW.
Wheel Arrangement: B-2.
Engine: Daimler Benz OM444LA 419 kW.
Transmission: Hydraulic.
Accommodation: –/62 (6) 1T.

Weight: 43.7 tonnes.
Length over Buffers: 25.42 m.
Maximum Speed: 120 km/h.

5047 001-2	**C**	KR	5047 009-5	**C**	KR	5047 017-8	**C**	KR
5047 002-0	**C**	KR	5047 010-3	**C**	KR	5047 018-6	**C**	KR
5047 003-8	**R**	KR	5047 011-1	**C**	VH	5047 019-4	**C**	KR
5047 004-6	**R**	KR	5047 012-9	**C**	KR	5047 020-2	**C**	KR
5047 005-3	**C**	KR	5047 013-7	**C**	KR	5047 021-0	**C**	KR
5047 006-1	**C**	KR	5047 014-5	**C**	KR	5047 022-8	**C**	KR
5047 007-9	**C**	KR	5047 015-2	**C**	KR	5047 023-6	**C**	KR
5047 008-7	**C**	KR	5047 016-0	**C**	KR	5047 024-4	**C**	VH

5047 025-1	C	KR	5047 051-7	C	WO	5047 076-4	C	WE
5047 026-9	C	KR	5047 052-5	C	WO	5047 077-2	C	WE
5047 027-7	C	VH	5047 053-3	C	WO	5047 078-0	C	WE
5047 028-5	C	VH	5047 054-1	C	WO	5047 079-8	C	WE
5047 029-3	C	NS	5047 055-8	C	WO	5047 080-6	C	WE
5047 030-1	C	NS	5047 056-6	C	WO	5047 081-4	C	WE
5047 031-9	C	NS	5047 057-4	C	WO	5047 082-2	C	WE
5047 032-7	C	NS	5047 058-2	C	WO	5047 083-0	C	WE
5047 033-5	C	VH	5047 059-0	C	WO	5047 084-8	C	WE
5047 034-3	C	NS	5047 060-8	C	KR	5047 085-5	C	NS
5047 035-0	C	NS	5047 061-6	C	WE	5047 086-3	C	NS
5047 036-8	C	NS	5047 062-4	C	WE	5047 087-1	C	WE
5047 037-6	C	GZ	5047 063-2	C	WE	5047 088-9	C	NS
5047 038-4	C	GZ	5047 064-0	C	WE	5047 089-7	C	NS
5047 039-2	C	KR	5047 065-7	C	WE	5047 090-5	R	NS
5047 040-0	C	KR	5047 066-5	C	WE	5047 091-3	C	NS
5047 041-8	C	KR	5047 067-3	C	WE	5047 092-1	C	NS
5047 042-6	C	NS	5047 068-1	C	WE	5047 093-9	C	NS
5047 043-4	C	NS	5047 069-9	C	WE	5047 094-7	C	NS
5047 044-2	C	VH	5047 070-7	C	WE	5047 095-4	C	NS
5047 045-9	C	VH	5047 071-5	C	WE	5047 096-2	C	NS
5047 046-7	C	VH	5047 072-3	C	WE	5047 097-0	C	NS
5047 047-5	C	NS	5047 073-1	C	WE	5047 098-8	C	NS
5047 048-3	C	WO	5047 074-9	C	WE	5047 099-6	C	NS
5047 049-1	C	WO	5047 075-6	C	WE	5047 100-2	C	WE
5047 050-9	C	WO						

Name: 5047 090-5 Manfred.

CLASS 5147   2-CAR UNITS

This is a two-car version of 5047 for use on local services around Wiener Neustadt and the Aspangbahn to Wien.

BD4VT (DMBSO).

Built: 1992.
Builder: JW.
Wheel Arrangement: B-2.
Engine: Daimler Benz OM444LA 419 kW.
Transmission: Hydraulic.

Weight: 43.7 tonnes.
Length over Buffers: 25.42 m.
Maximum Speed: 120 km/h.
Accommodation: –/62 (6) 1T.

5147 001-1	C	NS	5147 005-2	C	NS	5147 008-6	C	NS
5147 002-9	C	NS	5147 006-0	C	NS	5147 009-4	C	NS
5147 003-7	C	NS	5147 007-8	C	NS	5147 010-2	C	NS
5147 004-5	C	NS						

CLASS 5090   SINGLE UNITS

Single cars based on the VT30 design of the Steiermärkische Landesbahnen.

B4VT (DMSO).

Built: 1986.
Builder: Knotz.
Engine: 188 kW.
Accommodation: –/62.
Weight: 31.5 tonnes.

Gauge: 760 mm.
Wheel Arrangement: Bo-Bo.
Transmission: Electric.
Length over Couplings: 18.30 m.
Max. Speed: 70 km/h.

Non-Standard Livery: N 5090 001-8 and 5090 008-3 are in all over red.

5090 001-8	N	ZS	5090 007-5	C	ZS	5090 013-3	C	WH
5090 002-6	C	ZS	5090 008-3	N	ZS	5090 014-1	C	SP
5090 003-4	C	ZS	5090 009-1	C	WH	5090 015-8	C	SP
5090 004-2	C	SP	5090 010-9	C	WH	5090 016-6	C	SP
5090 005-9	C	SP	5090 011-7	C	WH	5090 017-4	C	SP
5090 006-7	C	ZS	5090 012-5	C	WH			

Name: 5090 015-8 RUPRECHTSHOFEN

1.5. NOSTALGIC FLEET

In the run up to the 150th Anniversary of railways in Austria which took place in 1987, ÖBB restored some of its older locomotives and railcars to original condition. Many of these were then still in capital stock. Since that time ÖBB has recognised the value of its restored stock and these locomotives and railcars having been withdrawn from normal service are now kept at dedicated depots for public excursions under the Nostalgic theme. ÖBB Nostalgie is part of ÖBB Personenverkehr AG being the GE Erlebnisbahn section. For convenience the ÖBB narrow gauge rack locos and railcars are included in this section.

STEAM LOCOMOTIVES

CLASS 52   2-10-0

By 1987 ÖBB had already sold out of service all its remaining Class 52s. A few years ago an opportunity arose to purchase a former Jugoslavian Class 33 at scrap price and overhaul it to working order. The overhaul was done at Knittelfeld works and it is believed the locomotive will normally be based in Steiermark.

Built: 1944.
Builder: MBA.
Driving Wheel Diameter: 1400
Length over Buffers: 22.975 m
Maximum Speed: 80 km/h.

Boiler Pressure: 1.38 MN/sq. m. (227 lb/sq.in).
Weight: 84.0 tonnes
Tractive Effort:
Cylinders: (2) 600 x 660.

52.4984   KD (ex JZ 33-227)

CLASS 298.2   0-6-2T

This two cylinder compound locomotive is the last of a class of three built for the Niederösterreichischen Landesbahnen (NÖLB) for use on the line from St. Pölten to Mariazell. It was based at Gmünd for many years for use on the narrow gauge network there, but has now returned to home territory.

Built: 1905.
Builder: Krauss, Linz.
Gauge: 760 mm.
Driving Wheel Diameter: 800 mm.
Length over Couplings: 7.804 m.

Boiler Pressure: 1.28 MN/sq. m. (185 lb/sq.in).
Weight: 27.5 tonnes.
Tractive Effort: 76.5 kN (17200lbf).
Cylinders: (2) 320 x 400 mm, 500 x 400 mm.
Maximum Speed: 35 km/h.

298.207   OG |

CLASS 399   0-8+4

ÖBB has transferred five locos of Class 399 to the Nostalgic fleet and promptly loaned them to supporting societies in their respective areas.

Built: 1906–08.
Builder: Krauss, Linz.
Gauge:760 mm.
Driving Wheel Diameter: 900 mm.
Length Over Couplings: 11.665 m

Boiler Pressure: 1.28 MN/sq.m. (185 lb/sq.in).
Weight: 45.1 tonnes
Tractive Effort: 80.4 kN (18080 lbf).
Cylinders: 410 x 450 mm.
Maximum Speed: 40 km/h.

399.01	ZS	399.03	GM	399.06	OG
399.02	GM (Z)	399.04	GM (Z)		

CLASS 0999.1   0-4-2RT

This class was built for the Schafbergbahn, but one now operates on the Schneebergbahn (p.91).

Built: 1896*–1900.
Builder: Krauss, Linz.
Boiler Pressure: 1.38 MN/m² (200 lb/sq.in).
Driving Wheel Diameter: 706 mm.
Rack Wheel Diameter: 575 mm.
Trailing Wheel Diameter: 520 mm.
Max. Speed: 12 km/h.
Non-standard liveries: N 0999 102/5 blue, 0999 104/6 green.

Gauge: 1000 mm.
System: Abt rack.
Cylinders (2): 320 x 600 mm.
Weight: 17.4 tonnes.
Length: 5.50 m.
Tractive Effort – Adhesion: 89.2 kN (20070 lbf).
Tractive Effort – Rack: 110.6 kN (24700 lbf).

0999 102-7	N	PB	Enzian
0999 103-5		PB	Erika
0999 104-3	N	PB	Bergprimel

0999 105-0	N	PB	Almrausch
0999 106-8	N	PB	Berganemone

CLASS 0999.2   0-4-2RT

This is a new design of oil-fired one man operated loco.

Built: 1991, 1995–.
Builder: SLM Wintertur.
Boiler Pressure: .
Driving Wheel Diameter: 705 mm.
Rack Wheel Diameter: .
Trailing Wheel Diameter: .
Max. Speed: .

Gauge: 1000 mm.
System: Abt rack.
Cylinders – Adhesion: (2) 320 x 440 mm.
– Rack: (2) 280 x 400 mm.
Weight: 17.4 tonnes.
Length: 5.50 m.

0999 201-7	PB
0999 202-5	PB

0999 203-3	PB
0999 204-1	PB

ELECTRIC LOCOMOTIVES

CLASS 1010   Co-Co

These main line locos were made surplus by the arrival of the Taurus fleet. ÖBB has retained some for use on its nostalgic trains whilst others have gone to preservation groups.

Built: 1955–58.
Builder – Mech. Parts: SGP.
Builder – Elec. Parts: BBC/Siemens/Elin.
One Hour Rating: 4000 kW.
Maximum Tractive Effort: 275 kN.
Wheel Diameter: 1300 mm.

Weight: 106 tonnes
Length over Buffers: 16.92 m.
Maximum Speed: 130 km/h.

1010 003	WN		1010 010	WN	

CLASS 1110   Co-Co

This class was the mountain 1010 with the 1110.5 version having rheostatic braking. All were rendered surplus by the arrival of the Taurus fleet, being withdrawn in 2004.

Built: 1956–60.
Builder – Mech. Parts: SGP.
Builder – Elec. Parts: BBC/Siemens/Elin.
One Hour Rating: 4000 kW.
Maximum Tractive Effort: 275 kN.
Wheel Diameter: 1300 mm.

Weight: 106 tonnes
Length over Buffers: 17.86 m.
Maximum Speed: 110 km/h.

1110 015		KD		1110 505	G	IN		1110 530		BL

CLASS 1018   1-Do-1

The 1018s were built in Austria during wartime as DRB E18 201–208. The class ended up working from Linz. The preserved loco is stored as it needs new wheelsets.

Built: 1939.
Builder – Mech. Parts: Floridsdorf.
Builder – Elec. Parts: AEG/Siemens.
One Hour Rating: 3340 kW.
Maximum Tractive Effort: 196 kN.
Driving Wheel Diameter: 1600 mm.

Weight: 110 tonnes
Length over Buffers: 16.92 m.
Maximum Speed: 80 km/h.

1018.05	G	WN

CLASS 1020   Co-Co

These locomotives are former DRB locos left in Austria after World War II or built there later. Towards the end of their lives they were allocated to Innsbruck, Bludenz and Salzburg. Normal operation of this class ceased in 1995 when the last of the 1044s entered service. A few have been retained for special trains.

Built: 1940–44.
Builder – Mech Parts: Kraus-Maffei/AEG.
Builder – Elec Parts: Siemens/AEG.
One Hour Rating: 3300 kW
Maximum Tractive Effort: 314 kN.
Wheel Diameter: 1250 m.

Weight: 118.5 tonnes
Length over Buffers: 18.60 m.
Maximum Speed: 90 km/h.

Former DRB numbers in parentheses.

1020.44	(E94.156)	**G**	IN	1020.47	**G**	FD

CLASS 1040   Bo+Bo

The 1040s were the first of the post-war electric locos and in effect folowed on from the pre-war designs being a development of the 1245 series. Latterly the class was used on local freight trips based on Selzthal which depot keeps one for nostalgic trains.

Built: 1950–52.
Builder – Mech. Parts: Floridsdorf.
Builder – Elec. Parts: Elin.
One Hour Rating: 2340 kW
Maximum Tractive Effort: 196 kN.
Wheel Diameter: 1350 mm.

Weight: 80 tonnes.
Length over Buffers: 12.92 m.
Maximum Speed: 90 km/h.

1040.01	**G**	SL	1040.09	Sigmundsherberg

CLASS 1041   Bo-Bo

This 1950s design was the follow-on from the 1040 and was latterly based at Attnang-Puchheim. This is yet another class pushed out of the way by the Taurus fleet.

Built: 1952–54.
Builder – Mech. Parts: SGP.
Builder– Elec. Parts: Siemens/BBC/AEG.
One Hour Rating: 2360 kW.
Maximum Tractive Effort: 196 kN.
Wheel Diameter: 1350 mm.

Weight: 83.8 tonnes.
Length over Buffers: 15.32 m.
Maximum Speed: 80 (100*) km/h.

1041.202   SL

CLASS 1141   Bo-Bo

A development of Class 1041 with similar duties.

Built: 1955–57.
Builder – Mech. Parts: Floridsdorf.
Builder – Elec. Parts: Siemens/AEG/Elin.
One Hour Rating: 2480 kW.
Maximum Tractive Effort: 196 kN.
Wheel Diameter: 1300 mm.

Weight: 83 tonnes.
Length over Buffers: 15.26 m.
Maximum Speed: 110 km/h.

1141 022	WN	1141 024	WN

CLASS 1045   Bo+Bo

A very early bogie locomotive which ended its days on local freight trips from Attnang-Puchheim where it is still based. Other locos survive on the Montafonerbahn.

Built: 1927–28.
Builder – Mech. Parts: Wiener Neustadt/Floridsdorf.
Builder – Elec. Parts: Elin.
One Hour Rating: 1140 kW.
Maximum Tractive Effort: 150 kN.
Wheel Diameter: 1300 mm.

Weight: 61.2 tonnes.
Length over Buffers: 10.40 m.
Maximum Speed: 60 km/h.

1045.09   **G**   AT

CLASS 1145   Bo+Bo

A development of Class 1045 the locos were last used in the Tirol but the preserved example has emigrated to Wien.

Built: 1927–31.
Builder – Mech. Parts: Floridsdorf/Krauss.
Builder – Elec. Parts: Elin.
One Hour Rating: 1200 kW   **Weight:** 70.6 tonnes
Maximum Tractive Effort: 175 kN.   **Length over Buffers:** 11.88 m.
Wheel Diameter: 1300 mm.   **Maximum Speed:** 70 km/h.
Electric Braking: Rheostatic.

1145.02   **G**   WS

CLASS 1245   Bo+Bo

A development of the Classes 1045 and 1145 latterly used on freight trip workings in Steiermark. 1245.525 finds regular employment ferrying vehicles from and to Knittelfeld Works.

Built: 1934 (1245.0), 1939–40 (1245.5).
Builder – Mech. Parts: Floridsdorf.
Builder – Elec. Parts: BBC/Elin/Siemens Wien/AEG.
One Hour Rating: 1840 kW   **Weight:** 83 tonnes
Maximum Tractive Effort: 196 kN.   **Length over Buffers:** 12.92 m.
Wheel Diameter: 1350 mm.   **Maximum Speed:** 80 km/h.
Electric Braking: Rheostatic.

1245.04   **G**   SA | 1245.05   **G**   SL | 1245 525   KD

CLASS 1046/4061   Bo-Bo

This original classification for this class was 4061 refelecting the fact that the locomotives had a luggage compartment and were basically motor luggage vans, i.e. EMU stock. They were reclassified as locomotives and became Class 1046, the luggage compartment eventually being removed. Some locos were rebuilt in the 1970s and 1980s with new bodies.

Built: 1956–59.
Builder – Mech. Parts: SGP/Floridsdorf.
Builder – Elec. Parts: Elin/AEG/Siemens.
One Hour Rating: 1600 kW   **Weight:** 67 tonnes
Maximum Tractive Effort: 118 kN.   **Length over Buffers:** 16.17 m.
Wheel Diameter: 1040 mm.   **Maximum Speed:** 125 km/h.

1046.019   WN | 4061.13   WN

CLASS 1062   C

These locomotives shunted the various stations and yards around Wien. One has been retained by ÖBB Nostalgie and is supposed to be active.

Built: 1955.
Builder – Mech. Parts: Floridsdorf.
Builder – Elec. Parts: AEG/Siemens.
One Hour Rating: 660 kW.   **Weight:** 68 tonnes.
Maximum Tractive Effort: 186 kN.   **Length over Buffers:** 10.82 m.
Wheel Diameter: 1140 mm.   **Maximum Speed:** 50 km/h.

1062.07   **G**   WN |

CLASS 1670   1A-Bo-A1

Built for the Salzburg–Innsbruck electrification these locos were always in the Tirol and Vorarlberg areas apart from an odd sortie to the Linz and Wien area. The class had gone from normal service by 1983.

Built: 1928–32.
Builder – Mech. Parts: Krauss (Linz), Floridsdorf.
Builder – Elec. Parts: Siemens.
One Hour Rating: 2350 kW.   **Weight:** 107/112* tonnes.
Maximum Tractive Effort: **Length over Buffers:** 14.46/14.68* m
Driving Wheel Diameter: 1350 mm.   **Maximum Speed:** 100 km/h.

| 1670.09 | **G** | SA | | 1670.25 | **G** | WN | | 1670.104 | **G** | * | BL |

CLASS 1072   1-B-1

Built for the Eisenbahn Wien–Pressburg (Bratislava) these locos remained working fron Wien to Wolfsthal right up to their withdrawal in the early 1970s. The preserved example still gets used on its old line from time to time.

Built: 1913.
Builder: Graz/AEG.
One Hour Rating: 600 kW.   **Weight:** 56.0 tonnes.
Maximum Tractive Effort: **Length over Buffers:** 10.526 m.
Driving Wheel Diameter: 1034 mm.   **Maximum Speed:** 60 km/h.

1072.01   **G**   WN

CLASS 1080   E

This class was built for the Arlberg electrification but in later days was well spread about the electrified areas ending up at Selzthal and Attnang Puchheim.

Built: 1924.
Builder – Mech Parts: Krauss, Linz.
Builder – Elec Parts: Siemens, Wien.
One Hour Rating: 1020 kW.   **Weight:** 77 tonnes.
Maximum Tractive Effort: 189 kN   **Length over Buffers:** 12.75 m.
Wheel Diameter: 1350 mm.   **Maximum Speed:** 50 km/h.

1080.01   **G**   SL

CLASS 1180   E

A more powerful 1080 also built for the Arlberg line where they stayed for most of their life.

Built: 1927.
Builder – Mech. Parts: Krauss, Linz.
Builder – Elec. Parts: Siemens-Wien.
One Hour Rating: 1300 kW.   **Weight:** 80.5 tonnes.
Maximum Tractive Effort: 197 kN   **Length over Buffers:** 12.75 m.
Wheel Diameter: 1350 mm.   **Maximum Speed:** 50 km/h.

1180.09   **G**   BL

CLASS 1189   1C + C1

Built 1926/7 for the Arlberg line but by the 1940s they had started to drift away to Salzburg and Attnang Puchheim. This latter shed was their last active depot being there from 1969 until withdrawal in the late 1970s. 1189.02 carries its BBÖ number 1100.102.

Built: 1926–27.
Builder – Mech. Parts: Floridsdorf.
Builder – Elec. Parts: BBC.
One Hour Rating: 1900 kW.   **Weight:** 118 tonnes.
Maximum Tractive Effort: **Length over Buffers:** 20350 m.
Driving Wheel Diameter: 1350 mm.   **Maximum Speed:** 75 km/h.

1189.02   (1100.102) **G**   WN

DIESEL LOCOMOTIVES

CLASS 2045   Bo-Bo

The first main line diesel loco all were latterly used on branch lines or as trip and shunt locos from their base at Krems where the preserved example remains.

Built: 1952–55.
Builder – Mech Parts: Simmering-Graz-Pauker.
Engine: SGP S12a of 760 kW (1020 h.p.)
Maximum Tractive Effort: 152 kN.
Driving Wheel Diameter: 960 mm.
Train Heating: Steam

Transmisson: Electric. Brown-Boveri.
Weight: 70.3 tonnes.
Length over Buffers: 14.80 m.
Maximum Speed.: 80 km/h.

2045. 020 **G**   KR

CLASS 2050   Bo-Bo

Locomotives of this class were all taken out of service towards the end of 2004 but the following have been retained for excursion trains.

Built: 1958–62.
Builder – Mech Parts: Henschel.
Engine: GM 567C of 1050 kW (1408 h.p.).
Maximum Tractive Effort: 179 kN.
Driving Wheel Diameter: 1040 mm.
Maximum Speed: 100 km/h.

Transmission: Electric.
Weight: 74.9 tonnes.
Length over Buffers: 17.76 m.
Train Heating: Electric (2050 002-1 only).

2050.02   **G**   WO | 2050 .04   **G**   Sigmundsherberg | 2050.09   **O**   WO

CLASS 2091   1-Bo-1

ÖBB has retained these two locomotives for use with Nostalgia trains at Gmünd and Waidhofen. Other examples have been preserved by preservation groups.

Built: 1936–40.
Builder: Simmering.
Engine: Simmering R8 of 155 kW (208 h.p.).
Gauge: 760 mm.
Maximum Tractive Effort: 34 kN.
Driving Wheel Diameter: 820 mm.

Transmission: Electric. Siemens.
Weight: 23.2 tonnes.
Length over Buffers: 10.80 m.
Maximum Speed: 50 km/h.

2091.07   GM | 2091.09   WH |

CLASS 2092   C

Previously station shunters, ÖBB has retained one at Obergrafendorf for such duties.

Built: 1943–44.
Builder: Windhoff.
Gauge: 760 mm.
Maximum Tractive Effort: 49 kN.
Driving Wheel Diameter: 700 mm.

Engine: Deutz 6 M517 of 100 kW (134 h.p.)
Transmission: Hydraulic.
Weight: 16.5 tonnes.
Length over Buffers: 5.325 m.
Maximum Speed: 25 km/h.

2092 .04   OG

ELECTRIC RAILCARS

CLASS 4041   Bo-2

These early electric railcars were built for the Arlberg line and most stayed all their life on home territory. All were withdrawn by the mid-1970s but several were retained as heating units or even shunt engines in the main works at Floridsdorf. Two Innsbruck units, 4041.01/05 fell into disuse and are now part of the Strasshof collection.

Built: 1929.
Builder – Mech Parts: Krauss (Linz).
Builder – Elec Parts: Elin.

Traction Motors: (410 kW)
Maximum Speed: 80 km/h.
Weight: 77.8 tonnes.

4041.03   FD

DIESEL RAILCARS/MULTIPLE UNITS
CLASS 5042   1A-A1

Introduced in 1935 these units were first used on fast connections between Wien and Graz, Villach, etc. After the war some were used on the Villach–Innsbruck corridor trains before all gathered in the Wien area for use on the branch lines to the north of the city. The survivor was restored in time for the 1987 celebrations.

Built: 1937.
Builder: Simmering.
Engine: Two Simmering R8 of 155 kW.
Seats: –/78 1T.
Weight: 56.8 tonnes.

Transmisson: Electric.
Length over Buffers: 22.44 m.
Maximum Speed.: 110 km/h.

5042.14   WN

CLASS 5145   B-2

These units were built for long-distance services and in their day worked such trains as the "Vindabona" and "Venezia". Latterly they were in use on branch lines in the Wien area. Staff at Wien Ost have taken great pride in restoring some cars to original condition.

Built: 1952–7.
Builder: Simmering.
Engine: SGP S 12a of 400 kW.
Transmisson: Hydraulic.

Maximum Speed.: 115 km/h.

Class 5145. BD4VT (DMBSO). Accommodation: –/56 1T. Weight: 47.3 tonnes. Length: 21.85 m.

| 5145 001-3 | WO | 5145 011-2 | WO | 5145 014-6 | WO |

Class 6545. BV4S (DTSO). Accommodation: –/80 1T. Weight: 28.2 tonnes. Length: 21.85 m.

6545 012-4   WO |

Class 6645. BV4S (DTSO). Accommodation: –/64 1T. Weight: 28.9 tonnes. Length: 21.85 m.

6645 002-4   WO |

Class 7645. AB4TI (CK). Accommodation: 30/31 1T. Weight: 28.0 tonnes. Length: 21.80 m.

7645 002-2   WO |

Class 6645. BV4S (DTSO). Accommodation: –/? 1T. Weight: 3409 tonnes. Length: 23.81 m.

7845 002-0   WO |

Now rebuilt as bar coach 80 81 97-32 941-6 (Blitz Express bar "Joanna")

CLASS 5099   2-B

These work exclusively on the Schafbergbahn.

Built: 1964.
Builder: SGP.
Engine: SGP S8 of 330 kW.
Transmisson: Hydraulic.
Maximum Speed: 12 km/h (rack), 20 km/h (adhesion).
Accommodation: –/78.

Gauge: 1000 mm.
System: Abt rack.
Weight: 32.9 tonnes.
Length over couplings: 14.89 m.

5099 001-9 **D** SW | 5099 002-7 **D** SW

▲ Class 1063 are used for shunting and trip working all over Austria. 1063 033-3 is seen at Wien Süd on 30 June 2003. **Horace Gamble**

▼ Class 1163 is the dual-voltage version of the 1063. The locos are painted in a distinctive non-standard orange and white livery. 1163 012-6 is seen shunting at Gmunden on 27 April 2004. **W.J. Freebury**

▲ Class 1822 consists of 15 kV AC/3000 V DC locos for working through Italy between Brennero and Lienz. They will be superceded by Class 1216. 1822 004-6 is seen at Steinach-in-Tirol with the 10.01 Innsbruck–Lienz on 22 July 2004.

▼ The sixteen 760 mm gauge locos of Class 1099 are now all over 90 years old, but still soldier on on the Mariazellerbahn. 1099 014-1 is seen at Laubenbachmühle with the 16.06 to St. Pölten on 19 July 2004.   **Brian Denton (2)**

▲ The two diesel-hydraulic Classes 2043 and 2143 are now being superceded by Class 2016. 2043 034-4 is seen at Linz Urfahr ready to head east with a freight on 1 May 2005.   **W.J. Freebury**

▼ Wien Ost depot on 13 February 2005. 2143 028-5 on the left is in standard livery whilst 2143.035 on the right has been restored to original blood orange livery.   **Brian Garvin**

▲ Class 2067 are small SGP shunters built between 1959 and 1977. 2067 061-8 iz seen on station pilot duties at Innsbruck Hbf on 21 July 2004.

▼ Class 2068 are more powerful diesel-hydraulic locos for shunting and trip work built in 1989. 2068 025-2 is seen on pilot duty at Wiener Neustadt. **Brian Denton (2)**

▲ Class 2070 from MaK are the latest loco for shunting and trip work built 2001–2004. 2070 044-9 is seen at Wien Westbf on 19 September 2003. **Dr. Iain C. Scotchman**

▼ ÖBB's standard 760 mm-gauge diesel loco is the Class 2095. 2095 015-0 is seen at St. Pölten Alpenbf on 19 July 2004. **Brian Denton**

Class 4010 were at one time ÖBB's prestige InterCity units, but some have now been withdrawn and all but two of the others have lost their restaurant cars. They are mainly used on secondary InterCity services. Set 4010 020-8 is seen behind Graz Hbf on 19 July 2005. **Peter Fox**

▲ Class 4020 are suburban EMUs mainly employed in the Wien area, but a dozen of them work local services in the Tirol and are allocated to Bludenz. 4020 103-0 is seen at Innsbruck on 19 September 2001 in S-Bahn livery with the 14.59 to Mittenwald. This unit is now at Floridsdorf and has been renumbered.   **Ian G. Feather**

▼ This class is now appearing in the standard local train livery of grey with red ends and white doors. Set 4020 296 is seen on the 17.12 Wien Westbf–Tullnerbach Pressbaum entering Wien Hütteldorf on 29 June 2005.   **Brian Garvin**

▲ The lastest EMUs are Bombardier "Talent" units and are built as both three-section (Class 4023) and four-section (Class 4024) units. 4024 010-3 is seen stabled for driver training at Wien Ostbf on 13 February 2005.

▼ Two EMUs of Class 4090 were built as prototypes for the 760 mm gauge Mariazellerbahn, but have not proved successful and no more were ordered. Power car 4090 003-7 awaits attention at St. Pölten works on 29 June 2005.   **Brian Garvin (2)**

▲ The latest ÖBB DMUs are Siemens desiros of Class 5022. 5022 009-4 awaits a Steiermärkische Landesbahn working to Weiz at Gleisdorf on 21 July 2005. **Peter Fox**

▶ The 5090 is the standard 760 mm gauge DMU. 5090 006-7 (right) and 5090 008-3 (bottom) are seen at Zell am See on 16 February 2004. 006 is in the standard livery for this class whereas 008 has been painted in all over red. **Ian Futers (2)**

▲ Class 5047 single unit railcar 5047 064-0 approaches Holzleithen with a Ried im Innkreis–Attnang-Puchheim service on 20 October 2004.   **Rail Photoprints**

▼ 5145.11, part of the ÖBB Nostaligic fleet heads a five-car "Blauer Blitz" formation at Wien Ost on 1 July 2005.   **Brian Garvin**

▲ 1020.044 arrives at Jenbach on 21 July 2004 with the 08.20 from Reutte-in-Tirol. **Brian Denton**

▼ 0-8+4T Engerth 399.01 prepares to leave Weitra with a test train to Gross Gerungs on 30 June 2005. The loco had only been outshopped from DB Dampflokwerk Meiningen the previous day! **Brian Garvin**

▲ X 432.001 is a test car for Indusi and LZB cab signalling based at Linz Hbf and is seen at Innsbruck Hbf on 3 August 2004.   **Horace Gamble**

▼ X 521 004 is a 1991-design Plasser two-axle overhead line inspection unit or "motor tower wagon". It is seen at Knittelfeld on 14 February 2005.   **Brian Garvin**

▲ X 552 031-7 is a four-axle Plasser vehicle with seperate cabin and centre platform for rebuilding of overhead line equipment. It is seen at Peggau on 2 February 2004. **Peter Fox**

▼ X 651 003 is a track test car of type EM-SAT 120 and is seen having a break at Knittelfeld shed on 14 February 2005. The red, white and blue livery is known as "Valousek design". **Brian Garvin**

▲ Class 2062 are now classified as Class X 262 as departmental stock. X 262 049-1 is seen shunting at Rosenbach on 2 April 2004.   **Dr. Iain C. Scotchman**

▼ Snowplough 80 81 9760 018-8 from Wörgl has arrived at Knittelfeld Works for attention. Note the wheels. The plough is built on the frame of a Class 52 2-10-0.   **Brian Garvin**

▲ Achenseebahn 0-4-0RT No. 1 "EBEN AM ACHENSEE" at Jenbach with the 09.15 to Achensee on 21 July 2004.   **Ian Futers**

▼ The GySEV Class 1047 is the same as the ÖBB Class 1116. 1047 504-4 is at Villach awaiting to work to Wien Süd on 12 February 2005.   **Brian Garvin**

▲ The GKB's fleet is now gaining full length UIC computer numbers as well as ordinary GKB numbers. DH1700.1 is seen shunting the yard at Graz Köflacher Bahnhof on 20 July 2005.

▼ A GKB 2-car DMU VT70.10 at Preding-Wieselsdorf with the 08.39 Graz–Wies-Eibiswald on 8 February 2005.   **Peter Fox (2)**

1.5. ÖBB DEPARTMENTAL STOCK

Numbering System

Recently details have come to light of the numbering system for departmental stock. The stock is identified by a three digit number preceded by X e.g. X534. The number breaks down as follows:

The hundred digit indicates:

1   Traction
2   Special Traction
3   Not used (originally rail automobiles)
4   Test vehicles
5   Overhead Line Vehicles (Motor Turm Wagen – MTW)
6   Light vehicles for track staff (Motor Bahn Wagen)
7   Draisines
8   Temporary numbers for vehicles on acceptance
9   Private stock

The ten digit indicates:

1   Mechanical transmission
3   Electric transmission

In the case of the 500 series vehicles (MTW) the last digit also details the engine used as follows

0   Vomag 113 hp engine
1   Saurer 118-150 hp engine
2   Oberhansli 100 hp engine
3   SGP G6 115 hp engine
4   Jenbach JW100 engine
5   Deutz engine

In the case of the 600 series vehicles the ten digit is either a 1 or 2 where 1 denotes the vehicle is not fitted with normal buffing gear and 2 indicates that normal buffing gear is fitted. The final digit is also related to engines as follows

0   Daimler 20 hp engine, light duty
1   Daimler 30 hp engine, heavy duty
2   Daimler 45 hp engine, heavy duty
3   Kromag 60 hp engine, heavy duty
4   JW 35 hp engine, heavy duty
5   JW 70 jp engine heavy duty
6   All others

The numbering of the private vehicles was also planned and here the last two digits in the 31-59 series denoted the firm concerned:

931, 941, 951 etc = AEG
932, 942, 952 etc = BBC
933, 943, 953 etc = Elin
934, 944, 954 etc = Siemens

This was the original system from the 1950s but no doubt now modified to cater for new firms (e.g. Balfour Beatty).

The remaining last two digits were grouped as follows:

60-69   Track Machines (Gleisbaumaschinen)
80   Other track machines
81   Road/rail vehicles
85   Road/rail vehicles with crane
86   Road/rail vehicles with digger/bulldozer
90   Trailer vehicle
92   Private MBW
94   Private MBW

Note: Many, but not all departmental vehicles now have computer check digits. These are shown in this section whether the vehicles carry them or not. To work out the check digit, the 'X' is replaced by a zero

HEATING UNITS

These are former locos used as stationary heating units. They cannot be used for traction.

Number	Formerly	Liv.	Location
01102	1280.10	G	MZ 2/05
01109	1073.17	G	Pöchlarn (?)
01111	1046 015		Penzing Yard 2/04
01112	1020 001		Innsbruck West 2/05 (Dumped)
01115	1670 001		bauzug in St. Ruprecht
01116	1670 020		Saalfelden (Not seen 2/05)
01117	1670 021	G	KD 2/05
01121	1670.06		MZ 2/05
01122	1670.26	G	NS 10/97 (Not seen 2/05)
01123	1670.28		Wolfurt 8/98
01124	1670.14		MZ 5/04
01127	1046 018		Bauzug 402
01130	1670.08	G	Kufstein
01132	1080 015		Bruck a.d. Mur (Not seen 2/05)
01133	1161 015		BO 2/05
?	1670.27		HW KD
01134	1245 513		Hohenau
01136	1245 008		Klein Reifling
01137	1146 002		Wulkersprodersdorf
?	1141 019		BO 3/05

Being transformers for carriage heating, the units are found in yards or stations where carriages stable.

SMALL SHUNTERS ('KLEINLOKS')

Computer Number	1957 No.	DRG System	Location	Type	Power (kW)
0170 001-2	(X 170.01)	Ks 4866	TS Floridsdorf	Bo ae	80
0170 002-0	(X 170.02)	Ks 4818	TS Floridsdorf	Bo ae	80

X 200 SERIES. SHUNTING LOCOS

The following sector codes are used in this section:

F	Fahrweg	T	Traktion
N	Netz	TS	Technische Services

X 260   B

These are Class 2060 shunters downgraded for departmental use.

Built: 1954–62.
Builder – Mech Parts: JW.
Engine: JW 200 of 150 kW (200 h.p.).
Transmission: Hydraulic. Voith L33 yUB.
Maximum Tractive Effort: 100 kN.
Wheel Diameter: 950 mm.
Maximum Speed: 60 km/h.

Weight: 27.0 tonnes.
Length over Buffers: 6.68 m.

Number	Sector	Location	Number	Sector	Location
X260 006-2	F	Gramatneusiedl	X260 082-3	T	WO
X260 012-0	TS	HW Linz	X260 086-4	T	WO
X260 013-8	T	LZ	X260 087-2	TS	AT
X260 014-6	F	LZ	X260 089-8	T	KR
X260 015-3	F	LZ Wegsheid	X260 090-6	T	WO
X260 037-7	TS	SB	X260 091-4	T	WO
X260 045-0	T	SL	X260 096-3	TS	WE
X260 051-8	T	LZ	X260 097-1	TS	LZ
X260 056-7	F	Zeltweg	X260 098-9	T	WE
X260 079-9	TS	SP	X260 100-3	T	SL

X 262   B

These are Class 2062 shunters downgraded for departmental use.

Built: 1958–66.
Builder – Mech Parts: JW.
Engine: JW 400 of 300 kW (400 h.p.).
Transmission: Hydraulic. Voith L26 St/A 100 KV.
Maximum Tractive Effort: 120 kN.   **Weight:** 32.3 tonnes.
Wheel Diameter: 950 mm.   **Length over Buffers:** 7.92 m.
Maximum Speed: 60 km/h.

Number	Sector	Location	Number	Sector	Location
X262 002-9	T	VH	X262 033-4	T	SP
X262 005-5	T	WE	X262 035-9	N	Mallnitz Obervellach
X262 006-0	T	SL	X262 036-7	T	SP
X262 008-6	T	KD	X262 047-4	T	VH
X262 009-4	N	Kolbnitz	X262 049-0	N	Rosenbach
X262 010-2	N	Landeck	X262 051-6	T	NS
X262 015-1	N	Böckstein	X262 051-7	T	NS
X262 016-9	T	KD	X262 056-5	TS	WS
X262 017-7	T	KD	X262 057-3	T	WO
X262 018-5	T	KD	X262 058-1	T	SB
X262 021-9	T	VH	X262 064-9	TS	BL
X262 026-8	T	SB			

X 400 SERIES. TEST VEHICLES

X 401   TUNNEL INSPECTION VEHICLE   B-2+2

This vehicle is based on an X552 unit permanently coupled to a driving trailer vehicle. The motorised vehicle also has a cab with observation windows, a messroom and sleeping space. Mounted between this area and the trailing driving cab is a hydraulic telescopic platform for use not only in tunnels but also for use when inspecting retaining walls as it can extend to 13 m.

Technical details as X 552 except:

Built: 1996   **Length over Buffers:** 25.43 m.
Builder: Plasser   **Weight:** 74 tonnes.
Engine: Deutz (V12) BF12L513C of 367 kW   **Transmission:** Hydraulic. Voith L26 St/A 100 KV.
Maximim Speed: 120 km/h.

X 401 001-3 **V**   Spratzern

X 432   LZB MESSWAGEN   2-B

This is a Plasser OBW 100 type vehicle and is used for testing 'LZB' cab signalling over the whole ÖBB network.

Built: 1991.   **Length over Buffers:** 15.85 m.
Builder: Plasser.   **Weight:** 43.4 tonnes.
Engine: Deutz (V12) BF12L513C of 367 kW   **Transmission:** Hydraulic. Voith L26 St/A 100 KV.
Maximum Speed: 140 km/h.

Non-Standard Livery: Red, yellow and blue.

X 432 001-6 **N**   Streckenleitung LZ

X 500 SERIES. SELF-PROPELLED OVERHEAD LINE INSPECTION UNITS ("MOTOR TOWER WAGONS")

These are overhead line maintenance units belonging to the electrical department and are allocated to various places for repairs or maintenance to the catenary. These depots can be found at substations or in specially constructed sheds near stations and yards. A common feature of all these units is the lifting platform found on top of the unit which can be adjusted in height or even revolved so that it sticks out over adjoining lines.

X 521   B

These four units were prototypes for replacing the X 534. The main frame and running gear is borrowed from X 628 (OBW 10) and thus the X 521 is also referred to as a MTW 10. Fitted with a pantograph, work platform and telescopic crane/grab.

Built: 1990–91.
Builder: Plasser & Theurer.
Engine: KHDF8L513 of 177 kW at 2300 r.p.m.   **Transmission:** Hydrodynamic.
Weight: 42 tonnes.   **Maximum Speed:** 80 km/h (100 towed).
Driving Wheel Diameter: 730 mm.   **Length over Buffers:** 11.94 m.

X 521 001-8	**YR**	Fahrleitungsbau Ost	X 521 003-4	**YR**	Fahrleitungsbau West
X 521 002-6	**YR**	Fahrleitungsbau Süd	X 521 004-2	**YR**	Fahrleitungsbau Süd

X 532.S (760 mm gauge)   Bo

This tower wagon is based on the now withdrawn standard gauge X532 design. Has a double-ended cab with a diesel engine in a box in front of the cab at one end. The pantograph is located on the edge of the roof above the motor.

Built: 1964.
Builder – Mech Parts: Franz Knotz, Tobisch.
Engine: JW 100 of 76 kW (102 h.p.)   **Transmission:** Electric.
Wheel Dia.: 940 mm.   **Weight:** 14.5 tonnes.
Length over Buffers: 7.86 m.   **Maximum Speed:** 45 km/h.

X 532.S.001-5 **RB** St. Pölten | X 532.S.002-3 **RB** St. Pölten

X 534   1-A

A total of 82 examples of this class were built between 1963 and 1983, based on the earlier X532. As with the X532.S there is a diesel engine in a box at one end and a pantograph above this box.

Built: 1963–78, 1970–83*, 1989§.
Builders: Bombardier, Tobisch, Knotz.
Engine: JW 200 of 122 kW (MAN D2566MTE of 147 kW*).
Transmission: Electric (BBC, ABB).
Wheel Diameter: 940 mm.   **Weight:** 20.5 tonnes.
Length over Buffers: 7.74 m.   **Maximum Speed:** 80 km/h.

X 534.101 is ex X 534.78.

Number		Area or Use	Location
X 534 032-8	**YR**	Innsbruck	Reutte in Tirol
X 534 054-2	**YR**	Landeck	Landeck
X 534 056-7	**YR**	Hütteldorf	Hütteldorf
X 534 062-5	**YR**	Feldkirch	Feldkirch
X 534 063-3	**YR**	Innsbruck	Innsbruck
X 534 064-1	**YR**	St. Veit a.d. Glan	St. Veit a.d. Glan
X 534 065-8	**YR**	Mallnitz	Mallnitz
X 534 066-6	**YR**	Linz Kleinmünchen	Linz Kleinmünchen
X 534 068-2	**YR**	Villach	Villach
X 534 069-0	**YR**	Tulln	Tulln
X 534 070-8	**YR** *	St. Pölten	St. Pölten

X 534 071-6	**YR** *	Selzthal	Selzthal
X 534 072-4	**YR** *	St. Johann in Pongau	St. Johann in Pongau
X 534 073-2	**YR** *	Linz Kleinmünchen	Linz Kleinmünchen
X 534 074-0	**YR** *	Wiener Neustadt	Wiener Neustadt
X 534 075-7	**YR** *	Wörgl	Wörgl
X 534 076-5	**YR** *	Graz	Graz
X 534 077-3	**YR** *	Wörgl	Wörgl
X 534 079-9	**YR** *	Ost	Bruck a.d. Leitha
X 534 080-7	**YR** *	Villach	Villach
X 534 081-5	**YR** *	Ost	Zentralfriedhof
X 534 082-3	**YR** *	Floridsdorf	Floridsdorf
X 534 083-1	**YR** *	St. Veit/Glan	St. Veit a.d. Glan
X 534 084-9	**YR** *	Wien Meidling	Wien Meidling
X 534 101-1	**YR** *	Fahrleitungsbau Ost	

X 551 MOTOR STEIGER WAGEN (MSW) 2-B

This is a solitary vehicle with a pointed cab front at one end. It has a hydraulic platform, telescopic crane and a trench digging arm at its rear end.

Built: 1983.
Builder: Plasser & Theurer.
Engine: Deutz KHD BF 12L 413 FC of 350 kW at 2500 r.p.m.
Length over Buffers: 15.34 m.
Maximum Speed: 100 km/h (own power), 120 km/h (hauled).

Transmission: Hydraulic.
Wheel Diameter: 710 mm.
Weight: 45 tonnes.

Number		*Area or Use*	*Location*
X 551 001-1	**YR**	Fahrleitungsbau Mitte	Linz

X 552 2-B

After five prototypes were built and evaluated ÖBB ordered more of these large overhead units. These are the real main line units and they cover large sections of the main lines which is reflected in their maximum speed. They have a 44 kW motor (KHD BR4L1011R) for the ancillary equipment.

CLASS X 552.0

These units feature a large workshop area, pantograph, work platform, telescopic crane/grab, and a mess room.

Built: 1990–1998.
Builder: Plasser & Theurer.
Engine: KHD Type BF12L513C of 367 kW at 2300 r.p.m.
Weight: 52–61 tonnes.
Maximum Speed: 120 km/h.

Transmission: Hydrodynamic.
Wheel Diameter: 840 mm.
Length over Buffers: 15.84 m.

Number		*Area or Use*	*Location*
X 552 001-0	**YR**	St. Pölten	St. Pölten
X 552 002-8	**YR**	Landeck	Landeck
X 552 003-6	**YR**	Villach	Villach
X 552 004-4	**YR**	Innsbruck	Innsbruck
X 552 005-1	**YR**	Wiener Neustadt	Wiener Neustadt
X 552 006-9	**YR**	Wörgl	Wörgl
X 552 007-7	**YR**	Linz Kleinmünchen	Linz Kleinmünchen
X 552 008-5	**YR**	Salzburg	Salzburg
X 552 009-3	**YR**	Floridsdorf	Floridsdorf
X 552 010-1	**YR**	Ost	Zentralfriedhof
X 552 011-9	**YR**	Hütteldorf	Hütteldorf
X 552 013-5	**YR**	St. Michael	St. Michael
X 552 014-3	**YR**	Attnang-Puchheim	Attnang-Puchheim
X 552 015-0	**YR**	St. Johann in Pongau	St. Johann in Pongau
X 552 016-8	**YR**	Tulln	Tulln
X 552 017-6	**YR**	Feldkirch	Feldkirch
X 552 018-4	**YR**	St. Veit a.d. Glan	St. Veit a.d. Glan
X 552 019-2	**YR**	Riedau	Riedau
X 552 020-0	**YR**	Wien Meidling	Wien Meidling
X 552 021-8	**YR**	Innsbruck	Innsbruck

X 552 022-6	**YR**	Graz	Graz
X 552 023-4	**YR**	Mallnitz	Mallnitz
X 552 024-2	**YR**	Selzthal	Selzthal
X 552 025-9	**YR**	Linz Kleinmünchen	Linz Kleinmünchen
X 552 026-7	**YR**	St. Pölten	St. Pölten
X 552 027-5	**YR**		Fahrleitungsbau Mitte
X 552 028-3	**YR**		Fahrleitungsbau West
X 552 029-1	**YR**		Fahrleitungsbau Ost
X 552 030-9	**YR**		Fahrleitungsbau Süd
X 552 031-7	**YR**	Graz	Bruck a.d. Mur
X 552 032-5	**YR**	Tulln	Göpfritz

CLASS X 552.1

Class X 552.1, have two separate cabins each housing a driving cab, with a work platform in the centre. Unlike the X552.0 there is no crane, but instead the work platform can be raised and lowered. Details as for Class X 552.1 except:

Weight: 61 tonnes.   **Length over Buffers:** 15.84 m.

Number		*Area or Use*	*Location*
X 552 101-8	**YR**	Landeck	Landeck
X 552 102-6	**YR**	Mallnitz	Leinz
X 552 103-4	**YR**	St. Michael	St. Michael
X 552 104-2	**YR**	Wiener Neustadt	Semmering
X 552 105-9	**YR**	Selzthal	Kleinreifling
X 552 106-7	**YR**	Attnang-Puchheim	Steeg
X 552 107-5	**YR**	Riedau	Wels
X 552 108-3	**YR**	Floridsdorf	Gänserndorf
X 552 109-1	**YR**	Innsbruck	Innsbruck
X 552 110-9	**YR**	Tulln	Brigittenau
X 552 111-7	**YR**	St. Johann/Pongau	Schladming
X 552 112-5	**YR**		
X 552 113-3	**YR**		
X 552 114-1	**YR**		
X 552 115-8	**YR**		
X 552 116-6	**YR**		
X 552 117-4	**YR**		
X 552 118-2	**YR**		
X 552 119-0	**YR**		
X 552 120-8	**YR**		
X 552 121-6	**YR**		
X 552 122-4	**YR**		

X 554/556 OVERHEAD REBUILDING TRAINS
FUMA/MAGE

These are two trains which can work anywhere on the network. The first is the *Fahrleitungs-umbaumaschine* (FUMA) (Overhead line equipment rebuilding machine) and the other is the *Maststellgerät* (MAGE) (mast-erecting machine).

FUMA-Zug

The FUMA-ZUG is made up of X 554 and X 556 vehicles into a train which is used for renewing the overhead. One vehicle can wind in the old wires (this is an X 501 un-powered vehicle) whilst another plays out the new wires. Work platforms are provided by X 552 vehicles. Wheel arrangement of X 556 001-6 is 2-B). The formation of a train at a worksite is likely to be X554.1, X 552, X 501, X556.0, X554.2.

X 554 101-5   X 501 001-2   X 556 001-6   X 554 201-4

MAGE-Zug

This train consists of X 556 101-4 (Wheel arrangement 3-C) which is the mast-erecting machine and X 556 201-2 which is a non-powered trailer. The train can work on its own or as part of a works train.

X 556 101-4   X 556 201-2

X 554.3   MGW   B

This class is built on an MTW/OBW 10 frame. Known as "Motorgerüstwagen" (literally scaffolding wagon), they are a variant of the X 552, with an exposed three-part engine and work cage between the two cabs. All three engines can be connected to electric and pneumatic hand tools. The vehicles work in pairs with their cabs at the outer ends.

Built: 2000–2001.
Builder: Plasser & Theurer.
Engine: 195 kW.

Length over buffers: 10.74 m.
Weight: 32 tonnes.
Maximum Speed: 90 km/h.

X 554 301-2 + X 554 302-0	**YR**	Fahrleitungsbau	Süd
X 554 303-8 + X 554 304-6	**YR**	Fahrleitungsbau	Ost
X 554 305-3 + X 554 306-1	**YR**	Fahrleitungsbau	West
X 554 307-9 + X 554 308-7	**YR**	Fahrleitungsbau	Mitte

X 600 SERIES. STAFF TRANSPORTERS FOR TRACK MAINTENANCE

BM SERIES STAFF TRANSPORTERS

The BM series are small staff transporters which can haul two or three lightweight trailers on which sleepers, ballast, gas cylinders etc can be transported. Many are also fitted with normal buffing gear and can be used as on-site shunting locos to move for example a wagon of ballast for unloading. Narrow gauge vehicles are numbered in the 9xx series. No technical details available.

X 616   TYPE BM35

Number		Area or Use	Location
X 616 905-6	**Y**	Schwarzenau	Langschlag

X 625   TYPE BM70

Number			Area or Use	Location
g		Fitted with GPS.		
X 625 901-4	**Y**	g	Waidhofen a.d. Ybbs	Waidhofen a.d. Ybbs
X 625 902-2	**Y**		Kirchberg/Pielach	Mariazell
X 625 903-0	**Y**	g	Kirchberg/Pielach	Mariazell

X 626   TYPE BM100

Built:
Weight: 7 tonnes.

Haulage capacity: 115 tonnes.
Maximum Speed: 50 km/h.

g   Fitted with GPS.
h   Hire vehicle.
t   Fitted with turntable.

Number			Area or Use	Location
X 626 101-0	**Y**		Tulln	Tulln
X 626 103-6	**Y**	h	Werke Wörth	Werke Wörth
X 626 104-4	**Y**		Schwarzach	Hofgastein
X 626 105-1	**Y**		Wiener Neustadt	Wiener Neustadt
X 626 106-9	**Y**		Bludenz	Langen am Arlberg
X 626 109-3	**Y**	g	St. Pölten	Neulengbach
X 626 110-1	**Y**		Linz Vbf	Rohrbach/Berg
X 626 111-9	**Y**		Villach-Süd	Fürnitz
X 626 112-7	**Y**	g	Gloggnitz	Mürzzuschlag
X 626 113-5	**Y**		Friedberg	Aspang
X 626 114-3	**Y**	g	Krems/Donau	Spitz/Donau
X 626 116-8	**Y**		Mallnitz	Kolbnitz
X 626 117-6	**Y**		Judenburg	Judenburg
X 626 118-4	**Y**		Hollabrunn	Hollabrunn
X 626 119-2	**Y**		Selzthal	Selzthal

X 626 120-0	Y		Schwarzach	Bruck Fusch
X 626 121-8	Y		Landeck	Landeck
X 626 122-6	Y		Wörgl	Wörgl
X 626 124-2	Y	g	Linz Vbf	Linz Vbf
X 626 125-9	Y		Hartberg	Hartberg
X 626 126-7	Y	h	Werke Wörth	Werke Wörth
X 626 127-5	Y		Bad Ischl	Bad Aussee
X 626 128-3	Y		Saalfelden	Saalfelden
X 626 129-1	Y		Klagenfurt	Klagenfurt
X 626 130-9	Y		Mallnitz	Böckstein
X 626 131-7	Y	g	Gloggnitz	Gloggnitz
X 626 133-3	Y		Villach-Süd	Fürnitz
X 626 134-1	Y		Landeck	Lermoos
X 626 136-6	Y		Selzthal	Hieflau
X 626 137-4	Y		Wiener Neustadt	Wiener Neustadt
X 626 138-2	Y		Klagenfurt	Wolfsberg
X 626 139-0	Y	g	Krems/Donau	Krems/Donau
X 626 140-8	Y		Wiener Neustadt	Lackenbach
X 626 141-6	Y		Bruck/Mur	Bruck a.d. Mur
X 626 142-4	Y	g	Wels	Sattledt
X 626 143-2	Y		Ried im Innkreis	Ried im Innkreis
X 626 144-0	Y	g	Bruck a.d. Leitha	Bruck a.d. Leitha
X 626 145-7	Y		Steyr	Kleinreifling
X 626 146-5	Y		Schwarzach	Schwarzach St.Veit
X 626 147-3	Y	g	Villach Hbf	Villach
X 626 148-1	Y		Wien West	Wien West
X 626 149-9	Y	g	Linz Hbf	Freistadt
X 626 150-7	Y		Wien Meidling	Wien Meidling
X 626 151-5	Y		Hartberg	Fürstenfeld
X 626 152-3	Y	g	Wien ZVB	Wien ZVB
X 626 153-1	Y		St.Veit a.d. Glan	Neumarkt
X 626 154-9	Y	g	Gänserndorf	Gänserndorf
X 626 155-6	Y	g	Leobersdorf	Leobersdorf
X 626 156-4	Y		Graz	Graz
X 626 157-2	Y		Innsbruck	Steinach/Brenner
X 626 158-0	Y		Friedberg	Friedberg
X 626 159-8	Y		Linz Hbf	Linz Hbf
X 626 160-6	Y		Attnang-Puchheim	Frankenmarkt
X 626 161-4	Y		Wien West	Wien West
X 626 162-2	Y		Wels	Wels Vbf
X 626 163-0	Y		St.Veit a.d. Glan	Friesach
X 626 164-8	Y	h	Werke Wörth	Werke Wörth
X 626 165-5	Y	g	Mistelbach	Dobermannsdorf
X 626 166-3	Y		Tulln	Tulln
X 626 167-1	Y		Schladming	Schladming
X 626 168-9	Y		Bruck/Mur	Bruck a.d. Mur
X 626 169-7	Y		Schwarzach	Bischofshofen
X 626 171-3	Y		Neumarkt Kalham	Schärding
X 626 172-1	Y	g	Wien ZVB	Wien ZVB
X 626 173-9	Y		Hall in Tirol	Hall in Tirol
X 626 174-7	Y	g	Sigmundsherberg	Sigmundsherberg
X 626 176-2	Y		Graz	Leibnitz
X 626 177-0	Y	g	Amstetten	Grein Bad Kreuzen
X 626 178-8	Y		Salzburg	Salzburg Gnigl
X 626 179-6	Y	g	Schwarzenau	Schwarzenau
X 626 180-4	Y		Neumarkt Kalham	Neumarkt Kalham
X 626 181-2	Y		St.Veit a.d. Glan	St.Veit a.d. Glan
X 626 182-0	Y		Villach	Feldkirchen/Kärnten
X 626 183-8	Y		Selzthal	Admont
X 626 185-3	Y		Steyr	St. Valentin
X 626 187-9	Y		Judenburg	Judenburg
X 626 188-7	Y		Landeck	Imst
X 626 189-5	Y		Signal-Systemtechnik Mitte	Salzburg
X 626 190-3	Y	h	Werke Wörth	Werke Wörth

X 626 192-9	Y	g	Mistelbach	Mistelbach
X 626 193-7	Y		Bad Ischl	Ebensee
X 626 194-5	Y		Hartberg	Feldbach
X 626 195-2	Y		Klagenfurt	Bleiburg
X 626 196-0	Y		Bad Ischl	Bad Ischl
X 626 197-8	Y		Floridsdorf	Floridsdorf
X 626 198-6	Y	g	Hainfeld	Hainfeld
X 626 199-4	Y		Steyr	Grossraming
X 626 200-0	Y		Salzburg	Hallein
X 626 202-6	Y		Attnang-Puchheim	Attnang-Puchheim
X 626 203-4	Y		Gramatneusiedl	Gramatneusiedl
X 626 205-9	Y		Schladming	Schladming
X 626 206-7	Y		Sigmundsherberg	Langau
X 626 208-3	Y	g	Schwarzenau	Zwettl
X 626 209-1	Y	g	Bruck a.d Leitha	Purbach/Neusiedlersee
X 626 215-8	Y		Wels	Lambach
X 626 216-6	Y		Stadlau	Stadlau
X 626 217-4	Y		Kirchdorf/Krems	Kirchdorf/Krems
X 626 218-2	Y		Spittal/Drau	Spittal/Drau
X 626 219-0	Y		Stadlau	Stadlau
X 626 220-8	Y	g	Hollabrunn	Hollabrunn
X 626 221-6	Y		Waidhofen a.d. Ybbs	Waidhofen a.d. Ybbs
X 626 222-4	Y		Wien Meidling	Wien Meidling
X 626 223-2	Y		Floridsdorf	Wien Nord
X 626 224-0	Y	t	Netz-Sicherheit	Mallnitz
X 626 226-5	Y	g	Linz Vbf	Linz Vbf
X 626 227-3	Y	h	Werke Wörth	Werke Wörth
X 626 228-1	Y	h	Werke Wörth	Attnang-Puchheim

TRACK MACHINES (OBERBAUWAGEN OBW)

This is the largest group of departmentals after the X 500 series o.l.e. units. They appear in many guises having various attachments to the main frame such as rotary snowploughs, ordinary snowploughs and are also used as ballast spreaders, hydraulic grabs, cranes, etc. They have normal buffing and coupling gear and can be used to haul wagons to engineering sites. Information is incomplete and details of observations welcomed.

X 627.0   TYPE OBW10   B

These vehicles have a crane and a ballast plough.

Built: 1981-1987.
Builder: Plasser & Theurer.
Engine: Deutz of 146 kW.
Weight: 27 tonnes.

Transmission: Hydraulic.
Wheel Diameter: 710 mm.
Length over Buffers: 9.70–10.13 m.
Maximum Speed: 90 km/h.

b   Fitted with ballast plough.
s   Fitted with sleeper grab.
t   Fitted with turntable.

Number			Area or Use	Location
X 627 021-9	Y	t	Bauzug 103	Amstetten
X 627 023-5	Y	t	Bruck a.d. Mur	Bruck a.d. Mur
X 627 031-8	Y	bst	Reserve	Knittelfeld
X 627 032-6	Y	bst	Wien Meidling	Wien Meidling
X 627 033-4	Y	bst	Selzthal	Selzthal
X 627 034-2	Y	bst	Graz	Graz
X 627 035-9	Y	t	Krems	Krems
X 627 036-7	Y	t	Wiener Neustadt	Wiener Neustadt
X 627 051-6	Y	s	Landeck	Landeck
X 627 052-4	Y	s	Kirchdorf/Krems	Kirchdorf/Krems
X 627 053-2	Y	bs	Wels	Wels
X 627 054-0	Y	bs	Bauzug 102	Strasshof
X 627 055-7	Y	bs	Portalkran	Unter-Purkersdorf

X 627.1   SHUNTER   B

No crane. Used for shunting.

Built: 1975.

Number	Area or Use	Location
X 627 101-9 **Y**	Linz Wegscheid	Linz Wegscheid

X 627.5   TYPE OBW10   B

These vehicles have a crane and winter fittings. Details as for X 627.0.

Built: 1978–84.
Builder: Plasser.

b   Fitted with ballast plough.
g   Fitted with sleeper grab.
p   Fitted with rotary snowplough.
t   Fitted with turntable.

Number		Area or Use	Location
X 627 501-0 **Y**	pt	St. Pölten	St. Pölten
X 627 511-9 **Y**	bpst	Stadlau	Wien ZVB
X 627 512-7 **Y**	st	Villach Hbf	Villach Hbf
X 627 513-5 **Y**	st	Villach Süd	Fürnitz
X 627 514-3 **Y**	st	Spittal-Millstättersee	Spittal-Millstättersee

X 627.7   TUNNEL EMERGENCY VEHICLES   B

Type OBW10-S2. vehicle. It is similar in appearance to the rest of the X 627 fleet but has a longer cab and no crane.

Built: 1987–8.
Builder: Plasser & Theurer.
Engine: MWM D232V12 of 165 kW.
Length over Buffers: 5.25 m.

Transmission: Hydraulic. Clark 13.7LHR.
Wheel Diameter: 710 mm.

Maximum Speed: 80 km/h.

Number	Area or Use	Location
X 627 701-6 **Y**	Netz Sicherheit	Hall in Tirol
X 627 702-4 **Y**	Netz Sicherheit	Pöchlarn

X 627.8   ULTRASONIC TEST CAR   B

This is an ultrasonic rail testing vehicle. It is similar in appearance to the rest of the X 627 fleet but has a longer cab and no crane.

Built: 1985.
Builder: Plasser & Theurer.
Engine: KHD F8L413F of 174 kW at 2500 r.p.m.
Length over Buffers: 12.64 m.

Transmission:
Wheel Diameter: 710 mm.

Maximum Speed: 80 km/h.

Number	Area or Use	Location
X 627 801-4 **V**	Messgruppe	Tulln Hbf

X 627.9   MULTI-PURPOSE VEHICLE   B-B

This is a narrow gauge version of Class X 627.5 and is a muti-purpose vehicle.

Built: 1986.
Builder: Plasser & Theurer.
Engine: KHD F8L413F of 174 kW at 2500 r.p.m.
Length over Buffers: 10.60 m.

Transmission: Hydraulic.
Weight: 46 tonnes.

Maximum Speed: 60 km/h.

Number	Area or Use	Location
X 627 951-7 **Y**	Kirchberg/Pielach	Kirchberg/Pielach

X 628 TYPE OBW10 B

These OBW 10 vehicles are used by the permanent way department as a multipurpose vehicle. Staff transport, shunting engine, trench digger, crane are some of the uses. The crane, indeed the whole vehicle can be remotely controlled by radio!

Built: 1989–96.
Builder: Plasser & Theurer.
Engine: KHD 12 cyl of 268 kW **Weight:** 42 tonnes.
Length over Buffers: 11.35 m. **Maximum Speed:** 90 km/h.

t Fitted with turntable.
* Equipped for winter operation.

Number			Area or Use	Location
X 628 001-0	Y	t*	Wörgl	Wörgl
X 628 002-8	Y	t*	Spittal-Millstättersee	Lienz
X 628 003-6	Y		Wolfurt	Wolfurt
X 628 004-4	Y	t*	Leoben	St. Michael
X 628 005-1	Y		Schnell Umbau Zug	Unter-Purkersdorf
X 628 006-9	Y		Wien Stadlau	Wien Stadlau
X 628 007-7	Y		Innsbruck	Innsbruck
X 628 008-5	Y		Salzburg	Salzburg
X 628 009-3	Y		Amstetten	Amstetten
X 628 010-1	Y		Attnang-Puchheim	Attnang-Puchheim
X 628 011-9	Y		Floridsdorf	Floridsdorf
X 628 012-7	Y		Wien West	Wien West
X 628 013-5	Y		Gloggnitz	Gloggnitz
X 628 014-3	Y		Bauzug 101	Wiener Neustadt
X 628 015-0	Y	*	Bauzug 402	Villach

X 629 TYPE OBW9 B

This is classed as OBW9 and is smaller than the OBW10. It is a development of the X628 with a more powerful motor. Other new features include an air-conditioned cab, low-level loading area, disc brakes and remote-controlled track pliers. An intermediate size of vehicle which will probably replace in time some of the X626 series. Staff compartment and telescopic crane/grab.

Built: 1990 (001–004), 1984 (009). **Transmission:** Hydromechanical.
Builder: Plasser & Theurer. **Wheel Diameter:** 730 mm.
Engine: KHD 6 cyl of 123 kW at 2500 r.p.m.
Length over Buffers: 9.24 m. **Weight:** 18 tonnes.
Maximum Speed: 90 km/h.

Number		Area or Use	Location
X 629 001-9	Y	St. Pölten Hbf	St. Pölten Hbf
X 629 002-7	Y	Attnang-Puchheim	Ried im Innkreis
X 629 003-5	Y	Steyr	Steyr
X 629 004-3	Y	Innsbruck	Innsbruck
X 629 005-0	Y	Gänserndorf	Gänserndorf

X 629.9 B

A narrow gauge version of X629.

Built: 1993–94 **Transmission:** Hydrodynamic.
Builder: Plasser & Theurer. **Wheel Diameter:**
Engine: KHD BF8L513 of 177 kW at 2300 r.p.m.
Length over Buffers: 9.10 m. **Weight:** 17 tonnes.
Maximum Speed: 60 km/h.

Number			Area or Use	Location
X 629 901-0	Y	t	Kirchberg/Pielach	Mariazell
X 629 902-8	Y	r	Schwarzach St. Veit	Furth Kaprun

X 630   B

This is a new series from the Robel firm of Freilassing in Germany. A large cabin has room not only for the driver but also up to six workmen and gives good all round visibility. Because of this the cabin is air conditioned and darkened glass used. Fitted with ZBF, PZB 90, Crane.

Built: 2001.
Builder: Robel, type 54.22-28.
Engine: Deutz BF 8M 1015CP of 440 kW.
Maximum Speed: 100 km/h.

Length over buffers: 11.90 m.
Wheel Diameter: 840 mm.
Weight: 27 tonnes.
Transmission: Hydraulic.

Number		Area or Use	Location
X 630 001-6	**0**	Bauzug 401	Leoben
X 630 002-4	**0**	Schwarzenau	Schwarzenau
X 630 003-2	**0**	Linz Hbf	Linz Hbf
X 630 004-0	**0**	Bludenz	Bludenz

X 631   B

These are former Class 2060 locomotives (later X 260) which have been re-engined with a KHD BF6M 1013 CP engine.

X 631 015-5 **0**   Linz Wegscheid | X 631 056-7 **0**   Zeltweg

X 651   **TRACK RECORDING CARS**   2-B

These are three track recording coaches also known as EM-SAT 120. They have a laser camera and a detachable battery-operated satellite which beams its lasers onto the camera. The EM vehicle being the main track recording unit which is connected to a "Satellite Trolley" which is the SAT part of the class description.

Built: 2000.
Builder: Plasser & Theurer.
Engine: Deutz BF8M 1015C of 400 kW.

Length over Buffers: 16.14 m.
Weight: 49.6 tonnes.
Maximum Speed: 120 km/h.

X 651 001-0 **V**   Wels | X 651 003-6 **V**   Villach Hbf
X 651 002-8 **V**   Spratzern |

X 651 004   **VIADUCT INSPECTION UNIT**   2-B

This is a bridge examination vehicle with a work platform and crane in the centre and cabins containing driving cabs at either end.

Built: 2000.
Builder: Plasser & Theurer.
Engine: Deutz

Length over Buffers: 18.80 m.
Weight: 89 tonnes.
Maximum Speed: 100 km/h (120 km/h hauled).

X 651 004-4 **YR**   Spratzern |

X 800 SERIES. VEHICLES ON ACCEPTANCE

X 890 & X 891   **TUNNEL RESCUE TRAINS**

These trains are being converted by ÖBB from DB Cargo Sprinters. Firm details are not yet available but it is likely that the trains will be scaled down versions of the DB NBS emergency trains. One power car will be fitted out as a fire fighting vehicle and this will be leading into a tunnel. The rear power car will be fitted out as a rescue vehicle the intention being to split the train and the rear part take people away from an incident. It is thought that the trains will be based at Bludenz, Böckstein, Mallnitz, Spittal/Drau and Villach Süd.

X 890 502-8 X 890 902-0 ex DB 690 502/002
X 890 503-6 X 890 903-8 ex DB 690 503/003
X 890 504-4 X 890 904-6 ex DB 690 504/004

X 891 501-9 X 891 901-1 ex DB 691 501/001
X 891 502-7 X 891 902-9 ex DB 691 502/002
X 891 503-5 X 891 903-7 ex DB 691 503/003

OTHER DEPARTMENTALS
CLASS 8081   DRIVER TRAINING UNITS   A-A

These are railbuses now used for road learning and previously Class 5081.

Built: 1964–67.
Builders: Uerdingen/JW/SGP.
Engine: Two Bussing U10 of 110 kW.
Weight: 21 tonnes.

Transmission: Mechanical.
Wheel Diameter: 900 mm.
Length over Buffers: 13.95 m.
Maximum Speed: 90 km/h.

8081 001-3	**B** WO		8081 021-1	**B** WE
8081 015-3	**B** WE		8081 055-9	**B** WE

SNOWPLOUGHS

The snowploughs detailed here have been generally built on the frames of old locomotives. Standard gauge snowploughs have been renumbered in the UIC wagon series.

Narrow Gauge: (760 mm).

Number	Depot	Formerly
985.02	SP	Converted wagon 1941
985.05	GM	Converted wagon 1941
985.50	ZS	
985.51	WH	

Narrow Gauge: (1000 mm)

986.10-4   PB   Built 1964 Diesel Rotary

Standard Gauge:

New No.	Old No.	Liv.	Converted	Frame	of Allocation
80 81 97-60 000-6	985.200	R	1954	52.765	Saalfelden
80 81 97-60 001-4	985.201	R	1955	52.458	VH
80 81 97-60 002-2	985.202	R	1955	52.1448	SP (Weinfeld)
80 81 97-60 003-0	985.203	R	1955	52.357	BO
80 81 97-60 004-8	985.204	N	1956	52.401	SB
80 81 97-60 007-1	985.207	R	1959	52.433	WL
80 81 97-60 009-7	985.209	R	1960	52.3602	SP
80 81 97-60 311-7	985.211	G	1961	52.6649	BL
80 81 97-60 312-5	985.212	R	1961	52.4943	GZ
80 81 97-60 013-9	985.213	R	1962	52.6940	SL
80 81 97-60 314-1	985.214	O	1966	52.3636	VH
80 81 97-60 016-2	985.216	R	1967	52.3174	WL (Saalfelden)
80 81 97-60 317-4	985.217	R	1968	52.1719	NS
80 81 97-60 019-0	985.219	G	1970	52.6969	Bruck a.d. Leitha
80 81 97-60 020-8	985.220	R	1971	52.7052	Spittal-Millstättersee
80 81 97-60 022-0	985.222	R	1974	52.3553	LZ
80 81 97-60 323-2	985.223	G	1975	52.6312	SL
80 81 97-60 324-0	985.224	G	1976	52.478	Schwarzenau
80 81 97-60 325-7	985.225	G	1977	52.3615	LZ
80 81 97-60 326-5	985.226	G	1978	52.3520	SA
80 81 97-60 027-9	985.227	G	1979	52.2374	VH
80 81 97-60 328-1	985.228	G	1980	52.7213	Klagenfurt
80 81 97-60 029-5	985.229	R	1981	52.2428	BL
80 81 97-60 030-3	985.230	R	1984	52.7100	IN
80 81 97-60 031-1	985.231	R		52.7595	IN (Reutte in Tirol)
80 81 97-60 032-9	-	R		52.1442	LK
80 81 97 60 033-7		R		52.7053	Wien ZVB
80 81 97-60 034 5	-	R		52.6428	AT

1.6.ÖBB SHIPS & BOATS

1.6.1. BODENSEE (LAKE CONSTANCE)

Vessel	Builder	Date	Displacement (empty)	Pass.	Power
MS Austria	Korneuburg	1939	352 tonnes.	1200	1270 kW
MB Dornbirn	Korneuburg	1956	40 tonnes.	100	300 kW
MB Feldkirch	Korneuburg	1955	40 tonnes.	100	300 kW
MB Montafon	Korneuburg	1957	42 tonnes.	160	300 kW
MS Osterreich	Korneuburg	1928	281 tonnes.	600	1200 kW
MS Vorarlberg	Korneuburg	1964	392 tonnes.	1000	1200 kW

1.6.2. WOLFGANGSEE

MS Elisabeth	1873	270 tonnes.	135 kW
MS Falkenstein	1959	270 tonnes.	150 kW
MS Kaiser Franz Josef	1872	225 tonnes.	115 kW
MS Osterreich	1984	365 tonnes.	173 kW
MS Salzkammergut	1973	300 tonnes.	170 kW
MB St. Wolfgang	1950	80 tonnes.	115 kW

PLATFORM 5 MAIL ORDER

PLATFORM 5 EUROPEAN HANDBOOKS

The Platform 5 European Handbooks are the most comprehensive guides to the rolling stock of selected European railway administrations available. Each book in the series contains the following information:

- Locomotives
- Preserved Locomotives, Museums and Museum Lines
- Railcars and Multiple Units
- Technical Data
- Depot Allocations (where allocated)
- Lists of Depots and Workshops

Each book is A5 size, thread sewn and includes colour illustrations.
Benelux Railways also includes details of hauled coaching stock. The following are currently available:

		TR Subs Price
No.1: Benelux Railways 4th edition. 176 pages. Published 2000	£14.50	£12.00
No.2a: German Railways Part 1: DB Locomotives & Multiple Units 4th edition. 176 pages. Published 2004	£16.95	£14.95
No.2b: German Railways Part 2: Private Railways & Museums. 224 pages. Published 2004	£16.95	£14.95
No.3: Austrian Railways 4th edition. 176 pages. Published 2005	£17.50	£15.50
No.4: French Railways 3rd edition. 176 pages. Published 1999	£14.50	£12.00
No.6: Italian Railways 1st edition. 160 pages. Published 1995	£13.50	£11.00
No.7: Irish Railways 2nd edition. To be Published in 2006	£11.95	£9.95

***TR subscriber* prices are only available to *Today's Railways* subscribers. Please see our advertisements on the inside covers of this book for further information.**

If you would like to be notified when new titles in this series are published, please contact our Mail Order Department. Alternatively, please see our advertisements in *Today's Railways* magazines for up to date publication information.

HOW TO ORDER

Telephone your order and credit/debit card details to our 24-hour sales hotline:
0114 255 8000 (UK) + 44 114-255-8000 (from overseas) or Fax: +44(0)114-255-2471.
An answerphone is attached for calls made outside of normal UK office hours.

Please state type of card, card number, issue no./date (maestro cards only), expiry date and full name & address of cardholder.
Or send your credit/debit card details, sterling cheque or British Postal order payable to Platform 5 Publishing Ltd. to:

**Mail Order Department (EHA), Platform 5 Publishing Ltd.,
3 Wyvern House, Sark Road, SHEFFIELD, S2 4HG, ENGLAND**
Please add postage & packing: 10% UK; 20% Europe; 30% Rest of World.

PLATFORM 5 MAIL ORDER

EISENBAHNATLAS DEUTSCHLAND 2005/2006
Schweers & Wall

The definitive colour atlas of Germany's railways in 1:300000 scale, completely revised and updated. Shows all lines with identification of double track, single track, narrow gauge, freight only, not in use, former line now removed, rack lines and lines under construction. Colours are used to show lines of different electrification voltages and German timetable numbers are shown beside passenger lines. Also shows all stations, halts, junctions, yards, freight facilities, preservation centres, museum lines, tramways and funiculars, plus many general geographical features including rivers and motorways. Includes enlargements of major centres, index maps and a full index to stations and other significant places. Key is in German, English, French and Dutch. 192 pages. Large format hardback. **£27.95.** *TR subscriber price £24.95.*

EISENBAHNATLAS SCHWEIZ
Schweers & Wall

The definitive atlas of Switzerland's railways in 1:150000 scale. Shows the same extensive detail as in Eisenbahnatlas Deutschland above, with additional identification of the operator of each line. Also includes diagrammatic tramway maps and a full list of railway companies with contact details. Key is in German, English, French and Italian. 96 pages. Large format hardback. Published 2004. **£21.95.** *TR subscriber price £18.95.*

EISENBAHN TASCHENATLAS
Deutschland Osterreich Schweiz

A useful rail atlas of Germany, Austria and Switzerland, showing all lines currently in use at a scale 1:750000 in Germany and Austria and 1:500000 in Switzerland. Shows all stations except in dense urban areas and distinguishes electrified lines, single track and narrow gauge lines. Also includes a full index to marked stations and a few colour illustrations. Combines a reasonable level of detail with a convenient carrying size. 96 pages (56 map pages). German text. **£11.50.** *TR subscriber price £9.50.*

BAHNPROFIL SCHWEIZ '05
Diplory Verlag

A complete set of gradient profiles, railway track diagrams and distance tables for the entire Swiss railway network. Includes a heading for every line with details of main operator, gauge, electrification voltage where applicable and Swiss timetable number. There then follows a gradient profile of each line, with adjacent track layout diagram and list of points on the route with distances in kilometres. The distances are shown 3 different ways – point to point, cumulative ascending and cumulative descending. Track layouts of major stations are shown separately. Also includes summaries of the number of lines and stations in each canton, subdivided by gauge, plus distance tables between major centres, a diagrammatic distance map and separate indices of tunnels, stations, railway operators and other listed locations. 142 pages. German/French text. **£23.95.** *TR subscriber price £21.50.*

Special note: Customers wishing to purchase this book should be aware that the price may seem rather high for a softback book, printed in black & white throughout. However, this is a reflection of the amount of work that has gone into compiling it, rather than the physical printing cost.

HOW TO ORDER

Telephone your order and credit/debit card details to our 24-hour sales hotline:

0114 255 8000 (UK) + 44 114-255-8000 (from overseas) or Fax: +44(0)114-255-2471.

An answerphone is attached for calls made outside of normal UK office hours.

Please state type of card, card number, issue no./date (maestro cards only), expiry date and full name & address of cardholder. Or send your credit/debit card details, sterling cheque or British Postal order payable to Platform 5 Publishing Ltd. to:

Mail Order Department (EHA), Platform 5 Publishing Ltd.,

3 Wyvern House, Sark Road, SHEFFIELD, S2 4HG, ENGLAND

Please add postage & packing: 10% UK; 20% Europe; 30% Rest of World.

2. INDEPENDENT RAILWAYS

Austria now has open access arrangements but German companies were the first to take the opportunity offered and there are many private trains now running from the München area through Austria to the Italian frontier at Brennero. Austria has several open access operators and more can be expected in the coming years.

CODES

Austria still has many private railways offering feeder services into the ÖBB network or simply providing local transport often in quite delightful backwaters. Most of these lines have retained the old style classifications which have a prefix letter to explain the type of traction:

E	(Elektrolokomotive)	Electric locomotive.
ET	(Elektrotriebewagen)	Electric railcar.
V	(Verbrennungsmotoren)	Diesel locomotive.
VT	(Verbrennungstriebwagen)	Diesel railcar.
X		Departmental.

On the Steiermarkische Landesbahnen some additional classifications exist whilst the GySEV uses the MAV (Hungarian State Railways) classification. Lines are standard gauge except where otherwise shown.

2.1. ACHENSEEBAHN   AB

Gauge: 1000 mm.
Route: Jenbach–Achensee.
Timetable: 311.

System: Riggenbach rack and adhesion.
Depot: Jenbach.
Internet: www.achenseebahn.at

This line is only open in the summer months. The locos propel their trains on the rack from Jenbach to Eben and then run round to haul their trains to the terminus.

STEAM LOCOMOTIVES

1–4   0-4-0RT

In recent years the Achenseebahn has been quite thriving and in 2005 has a surprise for visitors with locomotive No. 4 being added to traffic.

Built: 1899/2004*.
Builder: Floridsdorf
Wheel Diameter: 898 mm.
Length: 5.60 m.

Boiler pressure: 0.95 MN/sq. m. (135 lb/sq.in).
Weight: 18.3 tonnes.
Cylinders: 330 x 500 mm.
Maximum Speed: 20 km/h.

1	Eben am Achensee
2	Jenbach
3	Achenkirch
4*	

DIESEL LOCOMOTIVE.

D1   B

The Achenseebahn decided it needed a diesel shunting locomotive not only for shunting at the depot but also the odd small works train that can be run without having to light up a steam locomotive. The locomotive it acquired is interesting in that it is former Inselbahn Langeoog No.3 which was taken into stock in July 1995.

Built: 1949
Builder: Schöma
Engine: Deutz F4L514 of 59 kW.
Transmission: Hydraulic.

Wheel Diameter: 580 mm
Weight: 7.5 tonnes
Length: 5.00 m.
Maximum Speed:

D1

2.2. CARGO SERV

Cargo Serv is an open access operator and a subsidiary of VOEST Alpine Stahl, Linz GmbH. Under open access the steel works has taken over the movement of raw materials to the works in Linz. (Iron ore from Eisenerz and limestone from Steyrling). It also helps out other private operators. It is now moving finished products between Linz and Italy via the Tauern line.

CLASS V 1504   B-B

These locomotives are former Deutsche Reichsbahn V100s rebuilt by Adtranz in Kassel. Regretfully the original identities have not yet come to light.

Built: 19xx   **Wheel Diameter:** mm
Builder: LEW, Rebuilt 2001 by Adtranz, Kassel.   **Weight:** tonnes
Engine: CAT 3512 DITA of 1060 kW.   **Length:** 5.00 m.
Transmission: Hydraulic.   **Maximum Speed:** 100 km/h

V1504.01 | V1504.02 | V1504.03

CLASS ES64 U2   Bo-Bo

CargoServ also has four Dispoloks for use on the iron ore and finished products trains. ES64 U2 080/081 have remote radio control for shunting operations. Otherwise technical details are as ÖBB 1116. For full details of Dispolok please refer to the Platform 5 book on German Railways – Part 2 Private Lines.

ES64U2 005 | ES64U2 040 | ES64U2 080 | ES64U2 081

2.3. GRAZ KÖFLACHER BAHN   GKB

Routes: Graz–Wies Wibiswald/Köflach.
Depots: Graz GKB (Main Depot/Works). Wies Eibiswald, Köflach (Subsheds).
Timetable: 550.   **Internet:** www.gkb.at

The staple traffic of the GKB used to be coal but this has long since gone. Today the line is a busy commuter route using dmus and push-pull double-decker trains. Gone are the days of just a few passenger trains a day! Some freight traffic has been retained with timber now important with Holzindustrie Preding providing 150,000 tonnes per year. The GKB is a shareholder of LTE Logistik (q.v.). In recent years GKB has been adding a full UIC style number to its locomotives but the old number is still displayed.

STEAM LOCOMOTIVES

671   0-6-0

This loco is a grand old lady of the former Südbahn which ran on the GKB between 1878 and 1924 and stayed on when it became a private company once again. It was stored in the 1970s but has recently been fitted with a new boiler and is set to steam on for many more years. This locomotive is the oldest locomotive in service on a main line and has never been withdrawn from traffic in its long lifetime!

Built: 1860.
Builder: StEG.
Wheel Diameter: 1285 mm.
Length over Buffers: 14.25 m.
Power: 420 kW.

Boiler Pressure: 0.68 MN/sq. m. (110 lb/sq.in).
Weight: 65.6 tonnes.
Cylinders: 460 x 632 mm.
Maximum Speed: 45 km/h.

671   (98 45 0029 671-5)

CLASS 56   2-8-0

GKB once had 16 of these two-cylinder compound 2-8-0s which were all obtained from ÖBB after WW2 to strengthen its loco fleet as traffic picked up after the war. Being a major coal haulier at that time meant it had priority traffic. This locomotive is now retired from service and has been placed in a new museum at Lieboch station whilst funds are gathered for an overhaul.

Built: 1914.
Builder: Floridsdorf.
Driving Wheel Diameter: 1258 mm.
Length over Buffers: 17.70 m.
Power: 840 kW.

Boiler Pressure: 1.00 MN/sq. m. (140 lb/sq.in).
Weight: 68.1 tonnes.
Cylinders: 540/800 x 632 mm.
Maximum Speed: 60 km/h.

56.3115   (98 45 0563 115-5)

DIESEL LOCOMOTIVES
CLASS DH 80   B

The GKB has had this diesel in stock since 1968 but for many years it never appeared in the inventory. It is a typical German Köf that was used in industry before the GKB acquired it.

Built: 1938
Builder: BMAG
Engine: 85 kW
Transmission: Hydraulic.

Wheel dia.: 850 mm.
Weight: 16 tonnes.
Length over Buffers: 6.45 m.
Maximum Speed: 45 km/h.

DH 80.1

CLASS DM 100   A-1

These two "locomotives" are in fact track maintenance vehicles something akin to an OBW 10 but converted by GKB from two track machines; V100.1 was a former tamping machine whilst V100.2 was a lining machine.

Built: 19xx Rebuilt 1978, 1980.
Builder: GKB.
Engine: 76 kW
Transmission: Mechanical.

Driving Wheel Diameter:
Weight:
Length over Buffers:
Maximum Speed: 25 km/h

V100.1 | V100.2

CLASS DH 600 C

Typical Jenbach shunters but of a type not found on ÖBB.

Built: 1973.
Builder: JW.
Engine: Caterpillar CAT 3412C-DITA of 445 kW.
Length over Buffers: 10.50 m.
Transmission: Hydraulic.

Wheel Diameter: 950 mm.
Weight: 48 tonnes.

Maximum Speed: 60 km/h.

DH 600.1 (98 45 2 600 001-8)
DH 600.2 (98 45 2 600 002-6)

DH 600.3 (98 45 2 600 003-4)

CLASS DH 700 C

A one-off shunter which does not appear to have been second-hand.

Built: 1977.
Builder: MaK.
Engine: 6M282A of 515 kW.
Transmission: Hydraulic.

Wheel Diameter: 1000 mm.
Weight: 60 tonnes.
Length over Buffers: 9.86 m.
Maximum Speed: 60 km/h.

DH 700.01 (98 45 0700 001-1)

CLASS DH 1100 B-B

These are former DB Class 211s rebuilt with Caterpillar engines.

Built: 1961–62.
Builder: Henschel.
Engine: Caterpillar 3512D1 of 840 kW at 1500 r.p.m.
Transmission: Hydraulic.

Wheel Diameter: 950 mm.
Weight: 64 tonnes.
Length over Buffers: 12.10 m.
Maximum Speed: 110 km/h.

DH 1100.01 (98 45 0211 001-5, ex DB 211 170-6)
DH 1100.02 (98 45 0211 002-3, ex DB 211 182-1)

CLASS DH 1500 B-B

These locos were the first big diesel locos to be built for the line and brought about the demise of steam in the 1970s. After years of freight-only use they now appear on the modern double-deck passenger stock for which purpose they have been equipped for push-pull working.

Built: 1975–78.
Builder: JW.
Engine: MTU 12V396TC14 of 1200 kW at 1700 r.p.m.
Length over Buffers: 12.00 m.
Transmission: Hydraulic.

Wheel Diameter: 1000 mm.
Weight: 64 tonnes.

Maximum Speed: 100 km/h.

DH 1500.01 (98 45 0015 001-1)
DH 1500.02 (98 45 0015 002-9)
DH 1500.03 (98 45 0015 003-7)

DH 1500.04 (98 45 0015 004-5)
DH 1500.05 (98 45 0015 005-2)
DH 1500.06 (98 45 0015 006-0)

CLASS DH 1700 B-B

With open access giving more opportunities for traffic and heavier trains, GKB acquired a new locomotive from Vossloh in 2003.

Built: 2002.
Builder: Vossloh.
Engine: CAT 3512B-HD of 1700 kW.
Transmission: Hydraulic, Voith L620reU2

Wheel Diameter: 1000 mm .
Weight: 80 tonnes.
Length over Buffers: 15.2 m.
Maximum Speed: 100 km/h.

DH 1700.1 (98 45 0017 001-9)

DIESEL RAILCARS
CLASS VT 10 A-A

GKB got rid of steam off its main passenger trains at quite an early date when it obtained these railbuses in the mid 1950s. The arrival of double-deck sets meant that these vehicles are now spare.

Built: 1955/58.
Builder: Uerdingen WMD.
Engine: Büssing U10 of 110 kW.
Transmission: Mechanical.

Weight: 24 tonnes.
Length over Couplers: 13.30 m.
Maximum Speed: 90 km/h.
Accommodation: –/61.

VT10.03	(99 45 900 1003-3)	VT10.09	(99 45 900 1009-0)

CLASS VT 70 Bo-2-Bo

An articulated railcar built just a stone's throw from Graz GKB station! These DMUs started the turnaround in GKB passenger operations.

Built: 1980–85.
Builder: SGP Graz.
Engines: Two MAN D3256 BTYOE of 225 kW.
Transmission: Electric (BBC).

Weight: 54 tonnes.
Length over Couplers: 30.19 m.
Maximum Speed: 90 km/h
Accommodation: –/50 1T + -/54 (2).

VT 70.01	(98 45 5 070 001-2)	VT 70.01	(98 45 5 070 008-7)
VT 70.02	(98 45 5 070 002-0)	VT 70.01	(98 45 5 070 009-5)
VT 70.03	(98 45 5 070 003-8)	VT 70.01	(98 45 5 070 010-3)
VT 70.04	(98 45 5 070 004-6)	VT 70.01	(98 45 5 070 011-1)
VT 70.05	(98 45 5 070 005-3)	VT 70.01	(98 45 5 070 012-9)
VT 70.06	(98 45 5 070 006-1)	VT 70.01	(98 45 5 070 013-7)
VT 70.07	(98 45 5 070 007-9)		

2.4. GYÖR–SOPRON–EBENFURTI VASÚT GySEV
RAAB–OEDENBURG–EBENFURTER EISENBAHN

Routes: Györ–Sopron–Ebenfurth; Neusiedl–Fertöszentmiklós; Sopron–Szombathely.
Depots: Sopron (Main Depot/Works). Fertöszentmiklos, Györ (Subsheds).
Timetable: 512, 731. **Internet:** www.gysev.hu
Liveries: All GySEV stock now carries a green and yellow livery.

This is an international railway jointly owned by Austria and Hungary – a survivor of the old empire! It uses the Hungarian style of classification.

In recent years GySEV has been trading locos with MAV and lost its M43, M47 and M62 but gained more V43, M44 some M40s and the solitary M42. It has also joined the Taurus revolution and acquired some as Class 1047. Further Taurus locos are leased from ÖBB (q.v.).

DIESEL LOCOMOTIVES

M 40   Bo-Bo

Both these locomotives were acquired from MAV in 2001 when the Sopron–Szombathely line was taken over from MAV. The locos were previously M40 208/222.

Built: 1968/69.
Builder: Ganz Mavag.
Engine: Ganz 16VFE17/24 of 735 kW.
Transmission: Electric.

Wheel Diameter: 1040 mm .
Weight: 76 tonnes.
Length: 14.25 m.
Maximum Speed: 100 km/h.

M40 401 | M40 402

M 42   Bo-Bo

This locomotive was acquired from MAV where it had the same number. It is a one off being a prototype for a new series which never went into production as MAV decided to modernise its diesel locomotives rather than have new locomotives built.

Built: 1994.
Builder: Ganz Hunslet.
Engine: Deutz MWM TBD604BV12 of 640 kW.
Transmission: Electric.

Wheel Diameter: 1040 mm .
Weight: 66 tonnes.
Length: 14.64 m.
Maximum Speed: 80 km/h.

M42 401

M 44   Bo-Bo

These are standard MAV-type shunters some of which were obtained from MAV, some built for GySEV and the last three acquired from Hungarian industry. The type also exists in several former eastern-bloc countries.

Built: 1957–74.
Builder: Ganz Mavag.
Engine: Ganz 16JV 17/24 of 450 kW.
Transmission: Electric.

Wheel Diameter: 1040 mm.
Weight: 62 tonnes.
Length: 11.24 m.
Maximum speed: 80 km/h.

M44 301/2/5/8/9/10/11 were formerly MAV M44 001/025/525/008/018/073/122.
M44 312/13/14 were formerly ex Hungarian industrial locomotives A25-070/080/038.

M44 301	M44 304	M44 307	M44 309	M44 311	M44 313
M44 302	M44 305	M44 308	M44 310	M44 312	M44 314
M44 303	M44 306				

ELECTRIC LOCOMOTIVES
CLASS V43   Bo-Bo

These are standard 25 kV electric locos obtained from the MAV when GySEV electrified in 1984. In turn GySEV sold its M41 diesels to MAV, none of which now remain on the line. The former MAV numbers are in parentheses).

Built: 1963–68.
Builder-Mech. Parts: Ganz-Mavag.
Builder-Elec. Parts: Ganz.
One hour rating: 4300 kW.

Wheel dia.: 1180 mm.
Weight: 80 tonnes.
Length over Buffers: 15.70 m.
Maximum Speed: 130 km/h.

V44 320	(V43.1320)	V43 325	(V43.1325)	V43 330	(V43 1330)
V44 321	(V43.1321)	V43 326	(V43.1326)	V43 332	(V43 1164)
V44 322	(V43.1322)	V43 327	(V43.1327)	V43 333	(V43 1130)
V44 323	(V43.1323)	V43 328	(V43.1328)	V43 334	(V43 1267)
V44 324	(V43.1324)	V43 329	(V43.1329)	V43 335	(V43 1155)

CLASS 1047   Bo-Bo

GySEV and MAV joined forces to order a batch of Taurus electric locomotives which on MAV are 1047.0 whilst on GySEV they are 1047.5. Note that these locomotives would normally have been class V47 but because they work into Austria they are numbered as 1047s which fits into the ÖBB system perfectly. GySEV locomotives work Sopron to Budapest but also into Austria not only to Wien as expected but to balance up mileages there are daily workings from Wien to Villach. (MAV locos also work through to Linz and Wels).

Technical details as ÖBB Class 1116.

1047 501-0 | 1047 502-8 | 1047 503-6 | 1047 504-4 | 1047 505-1

DIESEL RAILCARS
CLASS Bamot   1A-A1

This unit was built new for MAV and obtained and rebuilt in 1970.

Built: 1962.
Builder: Györ.
Engine: Two Gabz JH13 5-17 of 110 kW.
Transmission: Hydraulic.

Weight: 37 tonnes.
Length over Buffers: 22.70 m.
Maximum speed: 90 km/h.
Accommodation: –/64.

Bamot 702

CLASS 5047

This class is the same as ÖBB class 5047 but built in 1995. See ÖBB Class 5047 for technical details

5047 501-1 | 5047 502-9

CLASS 5147

This is the same class as ÖBB 5147 built in 1996. See ÖBB class 5147 for technical details.

5147 511-9 | 5147 512-7

DEPARTMENTAL STOCK

Number	Built	Notes
FJ-001	1987	Overhead line unit with crane.
FJ-205	1987	Overhead line unit with crane.
VF 100		Heating unit, Sopron station. Ex-MAV V42 529.

2.5. HOHENBAHN REISSECK

Gauge: 600 mm.
Route: Schoberboden–Reisseck.
Timetable: .   **Internet:**

This is a difficult line for most people to visit being high in the mountains above Kolbnitz from where the access is by funicular. There are only two locos which are referred to by their works numbers. The locos are standard Jenbach types. In 1993 the line is understood to have received a new railcar which comprised two coaches either side of a Jenbach loco which generates the power.

Number	Type	Built	Power
2240	B dm	Jenbach 2240/1960	30 kW
2406	B dm	Jenbach 2406/1963	15 kW

2.6. LAVEMÜNDE BAHN BETRIEBS GmbH
LBB

This new company has taken over a closed ÖBB line. Local saw mills, the GKB, Lavemünde council and Nostalgie Bahnen im Kärnten are partners in moving timber traffic worked by one of the NBiK preserved diesel locomotives. NBiK are reported as having run some steam-hauled tourist trains over this line in 2004.

CLASS 383   C

This locomotive was built for the VOEST steel works in Linz but in 1983 was sold to a power station at Jenbach and later came into the hands of ÖDK Zeltweg. It was acquired by NBiK for preservation in 1995.

Built: 1957.
Builder: Mavag/VOEST
Engine: Deutz F4L514 of 510 kW.
Transmission: Hydraulic.

Wheel Dia.: mm
Weight: tonnes
Length: m.
Maximum Speed:

383.10

2.7. LTE LOGISTIK und TRANSPORT GmbH
LTE

LTE is an open access operator and a subsidiary of the Graz Köflacher Bahn and Porr Infrastruktor. LTE has also set up its own subsidiary company in Slovakia to permit through workings to that country. Traffic involvement at the time of writing is as follows:

Cement Marchegg to Liesing (2150); cement Kirchdorf – Liesing (2150); trips St. Valentin to oil sidings (2150, main train electric hauled ex Germany by Rail4Chem); coke from Burghausen (Germany)–Simbach–Marchegg–Ziar nad Hronom (Slovakia) (2170); container trains Graz–Duisburg (185, three trains per week, 7500 km for the 185 which works throughout). LTE is also involved in spot traffic and has been hauling newly built "Desiro" EMUs for South West Trains from Wien to Passau. In early 2005 LTE took delivery of 2016 903 so some more expansion is envisaged. LTE does not have a locomotive depot with servicing being carried out by mobile teams.

CLASS 185   Bo-Bo
This locomotive is a Bombardier DB Class 185 (33624/2003) taken off the production line in Kassel for LTE. It is certified for operation in Germany and Austria but interestingly has video camera fittings indicating that it might also be permitted in Switzerland or that Bombardier diverted a locomotive intended for Switzerland to LTE!

(Technical details as per DB 185 – see German Railways part1))

185 528-7

CLASS 2016   Bo-Bo
This locomotive was delivered as a standard 2016 (ex Dispolok ER20-009). After acceptance trials by LTE the locomotive is to have its electric train supply removed and the space used for greater fuel tank capacity.

See ÖBB 2016 for technical details.

2016 903-3

CLASS 2150   B-B
This class is the Vossloh/Mak type G1206. Originally purchased by LTE the locomotives now belong to Angel Trains Cargo and are now leased to LTE

Built: 2001.
Builder: VSFT (1001120, 1001123).
Engine: Caterpillar 3512B DI-TA-SC of 1500 kW.
Length: 14.7 m.
Transmission: Hydraulic. Voith L5r4ZU2

Wheel Diameter: 1000 mm .
Weight: 84 tonnes.

Maximum Speed: 100 km/h

2150 901-3 Birgit | 2150.902-1 Brigitte

CLASS 2170   B-B
This is another Vossloh/Mak product and is in fact the prototype locomotive that was exhibited at Innotrans in 2002.

Built: 2002
Builder: VSFT (1001159)
Engine: Caterpillar 3512 B-HD of 1700 kW.
Power: 1700 kW
Transmission: Hydraulic, Voith L620reU2

Wheel Diameter: 1000 mm
Weight: 80 tonnes
Length: 15.2 m.
Maximum Speed: 100 km/h

2170 001-8 Johanna

2.8. MONTAFONERBAHN AG   **MBS**

Route: Bludenz–Schruns.
Timetable: 420.
Depot: Schruns.
Internet: www.montafonerbahn.at

This 12.8 km line runs from the ÖBB junction at Blundenz to a terminal at Schruns, hence the abbreviation MBS. There are through passenger workings onto the ÖBB.

ELECTRIC LOCOMOTIVES
CLASS 1045   **Bo-Bo**

Obtained second hand from the ÖBB these locos have a long association with the Arlberg line.

Built: 1927–28.
Builder – Mech. Parts: Wiener Neustadt/Floridsdorf.
Builder – Elec. Parts: Elin.
One Hour Rating: 1140 kW
Maximum Tractive Effort: 150 kW
Wheel Diameter: 1300 mm.
Weight: 61.2 tonnes.
Length over Buffers: 10.40 m.
Maximum Speed: 60 km/h.

1045.01 | 1045.03

ELECTRIC RAILCARS

ET 10.103/4   **Bo-Bo**

These two units are former DB diesel railcars (VT 63) acquired in 1961 and rebuilt to Electric. Both these units were made spare in 2001 after the arrival of the new units from Stadler.

Built: 1935 Rebuilt 1965/74.
Builder – Mech. Parts: Lindner.
Builder – Elec. Parts: AEG Berlin.
Motors: Two of 370 kW.
Weight: 40 tonnes.
Length over Buffers: 22.08 m.
Maximum Speed: 100 km/h.
Accommodation: 8/56.

ET 10.103   (VT 63 905) | ET 10.104   (VT 63 907)

ET 10.107/8   **Bo-Bo+2-2**

These are Swiss built NPZ units.

Built: 1990/94.
Builder – Mech. Parts: FFA/SIG/SWP.
Builder – Elec. Parts: BBC (ABB).
One Hour Rating: 1650 kW
Weight: 70 t.
Length over Buffers: 25.00 m.
Maximum Speed: 140 km/h.
Accommodation: -/65 1T.

ET 10.107 | ET 10.108

ET10.109/110   **Bo-Bo**

These new units have allowed older stock to be stored.

Built: 2000.
Builder, Mechanical parts: Stadler.
Builder, Electrical parts: Adtranz
One Hour Rating: 800 kW.
Length: 23.514 m.
Weight: 46 tonnes.
Accommodation: –/56 1T.
Maximum Speed: 140 km/h.

ET10.109   Ernest Hemingway | ET10.110   Anita Wacter

DIESEL LOCOMOTIVE

CLASS V10   **D**

The line has only one diesel loco in stock and this is former KFBE V 51.

Built: 1956.
Builder: KHD.
Engine: Deutz T12M625 of 59 kW.
Transmission: Hydraulic.
Wheel Dia: 1120 mm.
Weight In Full Working Order: 60 t.
Length over Buffers:
Maximum Speed: 64km/h.

V 10.016

DEPARTMENTAL STOCK
CLASS X10

A former ÖBB Class 5081 converted into an overhead line maintenance unit.

Built: 1964-67
Builders: Uerdingen/JW/SGP.
Engine: Büssing U10.

Transmission: Mechanical.
Length over Buffers: 13.95 m.
Maximum Speed: 90 km/h.

X 10.903 (5081.12)

2.9. NIEDERÖSTERREICHISCHE SCHNEE-BERGBAHN GmbH   NÖSBB

Timetable: 523.
Internet: www.schneebergbahn.at

The ÖBB line from Puchberg to Hochschneeberg was privatised on 01/01/1997. The new company is 50% ÖBB and 50% NÖVOG (Niederösterreichische Verkehrs Organisations Gesellschaft); the infrastructure remains the property of ÖBB. The biggest change has been the acquisition of some rack fitted push-pull diesel trains.

STEAM LOCOMOTIVES

CLASS 999.0 & 999.1   0-4-2RT

Class 999.0 were built for and continue to operate this line. Class 999.1 were all built for the Schafbergbahn, but one now operates on the Schneebergbahn.

Built: 1893–94 (1896*).
Builder: Krauss, Linz.
Boiler Pressure: 1.40 MN/m^2 (200 lb/sq.in).
Driving Wheel Diameter: 706 mm.
Rack Wheel Diameter: 575 mm.
Trailing Wheel Diameter: 520 mm.
Max. Speed: 12 km/h.

Gauge: 1000 mm.
System: Abt rack.
Cylinders (2): 320 x 600 mm.
Weight: 18 (17.4*) tonnes.
Length: 5.55 (5.50*) m.
Tractive Effort – Adhesion: 89.2 kN (20070 lbf).
Tractive Effort – Rack: 110.6 kN (24700 lbf).

0999 001-1	0999 004-5
0999 002-2	0999 005-2
0999 003-7	0999 101-9* Schneeberg

RACK DIESEL LOCOS   B

These new trains were ordered in 1997 and delivered in 1999. The locomotives have a single cab and form a set with a trailer and a driving trailer. One locomotive is spare. The overall length of loco and carriages is 30.416 m whilst seating capacity is 119. The trailers are numbered 21, 22 whilst the driving trailers are 31, 32. The builders of the carriages are Waagner-Biró and Swoboda. These trains have a bizarre yellow and black colour scheme, hence their nickname of "Salamanders".

Built: 1999.
Builder: Hunslet Barclay.
Engine: Caterpillar 3412E DITTA JW 12 cyl.
Power: 544 kW at 1800 r.p.m.
Tractive Effort: 100 kN.

Wheel Diameter:
Weight: 15.25 tonnes
Length:
Maximum Speed: 15 km/h.
Transmission: Hydraulic.

11	FRANZ JOSEF
12	SISSI
13	LEO ARNOLDI

2.10. SALZBURGER LOKALBAHN   SLB
SALZBURGER EISENBAHN TRANSPORT
LOGISTIK GMbH   SETG

Routes: Salzburg–Lamprechtshausen, Bürmoos–Trimmelkam (35.3 km.)
System: 1000 V d.c.   **Depot/Works:** Salzburg Itzling.
Timetable: 210.   **Internet:** www.slb.at

This line is the remnant of a former light railway, the Salzburger Eisenbahn & Tramway Gesellschaft (SETG) which was formed in 1888. This ran from Berchtesgaden (with a branch to Königsee) in Germany. The line was taken over by the city in 1947 and was known as the Salzburger Stadtwerke Verkehrsbetriebe (SVB). Only the line from Salzburg to Lamprechtshausen remains plus the branch from Bürmoos to Trimmelkam which was taken over from Stern & Hafferl on 1st January 1994. Major alterations have taken place at the Salzburg end where the terminal station has been put underground. The line is now known as the Salzburger Lokalbahn, but is still owned by the city. The initials SETG are now in use again – see under diesel locomotives.

ELECTRIC LOCOMOTIVES

E 11   Bo

This small electric loco was obtained second hand in 1982 from Bahnen der Stadt Monheim (D) where it was No.14

Built: 1913.   **Wheel Diameter:** 900 mm.
Builder – Mech. Parts: AEG.   **Weight:** 48 tonnes.
Builder – Elec. Parts: AEG.   **Length over Buffers:** 6.25 m.
Power: 150 kW.   **Maximum Speed:** 30 km/h.

E 11

E 60   Bo-Bo

The first two locos were built for the line but the last two were obtained from SAKOG in 1974 and 1994 respectively.

Built: 1952.   **Wheel Diameter:** 900 mm.
Builder – Mech. Parts: SGP Graz.   **Weight:** 46 (* 44.8) tonnes.
Builder – Elec. Parts: BBC (Elin§).   **Length over Buffers:** 11.90 m.
Power: 380 kW (270 kW*, 292 kW§).   **Maximum Speed:** 60 km/h (*§ 50 km/h).

E 61 | E 62 | E 63   (E 27 002)* | E64   (E 27 001)§

E 71   Bo-Bo

Built new for the line to handle increasing freight tonnage that was getting too much for the older locos.

Built: 1986.   **Wheel Diameter:** 1000 mm.
Builder – Mech. Parts: Knotz.   **Weight:** 73 tonnes.
Builder – Elec. Parts: AEG.   **Length over Buffers:** 12.96 m.
Power: 600 kW.   **Maximum Speed:** 60 km/h.

E 71

DIESEL LOCOMOTIVES

SLB has obtained some diesel shunters in recent years which are involved in the open access arrangements. SLB has formed Salzburger Eisenbahn Transport Logistik GmbH (SETG) with Mittelweserbahn (MWB) in Germany. This joint company is involved mostly with timber products but also has some chemical traffic. MWB handles the long haul from Salzburg to the North Sea ports whilst SLB uses the diesels for shunting and trip working from Salzburg to final destinations such as Hallein and Hüttau.

V 81   B

This shunter was obtained second hand from the Wiener Lokalbahn where it was V 81. It is basically an ÖBB X262.

V 81

V 82   C

The SLB has obtained another diesel from the Wiener Lokalbahn, in this case the former WLB V 80.

Built: 1962.   **Wheel Diameter:** 950 mm.
Builder: JW.   **Weight:** 48 tonnes.
Engine: JW 600 of 445 kW.   **Length over Buffers:** 10.50 m.
Transmission: Hydraulic   **Maximum Speed:** 60 km/h.

V 82

V 83–87   B-B

The search for new locomotives coincided with ÖBB receiving its new 2070s and disposing of 2048s. SLB has some options for more as shown below. The locomotives are DB Class 211s that were re-engined by Layritz and became ÖBB Class 2048.

Built: 1962.   **Wheel Diameter:** 950 mm.
Builder: Layritz.   **Weight:** 64 tonnes.
Engine: Caterpillar type 351281 of 810 kW (1085 h.p.) at 1500 r.p.m.
Transmission: Hydraulic, Voith.   **Length over Buffers:** 12.10 m.
Maximum Speed: 100 km/h.

V 83   (ex MWB V 1101, ex ÖBB 2048 001-8 ex DB 211 297-7)
V 84   (ex ÖBB 2048 002-6 ex DB 211 084-9)
V 85   (ex ÖBB 2048 003-4 ex DB 211 099-7)
V 86   (ex ÖBB 2048 004-2 ex DB 211 100-3 (option))
V 87   (ex ÖBB 2048 018-2 ex DB 211 119-3 (on loan))

ELECTRIC RAILCARS

ET 1   Bo

Built for the Salzburger Lokalbahn then to Stern & Hafferl in 1954. Used on various lines but ended up at Bürmoos and passed back to SVB in 1994 when SVB took over the Bürmoos-Trimmelkam line. It has since regained its original number. Departmental car.

Built: 1908.   **Weight:** 18 tonnes.
Builder – Mech. Parts: MAN.   **Length over Buffers:** 9.31 m.
Builder – Elec. Parts: SSW.   **Maximum Speed:** 50 km/h.
Power: 138 kW.   **Accommodation:** –/32

ET 1 (StH 20.105)

MBC 3   Bo

This old railcar is now in "Nostalgic" service.

Built: 1908.   **Weight:** 17.8 tonnes.
Builder – Mech. Parts: MAN.   **Length over Buffers:** 9.37 m.
Builder – Elec. Parts: SSW.   **Maximum Speed:** 40 km/h.
Power: 126 kW.   **Accommodation:** 8/24

MBC 3 (ET 3)

ET 6–7 Bo

No. 6 is an original unit for the line but 7 was originally Konigl. Bayr. Staatsbahn No. 101 becoming DRB ET 184 01. In 1943 it became SETG MC 16 then MC 27 and ET 27 until 1981 when it became ET 7. Both in "Nostalgic" service.

Built: 1908, 1907.
Builder – Mech. Parts: MAN.
Builder – Elec. Parts: SSW.
Power: 306 kW.

Weight: 18 tonnes.
Length over Buffers: 9.37 m.
Maximum Speed: 60 km/h.
Accommodation: –/32.

ET6 Georg Rendl | ET7

ET 10 Bo

Another original Salzburg unit built as SETG MG1 later becoming ET 11 and from 1981 it was ET 1 but in 1994 then original ET 1 came back so it has now been renumbered yet again to ET 10! Now used as a breakdown train vehicle.

Built: 1919.
Builder – Mech. Parts: MAN.
Builder – Elec. Parts: SSW.
Power: 126 kW.

Weight: 16.6 tonnes.
Length over Buffers: 9.70 m.
Maximum Speed: 40 km/h.

ET 10

ET 33

Built for SVB. Now in "Nostalgic" service.

Built: 1951.
Builder – Mech. Parts: SGPG.
Builder – Elec. Parts: SSW.
Power: 612 kW.

Weight: 37.5 tonnes.
Length over Buffers: 16.90 m.
Maximum Speed: 60 km/h.
Accommodation: –/48.

ET 33

ET 41–54 Bo-2-Bo

These new articulated light rail-style vehicles were built over a period of 9 years and have transformed the line.

Built: 1983 (41–45), 1988 (46–50), 1992 (51–54).
Builder – Mech. Parts: SGP Graz.
Builder – Elec. Parts: AEG
Power: 600 kW.

Weight: 50.0 tonnes.
Length over Coupers: 28.40 m.
Maximum Speed: 80 km/h.
Accommodation: 32 (8) + 32 (8). 100 standees.

ET 41	Stadt Salzburg		ET 48	Göming
ET 42	Bergheim		ET 49	Stonnes. Gorgen
ET 43	Oberndorf		ET 50	Freilassing
ET 44	Bürmoos		ET 51	Berchtesgaden
ET 45	Lamprechthausen		ET 52	Dorfbeuern
ET 46	Anthering		ET 53	Stonnes. Pantaleon
ET 47	Nussdorf		ET 54	Laufen

ET 55–58 Bo-2-Bo

A development of ET 41–54 with swing-plug doors and a GPS-based information system.

Built: 2001–2002.
Builder – Mech. Parts: Siemens SGP.
Builder – Elec. Parts: Bombardier
Power: 600 kW.

Weight: 49.4 tonnes.
Length over Coupers: 28.40 m.
Maximum Speed: 80 km/h.
Accommodation: 32 (8) + 32 (8). 100 standees.

ET 55	Land Salzburg		ET 57	Ober Innviertel
ET 56	Land Oberösterreich		ET 58	Partnerstadt Dresden

2.11. STEIERMÄRKISCHE LANDESBAHNEN
StLB

The Austrian province of Steiermark has many standard and narrow gauge lines grouped together and run by the local government. There are some 47 km of standard gauge and 120 km of narrow gauge lines. Although managed by a central office, stock rarely changes from one line to another.
Internet: www.stlb.at

2.11.1. FELDBACH–BAD GLEICHENBERG

21 .2 km. Electrified at opening in 1931.

System: 800 V DC.
Depot: Feldbach.
Timetable: 532.

ELECTRIC LOCOMOTIVES

E 41   Bo-Bo

Built: 1930.
Builder – Mech. Parts: Graz.
Builder – Elec. Parts: AEG.
Power: 400 kW.

Wheel Diameter: 1000 mm.
Weight: 38.3 tonnes.
Length: 9.78 m.
Maximum Speed: 50 km/h.

E 41

ELECTRIC RAILCARS

ET 1/2   Bo-Bo

These two units also appear to be from the opening period but within the last 20 years both have been rebodied and rebuilt internally. (1978, 1990).

Built: 1930 Reb. 1978/90.
Builder – Mech. Parts: Graz.
Builder – Elec. Parts: Elin.
Power: 295 kW.

Weight: 35.3 tonnes.
Length over Buffers: 16.24 m.
Maximum Speed: 50 km/h.
Accommodation: –/45.

ET 1 | ET 2 |

DIESEL LOCOMOTIVE

RT 1   B

Built: 1963.
Builder - Mech. Parts: JW.
Builder - Elec. Parts: JW.
Power: 15 kW.
Transmission: Mechanical

Driving wheel dia:
Weight:
Length :
Maximum Speed:

RT 1

DEPARTMENTAL STOCK

X 51

2.11.2 GLEISDORF–WEIZ

Open access has allowed StLB to work trains off its own system to destinations far away and even into or via Hungary. For this purpose extra locomotives have been acquired. StLB also won the contract to do the shunting at the new container and freight terminal at Graz Süd (Werndorf) where DE 2 and D 3 are normally employed.

Depot: Weiz.   **Timetable:** 531.

DIESEL LOCOMOTIVES

DE 1/2   Co

DE 1 usually shunts at Weiz whilst DE 2 is spare at Graz Süd Cargo Centre.

Built: 1964–65.
Builder – Mech. Parts: ÖAM.
Builder – Elec. Parts: BBC.
Engine: MTU 8V396TC II of 550 kW.
Transmission: Electric.

Wheel Diameter: 1000 mm.
Weight: 48 tonnes.
Length over Buffers: 9.50 m.
Maximum Speed: 60 km/h.

DE 1   DE 2

D 3   B-B

StLB surprised everyone in 1993 by acquiring a new loco from Germany and not from a local manufacturer. Like all modern shunting locos it is capable of remote radio control. Normally used at Graz Süd Cargo Centre.

Built: 1993.
Builder : Käble/Gmeinder.
Engine: 1100 kW.
Transmission: Hydraulic

Wheel Diameter:
Weight: 72 tonnes.
Length over Buffers: 12.90 m.
Maximum Speed: 100 km/h.

D 3

D 4–D 6   B-B

These modern locomotives were obtained for open access trains. They are capable of remote control by radio and are fitted with automatic shunting couplers. Like some other lines UIC style numbers are starting to appear. D 4 and D 6 work trips between Weiz and Gleisdorf whilst D 5 shunts at Graz Süd Cargo Centre.

Built: 1999 (D 4), 2002
Builder: Gmeinder
Engine: MTU V12 4000 R20 of 1500 kW.
Transmission: Hydraulic – Voith L5r4zseU2

Wheel Diameter: 1000 mm
Weight: 72 tonnes.
Length over Buffers: 13.93 m
Maximum Speed: 60/120 km/h

D 4   (UIC 90 34 0020 004-9)   D 6   (UIC 90 34 0020 006-4)
D 5   (UIC 90 34 0020 005-6)

D 45   B-B

This locomotive was acquired second hand from an industrial concern in Romania. It is a standard FAUR product but appears to have seen little use since arriving at Weiz. It was LDH45-051 in Romania. Currently stored at weiz.

Built: 1970
Builder: U23A
Engine: 331 kW
Transmission: Hydraulic.

Wheel Diameter: mm
Weight: tonnes.
Length over Buffers:
Maximum Speed:

D45 03

V60 D

This locomotive is another second hand acquisition but did not have to travel far being obtained from the ELIN factory in Weiz. It is a standard DR V60D later DB class 346. (Technical spec as a DB 346 – see German Railways Part 1.)

V 60

CLASS 2016 Bo-Bo

The need for more locomotives intensified as ÖBB was receiving the last of its 2016s. The loco intended to be 2016 090 was diverted to StLB becoming 2016 901! Both locos are normally used in multiple on an overnight freight from Weiz to Wiener Neustadt and return. For technical details see ÖBB 2016.

2016 901-7 | 2016 902-5

SHUNTING ROBOTS

StLB needed some more shunting engines so that main line locomotives could be used elsewhere. This was at the time when ÖBB was disposing of surplus class 2060 diesel shunting locomotives. They have had their diesel engines and transmissions removed and converted to battery electric operation. The locomotives shunt at various sidings on the line. They have a pantograph fitted for use when recharging the batteries.

Built: 1998
Builder – Mech. Parts: StLB Weiz
Builder – Elec. Parts: WB Antriebstechnik Waltrop, Germany
Length over Buffers: 6.68 m.
Maximum Speed: 7.5 or 15 km/h.
Wheel Diameter: 950mm
Weight: 25tonnes.
Power: 32 kW (54 kW for max. 5 minutes)
Transmission: Electric

RE 01 (2060 008-6)
RE 02 (2060 001-1)
| RE 03 (2060 007-8)
| RE 04 (2060 030-0)

DIESEL RAILCARS

VT 51/2 B-2

ÖBB Class 5047 vehicles bought by StLB in 1992.

Built: 1987.
Builder: JW.
Engine: Daimler Benz OM444LA of 419 kW.
Transmission: Hydraulic.
Weight: 45 tonnes.
Length over Buffers: 25.42 m.
Maximum Speed: 120 km/h.
Accommodation: –/62 (6) 1T.

VT 51 (5047 401-4) WEIZ | VT 52 5047 402-2) GLEISDORF

Other vehicle:

X 41

2.11.3. PEGGAU–ÜBELBACH

(10.25 km)

System: 15 kV AC 16.7 Hz.
Depot: Übelbach.
Timetable: 540.

ELECTRIC MULTIPLE UNITS

ET 14 Bo-Bo+2-2

A secondhand acquisition from Switzerland being ex SZU BDe4/4 91 + Bt 191.

Built: 1955.
Builder: SWS/MFO.
Power: 520 kW.
Accommodation: –/34 + –/60
Weight: 25 + 19 tonnes.
Maximum Speed: 70 km/h.
Length: 20.60 +20.60 m.

ET 14 + ES 24

ET 15 Bo-Bo+2-2

Another secondhand acquisition from Switzerland, these cars still carry their former numbers (SZU BDe4/4 593 + Bt 994.

Built: 1955.
Builder: SWS/MFO.
Power: 520 kW.
Accommodation: –/48 + –/72

Weight: .
Maximum Speed: 70 km/h.
Length: 22.35 +22.12 m.

ET 15 + ES 25

2.11.4. MIXNITZ–ST. ERHARD

This freight-only 10.4 km line has its own standard gauge shunters for transfer work at the main-line junction.

Gauge: 760 mm.
Depot: Mixnitz.

System: 800 V DC.

DIESEL LOCOMOTIVES

VEL 1 Bo

Built: 1956.
Builder: Gebus.
Engine: ?
Power: 48 kW.
Transmission: Electric.

Wheel Diameter: 950 mm.
Weight: 20 tonnes.
Length: 6.56 m.
Maximum Speed: 18 km/h.
Gauge: 1435 mm.

VEL 1

VHL 2 B

Built: 1967.
Builder: JW.
Engine: JW 200
Power: 150 kW.
Transmission: Hydraulic.

Wheel Diameter: 950 mm.
Weight: 27 tonnes.
Length: 6.64 m.
Maximum Speed: 60 km/h.
Gauge: 1435 mm.

VHL 2

E 1/2 Bo

Built: 1913.
Builder: AEG.
Engine: AEG.
Power: 122 kW.
Gauge: 760 mm.

Wheel Diameter: 950 mm.
Weight: 15 tonnes.
Length: 5.51 m.
Maximum Speed: 30 km/h.

E 1 | E 2 |

E 3/4 Bo-Bo

Built: 1957/63.
Builder: ÖAM.
Engine: BBC.
Power: 150 kW.
Gauge: 760 mm.

Wheel Diameter: 840 mm.
Weight: 30 tonnes.
Length: 9.60 m.
Maximum Speed: 40 km/h.

E 3 | E 4 |

2.11.5. UNZMARKT–TAMSWEG (MURTALBAHN)

This line is 65. 5 km long and used to go through to Mauterndorf.

Gauge: 760 mm.
Depots: Murau-Stozalpe (Main depot & works), Unzmarkt, Tamsweg (Sub-sheds).
Timetable: 630.

STEAM LOCOMOTIVES

Stainz 2 0-4-0T

As the name suggests this loco originated on the Stainz system which once connected into the GKB but became part of the StLB in the 1920s. Its current use is for amateur driving.

Built: 1892.	**Boiler Pressure:** 1.00 MN/sq. m. (165 lb/sq.in).
Builder: Krauss Linz.	**Weight:** 12 tonnes.
Wheel Diameter: 760 mm.	**Cylinders:** 225 x 350 mm.
Length over Buffers: 5.35 m.	**Maximum Speed:** 25 km/h.

Stainz 2

CLASS U 0-6-2T

The "U" in the classification stands for Unzmarkt - the line which the first locos of this type were built for and all subsequent locos of the same type were classed "U". Of these locos U40 was in fact built for the Trieste–Parenzo line and also saw service in Jugoslavia before coming to the StLB lines. U43 was built for the Unzmarkt line. As far as it is known both locos have never been withdrawn from service and simply graduated from normal service into tourist train use.

Built: 1894, 1908, 1913.	**Boiler Pressure:** 1.00 MN/sq. m. (165 lb/sq.in).
Builder: WrN, KrL.	**Weight:** 24.5 tonnes.
Driving Wheel Diameter: 800 mm.	**Cylinders:** 290 x 400 mm.
Length over Buffers: 7.54 m.	**Maximum Speed:** 45 km/h.
Tractice Effort: 160 kW.	

U 11 | U 40 | U 43 |

DIESEL LOCOMOTIVES

VL 6 B

Another import from Germany oiginating on the Rhein Sieg Eisenbahn (V 13) then passing to the Zillertalbahn in 1969 (D11) and then the StLB in 1974.

Built: 1959.	**Wheel Diameter:** 700 mm.
Builder: OK.	**Weight:** 18 tonnes.
Engine: OK316V6D of 104 kW.	**Length over Buffers:** 5.50 m.
Transmission: Hydraulic.	**Maximum Speed:** 20 km/h.

VL 6

VL 12–16 Bo-Bo

These locos were all built for the StLB lines and continue to see use on what freight trains still run. VL 14–16 are on the Weiz–Birkfeld line.

Built: 1966-7.	**Wheel Diameter:** 840 mm.
Builder – Mech. Parts: ÖAM.	**Weight:** 31 tonnes.
Builder – Eelc. Parts: BBC.	**Length over Buffers:** 9.80 m.
Engine: 260 kW (315 kW*).	**Maximum Speed:** 50 km/h.
Transmission: Electric.	

VL 12   EHRENFRIED | VL 13   FERDINAND

DIESEL RAILCARS

CLASS VT 30   Bo-Bo

These modern railcars from which the ÖBB Class 5090 were developed reinvigorated passenger services on the line and allowed bus services to be taken off!

Built: 1980/81 (1998*).
Builder: Knotz/BBC.
Engine: MAN D3256BTYVE of 250 kW.
Transmission: Electric.

Weight: 28.8 tonnes.
Length: 18.30 m.
Maximum Speed: 70 km/h.
Accommodation: –/56.

| VT 31 | VT 32 | VT 33 | VT 34 | VT 35* | |

CLASS VS 40   2-2

Trailers to work with Class VT 30.

Built: 1980/81.
Builder: Knotz/BBC
Maximum Speed: 70 km/h.

Weight: tonnes.
Length: 17.80 m.
Accommodation: –/52 1T.

Note: Some or all of these traiilers are now –/34 1T plus a bicycle stowage area.

| VS 41 | VS 42 | VS 43 | VS 44 | |

DEPARTMENTAL STOCK

X 42
X 45
X 52

2.11.6. WEIZ–OBERFEISTRITZ (FEISTRITZTALBAHN)

This line is 13 km long and is freight-only but with steam-hauled tourist trains in the summer. The section from Oberfeistritz to Birkfeld is owned and operated by the preservation group "Club U44".

Gauge: 760 mm. **Depot & Works:** Weiz.

STEAM LOCOMOTIVES

Kh 101 0-10-0T

The K in the classification denotes the type originated on the Kuhnsdorf system, the h means superheated (heissdampf). The loco has wondered about the StLB lines being used at first on the Unzmarkt system and was at Kapfenberg before coming to Weiz.

Built: 1926. **Boiler Pressure:** 1.00 MN/sq. m. (165 lb/sq.in).
Builder: KrL. **Weight:** 33.3 tonnes.
Driving wheel dia: 800 mm. **Cylinders:** 400 x 400 mm.
Length: 8.72 m. **Maximum Speed:** 45 km/h.
Power: 280 kW.

Kh 101

U 8/44 0-6-2T

U8 is one of the original locos built for the Unzmarkt line whilst U44 was built much later for the same system.

Built: 1894 (*1922). **Boiler Pressure:** 1.00 MN/sq. m. (165 lb/sq.in).
Builder: Krauss L. **Weight:** 24.5 tonnes.
Driving wheel dia: 800 mm. **Cylinders:** 290 x 400 mm.
Length: 7.54 m. **Maximum Speed:** 45 km/h.
Power: 160 kW.

U 8 | U 44*

DIESEL LOCOMOTIVES

VL 4 C

This little shunter is a former Wehrmacht HF 130C type obtained second-hand from a paper factory.

Built: 1942. **Wheel Diameter:** 750 mm.
Builder: Gmeinder. **Weight:** 16.5 tonnes.
Engine: 100 kW. **Length:** 5.58 m.
Transmission: Hydraulic. **Maximum Speed:** 25 km/h.

VL 4

VL 8 B

This locomotive came second hand from Judenburg Stahlwerk.

Built: 1966 **Wheel Diameter:** mm
Builder: Jung, 13989 **Weight in full working order:** 16tonnes.
Engine: 110 kW **Length over Buffers:**
Transmission: Hydraulic. **Maximum Speed:** 20 km/h

VL 8

VL 14–16 Bo-Bo

Built 1967 for StLB lines. For details see VL 12–13 on Unzmarkt System.

VL 14 | VL 15 | VL 16*

VL 22–24   Bo-Bo

These three locos were acquired from Yugoslavia in 1980 after that country had closed down the major parts of its 760 mm gauge lines. StLB then spent some 4–6 years converting the locos to suit their requirements. The locos have been modified for radio remote control.

Built: 1972.
Builder: Djuro Djakovic.
Engine: MTU 6V396 Tc12 of 485 kW.
Transmission: Hydraulic.

Wheel Diameter: 850 mm.
Weight: 32 tonnes.
Length: 12.85 m.
Maximum Speed: 50 km/h.

VL 22 | VL 23 | VL 24 (ex 740-106)

RT 3   B

There is a talcum factory on the Weiz system at Oberfeistritz where this loco shunts. It was acquired in 1980 from Braubach am Rhein (Lok I).

Built: 1957.
Builder: Deutz.
Engine: 41 kW.
Transmission: Hydraulic.

Wheel Diameter: ?
Weight: ?
Length over Buffers: ?
Maximum Speed: 25 km/h.

RT 3

2.12 STERN & HAFFERL   StH

This organisation runs several lines in Oberösterreich. Many of these lines use second-hand tramway equipment and offer a quaint way of travel through some backwater routes. The lines are owned by Stern & Hafferl, but are operated by subsidiaries.

NUMBERING SYSTEM

The second digit of the numbering system denotes the owning company and the third digit denotes the type as follows:

Second digit:

20000	Stern und Hafferl	24000	LV
22000	LILO	25000	LH
23000	GV	26000	VA

Third digit:

This is 0 for a locomotive, 1 for a railcar and 2 for a trailer.

Note that vehicles are often, but not always, renumbered when transferred between lines. On renumbering, the last two digits are generally unaltered unless this would cause duplication. Renumberings shown are those which have occurred since the first edition of this book.

Details of the lines operated, which are all electrified at 800 V DC, are as follows:

STANDARD GAUGE LINES
2.12.1. LINZER LOKALBAHN   LILO

A commuter line with some freight traffic. The Neumarkt–Waizenkirchen–Peuerbach line was a seperate undertaking but was assimilated into LILO in 1998.

Routes: Linz–Peuerbach. Waizenkirchen–Niederspaching–Neumarkt-Kalham.
Depots: Eferding, Waizenkirchen.
Length: 58.9 km.   **Timetable:** 143.

ELECTRIC LOCOMOTIVES
E 22 001   Bo-Bo

This loco is from Wöllersdorf which LILO acquired in 1935.

Built: 1915.	**Wheel Diameter:** 900 mm.
Builder – Mech. Parts: Ganz.	**Weight:** 30 tonnes.
Builder – Elec. Parts: Ganz.	**Length over Buffers:** 11.70 m.
Power: 200 kW.	**Maximum Speed:** 40 km/h.

22 001

E 22 002   Bo

An original LILO loco.

Built: 1912	**Wheel Diameter:** 900 mm.
Builder – Mech. Parts: Ganz.	**Weight:** 19 tonnes.
Builder – Elec. Parts: SSW.	**Length over Buffers:** 6.90 m.
Power: 80 kW.	**Maximum Speed:** 25 km/h.

22 002

E 22 004/5 — Bo-Bo

These are two steeple cab locos. 22.004 was on the Pressburgerbahn as Eg6 being obtained in 1945, whilst 22 005 is from the Wöllersdorf amunition factory (No. 11) and was obtained in 1947.

Built: 1915/26.
Builder – Mech. Parts: Ganz.
Builder – Elec. Parts: Ganz.
Power: 200 kW.

Wheel Diameter: 900 mm.
Weight: 30 tonnes.
Length over Buffers: 11.70 m.
Maximum Speed: 40 km/h.

E 22 004 | E 22 005

E 22 006 — Bo-Bo

Acquired in 1980 from Wuppertal Stadtwerke (3609).

Built: 1912
Builder – Mech. Parts: Maffei.
Builder – Elec. Parts: SSW.
Power: 600 kW.

Wheel Diameter: 1000 mm.
Weight: 60 tonnes.
Length over Buffers: 10.90 m.
Maximum Speed: 40 km/h.

E 22 006

ELECTRIC RAILCARS

ET 22 105 — Bo

This wooden-bodied unit has been reinstated as a museum car having spent some time in the tramway museum at Mariazell.

Built: 1951.
Builder – Mech. Parts: Graz.
Builder – Elec. Parts: AEG.
Accommodation: –/55

Power: 100 kW.
Weight: 17.5 tonnes.
Length over Buffers: 11.50 m.
Maximum Speed: 50 km/h.

22 105 (also carried 25 105 previously)

ET 22 106/7 — Bo-Bo

Buit new for LILO. 22 106 also carried 20 112 and 21 106 previously.

Built: 1951.
Builder – Mech. Parts: SGP Graz.
Builder – Elec. Parts: Elin.
Accommodation: –/54

Power: 376 kW.
Weight: 39 tonnes.
Length over Buffers: 16.90 m.
Maximum Speed: 60 km/h.

22 106 | 22 107 |

ET 22 108 — Bo-Bo

This unit is ex-SVB ET 32 in 1994.

Built: 1952.
Builder – Mech. Parts: SGP Graz.
Builder – Elec. Parts: BBC.
Accommodation: –/48

Power: 376 kW.
Weight: 37.5 t.
Length over Buffers: 18.07 m.
Maximum Speed: 60 km/h.

22 108

ET 22 109 — Bo

An original NWP unit now classed as a museum car and retained for excursion use.

Built: 1908.
Builder – Mech. Parts: Graz.
Builder – Elec. Parts: AEG.
Accommodation: –/32

Power: 108 kW.
Weight: 17.0 tonnes.
Length over Buffers: 17.00 m.
Maximum Speed: 50 km/h.

22 109   (21 150)

ET 22 134–137/ES 22 234–237   Bo-Bo + 2-2

This batch of units were all acquired from KFBE in the early 1970s and entered service on the Linz system in the next 13 years. 137 is a single car with two cabs and acted as a strengthening unit. At present stored now that the new dual-voltage units have arrived. Two units of this type have been transferred to the Lambach–Vorchdorf line.

Built: 1953–54.
Builder – Mech. Parts: Westwaggon.
Builder – Elec. Parts: Kiepe.
Accommodation: –/49 + –/49 (–/49*).

Power: 240 kW.
Weight: 24.1 t + 18.1 tonnes.
Length over Buffers: 15.75 + 15.75 m.
Maximum Speed: 60 km/h.

22 134 + 22 234	(KFBE 1292 + 2292)	22.137* (KFBE 1289)
22 135 + 22 235	(KFBE 1291 + 2291)	

ET 22 141–143ab   Bo-Bo + 2–2

These units were also obtained from the Köln area being from the KBE (Köln–Bonner Eisenbahn) in 1987. All now stored at Eferding.

Built: 1954–56.
Builder – Mech. Parts: Westwaggon.
Builder – Elec. Parts: SSW.
Accommodation: –/60 + –/69.

Power: 272 kW.
Weight: 60.7 tonnes.
Length over Buffers: 19.34 + 19.34 m.
Maximum Speed: 60 km/h.

22141   (KBE ET 60) | 22 142 (KBE ET 59) | 22 142 (KBE ET 55)

ET 22 151–158   2-Bo-2

These are new units of type GTW 2/6. 22 151 was delivered as dual voltage and the others are being retrospectively converted to dual voltage.

Built: 2000
Builder – Mech. Parts: Stadler.
Builder – Elec. Parts: Bombardier.
Accommodation: –/54(6) + –/48 (6) 1TD.

Power: 520 kW.
Weight: 56 tonnes.
Length over Buffers: 38.20 m.
Maximum Speed: 80 km/h.

22 151	22 153	22 155	22 156	22 157	22 158
22 152	22 154				

ET 22 159–164   2-Bo-2

These are new dual voltage units of type GTW 2/6. .

Built: 2005.
Power: 520 kW.
Builder – Mech. Parts: Stadler.
Builder – Elec. Parts: Bombardier.
Accommodation: –/66 + –/52 (6) 1TD.

System: 800 V DC/15 kV 16.7 Hz AC.
Weight: 60 tonnes.
Length over Buffers: 38.20 m.
Maximum Speed: 80 (DC), 130 (AC) km/h.

22 159	22 160	22 161	22 162	22 163	22 164

TRAILERS   2-2

Built: 1950
Builder: SGP.
Accommodation: –/?
Maximum Speed:

Wheel dia:
Weight:
Length over Buffers:

B 22.209 (B) | 22.254 (BD)

4.12.2. LAMBACH–HAAG. LH

This line shares some tracks with the ÖBB which is electrified at 15 kV a.c. Two transformer vehicles are included in the fleet which are attached to old trains before reaching ÖBB lines and detached on the return journey!

Depot: Haag.
Length: 26.3 km.
Timetable: 162.

ELECTRIC LOCOMOTIVE

E 20 007 Bo-Bo

Built for LILO, this loco passed to the Bürmoos–Trimmelkam line in 1980, moving to LVE in 1994 when the Trimmelkam line became part of SVB.

Built: 1956
Builder – Mech. Parts: SGP Graz.
Builder – Elec. Parts: BBC.
Power: 492 kW.

Wheel Diameter: 1000 mm.
Weight: 48 tonnes.
Length over Buffers: 12.20 m.
Maximum Speed: 40 km/h.

E 20.007

DIESEL LOCOMOTIVES

V 20 011 B-B

This loco was former Tegernseebahn (Germany) No. 14.

Built: 1982.
Builder: MaK (G1203 BB)
Engine: MTU 8V396 TC13 of 745 kW at 1800 r.p.m.
Transmission: Hydraulic. Voith L4r4zU2.
Length over Buffers: 12.50 m.

Wheel Diameter: .1000 mm.
Weight: 80 tonnes.

Maximum Speed: 70 km/h.

V 20.011

V 20 012 B-B DIESEL

This locomotive was the formerly GKB DH 1500.7.

Built: 1992.
Builder – Mech. Parts: MaK.
Transmission: Hydraulic.
Power: 1100 kW.

Wheel Diameter: 1000 mm.
Weight: 72 tonnes.
Length over Buffers: 12.80 m.
Maximum Speed: 100 km/h.

V 20.012

DUAL-VOLTAGE TRANSFORMER UNITS 1A

These two rectifier vehicles were home-built by Stern & Hafferl with local equipment from Linz. They are now spare and only used with the old stock on tourist trains.

Built: 1950–52.
Builder – Mech. Parts: StH.
Builder – Elec. Parts: Linz.
Power: 44 kW.

System: 15 kV 16.7 Hz AC.
Weight: 21 t (20 t*).
Length over Buffers: 9.50 m.
Maximum Speed: 50 km/h.

EGL 25.051   LH |EGL 25 052*   LH

ELECTRIC RAILCARS

ET 24 104   Bo-Bo

Built: 1950.   **Power:** 185 kW.
Builder – Mech. Parts: Graff.   **Weight:** 30.0 tonnes.
Builder – Elec. Parts: Lindner. **Length over Buffers:** 18.47 m.
Accommodation: –/58.   **Maximum Speed:** 75 km/h.

24 104

ET 25 102   Bo

An original LH unit now retained for excursion use.

Built: 1932.   **Power:** 212 kW.
Builder – Mech. Parts: Graz.   **Weight:** 20.0 tonnes.
Builder – Elec. Parts: SSW.   **Length over Buffers:** 11.00 m.
Accommodation: –/46   **Maximum Speed:** 50 km/h.

25 102

ET 25 103/104   Bo-Bo

These modern units are dual voltage thus allowing through workings to Wels on the ÖBB main line. Classified 4855 by ÖBB.

Built: 1989.   **Systems:** 800 V DC/15 kV 16.7 Hz AC.
Power: 480 kW.
Builder – Mech. Parts: Bombardier Rotax.   **Weight:** 58.0 tonnes.
Builder – Elec. Parts: Elin.   **Length over Buffers:** 24.43 m.
Accommodation: –/64.   **Maximum Speed:** 120 km/h.

25 103 (4855 001-6) | 25 104 (4855 002-4)

2.12.3. LAMBACH–VORCHDORF   LV

Known as the "Vorchdorferbahn".
Depot: Vorchdorf Eggenburg (shared with the narrow-gauge GV line).
Length: 15.5 km.   **Timetable:** 160.

LOCOMOTIVE

E 24 010   Bo-Bo

Another good second-hand loco acquired in 1980 from Wuppertal Stadtwerke (3608).

Built: 1910   **Wheel Diameter:** 900 mm.
Builder – Mech. Parts: Maffei.   **Weight:** 33 tonnes.
Builder – Elec. Parts: SSW.   **Length over Buffers:** 8.81 m.
Power: 300 kW.   **Maximum Speed:** 40 km/h.

24 010

ELECTRIC RAILCARS

ET 20 109   Bo

This rebodied unit was acquired in 1970 from the German Extertalbahn and was used on the Bürmoos–Trimmelkam line which is now part of the Salzburger Lokalbahn.

Built: 1953.   **Power:** 203 kW.
Builder – Mech. Parts: Westwaggon.   **Weight:** 25.4 tonnes.
Builder – Elec. Parts: AEG.   **Length over Buffers:** 16.75 m.
Accommodation: –/32.   **Maximum Speed:** 70 km/h.

20 109   (21 001, 21 150, 22 109)

ET 20 111   Bo-Bo

This rebodied unit was also acquired in 1970 from the German Extertalbahn.

Built: 1953..   **Power:** 320 kW.
Builder – Mech. Parts: Westwaggon.   **Weight:** 26.5 tonnes.
Builder – Elec. Parts: AEG.   **Length over Buffers:** 17.30 m.
Accommodation: –/60.   **Maximum Speed:** 70 km/h.

20 111

ET 22 133/136   Bo-Bo + 2-2

For details see LILO 22.134/135.

22 133 + 22 233   (KFBE 1288 + 2288) | 22 136 + 22 236   (KFBE 1290 + 2290)

ET 24 101   Bo

A museum unit.

Built: 1931.   **Power:** 106 kW.
Builder – Mech. Parts: Graz.   **Weight:** 17 tonnes.
Builder – Elec. Parts: SSW.   **Length over Buffers:** 11.01 m.
Accommodation: –/46.   **Maximum Speed:** 50 km/h.

24 101

ET 24 103   Bo

A museum unit.

Built: 1912.   **Power:** 108 kW.
Builder – Mech. Parts: Graz.   **Weight:** 20 tonnes.
Builder – Elec. Parts: SSW.   **Length over Buffers:** 12.70 m.
Accommodation: –/60.   **Maximum Speed:** 50 km/h.

24 103

METRE GAUGE LINES
2.12.4. GMUNDEN–VORCHDORF   GV

Known as the "Traunseebahn".

Length: 14.6 km.
Depot: Vorchdorf Eggenburg.   **Timetable:** 161..

ELECTRIC RAILCARS
ET 23 103   Bo

A museum unit.

Built: 1921.   **Wheel Diameter:** 850 mm.
Builder – Mech. Parts: Graz.   **Weight:** 13.0 tonnes.
Builder – Elec. Parts: AEG.   **Length over Buffers:** 10.40 m.
Power: 110 kW.   **Maximum Speed:** 30 km/h.
Accommodation: –/40.

23 103

ET 23 105/106   Bo-Bo

Acquired in 1978 from the Swiss Trogener Bahn where they were Nos. 5 and 4 respectively. No. 3 was also acquired but was used for spares. Originally built for Lausanne Tramways.

Built: 1954.   **Wheel Diameter:** 720 mm.
Builder – Mech. Parts: ACMV Vevey.   **Weight:** 28.0 tonnes.
Builder – Elec. Parts: BBC.   **Length over Buffers:** 17.10 m (17.40 m*).
Power: 320 kW.   **Maximum Speed:** 50 km/h.
Accommodation: –/40 (–/38*).

23 105   (Basel BDe 4/4 5) | 23 106*   (Basel BDe 4/4 4)

ET 23 111/112   Bo-Bo

Acquired in 1994 from WSB.

Built: 1954.   **Wheel Diameter:** mm.
Builder – Mech. Parts: SWS.   **Weight:** 28.5 tonnes.
Builder – Elec. Parts: BBC.   **Length over Buffers:** 17.15 m.
Power: 326 kW.   **Maximum Speed:** 75 km/h.
Accommodation: –/48.

23 111 (WSB Be4/4 7) | 23 112 (WSB Be4/4 8)

TRAILERS   2-2

Various trailers

20.224 (VBW 8)	1916	12.8 t	–/54.	15.25 m.
20.225 (VBW 9) buffet	1926	14.0 t	–/54.	15.24 m.
20.227 (VBW 10)	1942	11.3 t	–/54.	14.50 m.
23.221	1899			

2.12.5. VÖCKLAMARKT–ATTERSEE   VA

Known as the "Atterseebahn".

Length: 13.4 km.
Depot: Attersee.   **Timetable:** 180.

ELECTRIC RAILCARS

ET 26.104   Bo

A Ganz 4-wheeled railcar built for the Pressburgerbahn and regauged after acquisition in 1941, now in museum use.

Built: 1913   **Wheel Diameter:** 850 mm.
Builder – Mech. Parts: Ganz.   **Weight:** 13.0 tonnes.
Builder – Elec. Parts: Ganz.   **Length over Buffers:** 9.50 m.
Power: 108 kW.   **Maximum Speed:** 30 km/h.
Accommodation: –/46.

26 104 (20 104)

ET 26 109/110   Bo-Bo

These railcars were built for the Swiss Sernftalbahn (Schwanden–Elm) moving in 1969 to the Aigle–Ollon–Monthey–Champéry line before coming to Austria in 1985.

Built: 1949   **Wheel Diameter:**
Builder – Mech. Parts: SWS.   **Weight:** 25.0 tonnes.
Builder – Elec. Parts: MFO.   **Length over Buffers:** 15.92 m.
Power: 320 kW.   **Maximum Speed:** 50 km/h.
Accommodation: –/40.

26 109   (AOMC BDe 4/4 112)   ST. GEORGEN AM ATTERSEE
26 110   (AOMC BDe 4/4 111)

ET 26 111/112   Bo-Bo

These are more former Swiss railcars being built for the Birsigtalbahn (now part of Baselland Transport) and acquired by Stern & Hafferl in 1989. They were previously used on the GV line as ET 23 109/10. 26 112 is stored at Vorchdorf with severe accident damage.

Built: 1951   **Wheel Diameter:**
Builder – Mech. Parts: SWP.   **Weight:** 25.0 tonnes.
Builder – Elec. Parts: .   **Length over Buffers:** 15.92 m.
Power: 320 kW.   **Maximum Speed:** 50 km/h.
Accommodation: –/48.

26 111   (BLT BDe 4/4 8) | 26 112   (BLT BDe 4/4 9)

Trailers

B 20.220	2	1907	Museum stock. Ex Gmunden 7.
B 20.222	2	1907	Museum stock. Ex Stonnes. Florian 1.
B 20.223	2-2	1914	Ex VBW (Switzerland) 7. Buffetonnes.
B 20.226	2-2	1914	Ex VBW (Switzerland) 10.
B 20.228	2-2	1914	Ex VBW (Switzerland) 15.
B 26.201	2	1912	

2.13. SÜDBERGENLANDISCHE REGIONALBAHN

This organisation has taken over the former ÖBB lines Oberwart–Oberschutzen and Unterwart-Rechnitz. It moves some freight traffic and in the tourist season operates museum trains.

Depot: Grosspetersdorf.

STEAM LOCOMOTIVE

CLASS 93   2-8-2T

This typical Austrian branch line loco spent some time as part of the Brenner & Brenner fleet before passing to the SRB. Used on weekend excursions.

Built: 1928.
Builder: Floridsdorf
Driving Wheel Diameter: 1140 mm.
Length over Buffers: 11.96 m.
Maximum Speed: 60 km/h.

Boiler Pressure: 1.35 MN/sq. m. (195 lb/sq.in)
Weight: 66.5 tonnes.
Tractive Effort: 575 kW.
Cylinders (2): 450 x 570 mm.

93.1422

DIESEL LOCOMOTIVES

CLASS 242   B

This shunting loco was built for the Linz steelworks who sold it to Schleppbahn Liesing (Wien) in 1982, passing it on to SRB from there early in the 1990s.

Built: 1962.
Builder: SGP F.
Engine: SGP of 182 kW.
Transmission: Hydraulic.

Wheel Diameter: .
Weight:
Length over Buffers:
Maximum Speed:

242.01

CLASS M 31   C

These are standard MAV shunters and retain their MAV numbers.

Built: 1958–60.
Builder: Ganz Mavag.
Engine: Ganz Mavag 12 Jv 17/24 of 330 kW.
Transmission: Hydraulic.

Wheel Diameter: 1225 mm.
Weight: 45.0 tonnes.
Length over Buffers: 10.95 mm.
Maximum Speed: 62 km/h.

M31.2013 | M31.2020 |

2.14. WIENER LOKALBAHN   WLB

A light rail line from Wien to Baden which also runs freight trains. The trams run along Wiener Linien tracks to the terminus at Wien Oper. The company is now also an open access freight operator.

Length: 30.3 km.
Depots: Wien Wolfganggasse. Leesdorf.
Timetable: 515.

System: 850 V DC
Works: Inzersdorf.

DIESEL LOCOMOTIVES

V 82/3   C

These are standard Jenbach shunters but are more powerful than those on ÖBB.

Built: 1976, 1980.
Builder: JW.
Engine: JW 600 of 445 kW.
Power: 445 kW.
Transmission: Hydraulic

Wheel Diameter: 950 mm.
Weight: 54.0 t.
Length over Buffers: 10.50 m.
Maximum Speed: 60 km/h.

V 82 | V 83

V 90–92   C

WLB got itself into open access and acquired some main line diesel locomotives. These are former DB Class 201/202 locos modernised by Adtranz at Kassel. Unfortunately the original identifications are not known. They have Zugfunk ZFM90, Indusi I60R (PZB 90), remote radio control and automatic shunting couplers.

Built/rebuilt: 19xx/2001–02.
Builder: LKM rebuilt Adtranz, Kassel.
Engine: Caterpillar BDI-TA, 12-cyl 4-stroke.
Power: 1060 kW.
Transmission: Hydraulic

Wheel Diameter: 1000 mm.
Weight: 74.0 t.
Length over Buffers: 14.36 m.
Maximum Speed: 100 km/h.

90   (98 37 0000 090-1)
91   (98 37 0000 091-9)

92   (98 37 0000 092-7)

ELECTRIC LOCOMOTIVES

In connection with the open access activities there are some leased locomotives from Siemens Dispolok. They are the same type as ÖBB Class 1116 and carry the WLB blue and cream livery and WLB logos.

ES64U2-020
ES64U2-021
ES64U2-024

ES64U2-027
ES64U2-033

TRAMS
3-SECTION CARS   B-2-2-B

These modern trams were built in batches between 1979 and 1993 and allowed the former KBE units which the company used to operate to be withdrawn. All these cars are named after staff on the system, but these are being removed when the trams are re-liveried.

Built: 1979–93.
Builder-Mech. Parts: SGP Simmering.
Builder-Elec. Parts: AEG, Kiepe, SSW.
Accomodation: 64 seats 130 standees.

Power: 380 kW.
Weight: 36 t.
Length over Couplers: 26.75 m.
Maximum Speed: 80 km/h.

101	Erich	111	Inge	119	Margot
102	Karl	112	Reni	120	Michaela
103	Theo	113	Vera	121	Erika
104	Rudi	114	Franziska	122	Elfriede
105	Toni	115	Andrea	123	Harald
106	Loisl	116	Wilhelm	124	Cladia
108	Ernst	117	Josef	125	Susanne
109	Hans	118		126	Robert
110	Herta				

3-SECTION CARS   CITY TRAM   Bo+2+2+Bo

These trams are based on those ordered by Wiener Linien for use on line U6 (the former Stadtbahn), but have cabs at both ends and a differnt seating layout. 407–410 are under construction.

Built: 2001/2005.
Builders-Mech. Parts: Bombardier Wien.
Builder-Elec. Parts: Bombardier.
Traction motors: 4 of 100 kW.
Accommodation: 70 seats 118 standees.
Weight: 35.7 tonnes.
Floor height: 440/525 mm.

Systems: 600/850 V DC.

Length over Couplers: 26.94 m.
Width: 2.50 m.
Maximum Speed: 80 km/h.

401	403	405	407	409	410
402	404	406	408		

MUSEUM CARS

All these are bogie cars.

200	Graz 1899.	Imperial saloon.
223	Graz 1927.	Ex 23.
230	Graz 1928.	Ex 34.
231	Graz 1928.	Ex 31.

2.15 ZILLERTALBAHN ZB

Gauge: 760 mm.
Route: Jenbach–Mayrhofen (31 km).
Timetable No. 310.

Depots: Jenbach (main), Mayrhofen (subshed).
Internet: www.zillertalbahn.at

STEAM LOCOMOTIVES

2 0-6-2T

Built/rebuilt: 1900.
Builder: Krauss Linz.
Driving Wheel Dia.: 800 mm.
Length over Buffers: 7.19 m.
Maximum Speed: 35 km/h.

Boiler Pressure: 1.00 MN/sq. m. (165 lb/sq.in).
Weight: 21.9 tonnes.
Power: 160 kW.
Cylinders: 290 x 400 mm.

2 ZILLERTAL

3 0-6-2T

Built: 1902.
Builder: Krauss Linz.
Driving Wheel Dia.: 800 mm.
Length over Buffers: 7.84 m.
Maximum Speed: 35 km/h.

Boiler Pressure: 1.25 MN/sq. m. (180 lb/sq.in)
Weight: 25.4 t.
Power: 225 kW.
Cylinders: 320/500 x 400 mm.

3 TIROL

4 0-8-2

This locomotive has been acquired on a 10 year lease from Club 760. It is in fact JZ 83-076 and has taken a blank ZB number as the original No. 4 was sold off many years ago. The tourist traffic on the ZB was getting so heavy that double headed trains had to be run. Now this powerful loco means one engine only on these trains. The 10 year hire is about to expire; it is not known whether a further period of hire has been agreed. In February 2005 the locomotive was nearing the end of a major overhaul.

Built: 1909.
Builder: Krauss Linz.
Driving Wheel Dia.: 900 mm.
Length over Buffers: 13.70 m.
Maximum Speed: 35 km/h.

Boiler Pressure: 1.25 MN/sq. m. (180 lb/sq.in)
Weight – Locomotive: 36 tonnes
– Tender: 16 tonnes.
Cylinders: 430 x 450 mm.

4

5 0-6-2T

Built: 1930.
Builder: Krauss Linz.
Driving Wheel Dia.: 800 mm.
Length over Buffers: 8.02 m.
Maximum Speed: 40 km/h.

Boiler Pressure: 1.25 MN/sq. m. (180 lb/sq.in)
Weight: 28.1 tonnes.
Power: 250 kW.
Cylinders: 350 x 400 mm.

5 GERLOS

6 0-4-0T

This little loco was acquired from the Böhler steelworks in Kapfenberg in 1972 and is used for driving lessons for the public as part of the tourist steam operations.

Built: 1916.
Builder: Krauss München.
Driving Wheel Dia.: 600 mm.
Length over Buffers: 5.70 m.
Maximum Speed: 20 km/h.

Boiler Pressure: ?
Weight: 10.9 tonnes.
Power: ?
Cylinders: 210 x 300 mm.

6

DIESEL LOCOMOTIVES

D 8/9   D

These two locos were built new for the line.

Built: 1967.
Builder: OK.
Engine: JW 600 of 397 kW.
Transmission: Hydraulic.

Wheel Diameter: 750 mm.
Weight: 36.0 tonnes.
Length over Buffers: 9700 mm.
Maximum Speed: 50 km/h.

D 8 | D 9

D 10   B-B

This is former JZ 740-007 acquired in 1980 and rebuilt by Jenbach to ZB requirements and in service on ZB since 1982. In 1995 it was converted to push-pull operation in order to replace railcars in emergency.

Built: 1970, rebuilt 1962.
Builder: DD JW.
Engine: JW 600 of 440 kW.
Transmission: Hydraulic.

Wheel Diameter: 850 mm.
Weight: 32 tonnes.
Length over Buffers: 12.05 m.
Maximum speed: 60 km/h.

D 10

D 11/12   B

Both bought from the Rhein-Sieg Eisenbahn (D) in 1969. In 1995 these locos were fitted with radio remote control.

Built: 1958/60.
Builder: OK.
Engine: OK 316U6D of 104 kW.
Transmission: Hydraulic..

Wheel Diameter: 700 mm.
Weight: 18.0 tonnes.
Length over Buffers: 5.50 m.
Maximum Speed: 20 km/h.

D 11 | D 12

D13/14   B-B

These two new locomotives were acquired in 2004 to deal with heavy freight traffic. The timber industry along the Zillertalbahn is thriving causing the diesel fleet to be augmented. The locomotives have been constructed so that they are gauge convertible should the ZB put in dual gauge down to the main saw mills. The locomotives have remote radio control for shunting operations and can work in multiple with railcar trailers VS3/4.

Built: 2004
Builder: Gmeinder (Type D75 BB-SE)
Engine: Caterpillar 3412 E DI-TTA of 746 kW at 2100 r.p.m..
Transmission: Hydraulic, Voith L3r4zseU2
Maximum speed: 70 km/h

Wheel Diameter: 920 mm
Weight: 50 tonnes

Length: 14.53 m

D 13 | D 14

DIESEL RAILCARS/MUs

VT 3–4   B-B + 2-2

Built: 1984.
Builder – Mech. Parts: Knotz.
Builder – Elec. Parts: BBC.
Engine: 228 kW.
Accommodation: –/64 + –/46.

VT 3

Transmission: Electric.
Weight: 28.6 + 17.5 tonnes.
Length over Buffers: 16.875 + 16.605 m.
Maximum speed: 70 km/h.

| VT 4   RAIMUND RAINER

VT 5–8   B-B

Built: 1992/3 (VT 5/6), 1998 (VT 7/8)
Builder – Mech. Parts: JW.
Builder – Elec. Parts: ABB.
Engine: MAN D2866 LUE of 250 kW.
Accommodation: –/64.

VT 5   ADOLF TRAPPMAIR
VT 6

Transmission: Electric
Weight: 31 tonnes.
Length: 16.88 m.
Maximum speed: 70 km/h.

| VT 7
| VT 8

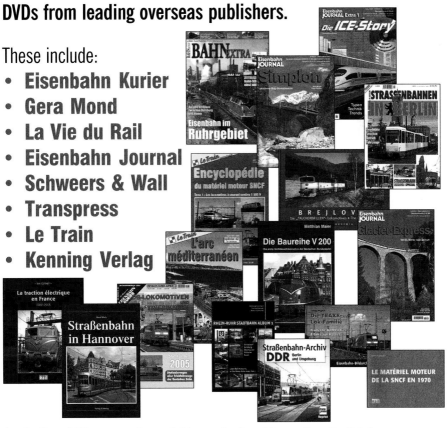

3. TRAMWAY SYSTEMS

There are four cities in Austria which have tramway systems plus the single line in Gmunden which is advertised as the smallest tramway in the world. Trams in Austria go by the nickname of "Bim", after the sound of their bells.

Special Note: Tramway museums, nor the numerous historic vehicles of Wiener Linien are not within the scope of this book. For details of these please consult the book "Tramways and Light Railways of Switzerland and Austria", published by the Light Rail Transit Association and available from Platform 5 mail order. Note that historic trams from museums in Innsbruck, Graz and Wien operate over the city networks.

3.1. GMUNDEN

This small tramway connects the town of Gmunden with the ÖBB station and is owned by Stern und Hafferl. Full details of the cars not available. All are bidirectional.

Length: 2.3 km.   **Depot:** Gmundner Keramik.
Livery: Red and white.

5   MUSEUM CAR

Built: 1911   **Weight:**
Builder: Graz   **Wheel arrangement:** Bo.
Power: **Length:** 9.08 m.
Accommodation: **Max. Speed:**

5

8

Built: 1962.   **Weight:**
Builder: Lohner   **Wheel arrangement:** Bo-Bo.
Power: **Length:** 13.40 m.
Accommodation: 34 seats 32 standees.   **Max. Speed:**

8

9/10

These two cars were from the former Vestische Strassenbahn in Germany. They were obtained in 1974 and put into service in 1977 and 1983 respectively.

Built: 1951–52.   **Weight:**
Builder: Lohner.   **Wheel arrangement:** Bo-Bo.
Power: **Length:** 14.10 m.
Accommodation: **Max. Speed:**

9   (VS 347) | 10 (VS 341)

100   MUSEUM CAR

This open-sided museum car was obtained from the Postlingbergbahn in Linz in 1995.

Built: 1898.   **Weight:**
Builder: Graz.   **Wheel arrangement:** Bo.
Power: **Length:** 6.80 m.
Accommodation: **Max. Speed:**

100

3.2. GRAZER VERKEHRSBETRIEB   GVB

Gauge: 1435 mm.   **Voltage:** 600 V DC.
System Length: 29.7 km.
Depots: Remise I (Steyrergasse), Remise III (Eggenberger Strasse).
Livery: Green and cream.

Graz has a network of six routes which are operated in traditional manner in the centre of the street. The tracks are quite close together so the trams have to be very narrow. All cars are unidirectional. Various extensions are being built at present and a new batch of trams will be ordered in late 2005.

260 SERIES   2-SECTION CARS

23 trams of this class of two-section cars were built, but only seven now survive.

Built: 1965.
Builders – Mech. Parts: Lohner (261–265), SGP (266–273).
Builder – Elec. Parts: Siemens.
Wheel arrangement: Bo-2-Bo.
Traction motors: 4 Siemens of 55 kW.   **Length:** 19.35 m.
Accommodation: 38 seats 70 standees.   **Width:** 2.24 m.
Weight: 24.1 tonnes.   **Maximum speed:** 60 km/h.

263	267	268	271	278	279
265					

500 SERIES   3-SECTION CARS

This class of three-section cars was based on a Duewag design for Duisburg.

Built: 1978.
Builders – Mech. Parts: SGP.
Builder – Elec. Parts: Duewag.
Wheel arrangement: B-2-2-B.
Traction motors: 2 x Duewag of 150 kW.   **Length:** 25.35 m.
Accommodation: 52 seats 82 standees.   **Width:** 2.26 m.
Weight: 32.2 tonnes.   **Maximum speed:** 60 km/h.

501	503	505	507	509	510
502	504	506	508		

520 SERIES   3-SECTION CARS

These trams were obtained second-hand from Duisburg and went into service in Graz 1988–94. They have traditional diamond pantographs.

Built: 1971–74.
Builders – Mech. Parts: Duewag.
Builder – Elec. Parts: Duewag.
Wheel arrangement: B-2-2-B.
Traction motors: 2 Duewag of 120 kW.   **Length:** 25.90 m.
Accommodation: 63 seats 164 standees.   **Width:** 2.29 m.
Weight: 32.2 tonnes.   **Maximum speed:** 60 km/h.

Former Duisberg numbers in parentheses.

521	(1077)	527	(1083)	531	(1087)	535	(1091)
524	(1080)	528	(1084)	532	(1088)	536	(1092)
525	(1081)	529	(1085)	533	(1089)	537	(1093)
526	(1082)	530	(1086)	534	(1090)		

580 SERIES   3-SECTION CARS

These four trams are rebuilds of 260 series cars with centre sections from withdrawn ex-Wuppertal cars. They have a strange appearance since the centre sections have a different type of window to the end cars.

Rebuilt: 1996–97.
Builders – Mech. Parts: SGP Graz/Duewag.
Builder – Elec. Parts: Siemens
Wheel arrangement: Bo-2-2-Bo.
Traction motors: 4 Siemens of 55 kW.   **Length:** 26.20 m.
Accommodation: 58 seats 97 standees.   **Width:** 2.24 m.
Weight: 26.90 tonnes.   **Maximum speed:** 60 km/h.

The first number in parentheses is the former 260 series number whilst the second number is the GVB number of the ex-Wuppertal car from which the centre section was taken with the number in square brackets being its former Wuppertal number.

581 (273/552[3809]) | 582 (270/570[3819]) | 583 (276/559[3808]) | 584 (266/560[3807])

600 SERIES   3-SECTION CARS

These trams were built as 2-section cars but all were fitted with new low-floor centre sections in 1999 with bogies from withdrawn ex-Wuppertal cars.

Built: 1986.
Builders –Mech. Parts: SGP Graz.
Builder – Elec. Parts: Siemens
Wheel arrangement: B-2-2-B.
Traction motors: 2 Duewag of 150 kW.   **Length:** 26.30 m.
Accommodation: 40 seats 126 standees.   **Width:** 2.24 m.
Weight: 33.95 tonnes.   **Maximum speed:** 60 km/h.
Floor height of low-floor section: 300 mm.

601	603	605	607	609	611
602	604	606	608	610	612

650 SERIES   CITYRUNNER   5-SECTION CARS

These new 100% low floor cars are seeing the demise of the 260 and 521 series.

Built: 2000–01.
Builders –Mech. Parts: Bombardier Wien.
Builder – Elec. Parts: Kiepe.
Wheel arrangement: Bo+2+Bo.
Traction motors: 6 Kiepe of 145 kW.   **Length:** 27.00 m.
Accommodation: 53 (4) seats 93 standees.   **Width:** 2.20 m.
Weight: 32.00 tonnes.   **Maximum speed:** 70 km/h.
Floor height: 290 mm.

651	654	657	660	663	666
652	655	658	661	664	667
653	656	659	662	665	668

3.3 INNSBRUCKER VERKEHRSBETRIEBE UND STUBAITALBAHN GmbH IVB

Gauge: 1000 mm.
System Length: 35.8 km.
Livery: Red and beige.

Voltage: 600 V DC.
Depot: Wilthen.

Innsbruck has three city tram lines plus the former AC Stubaitalbahn which was incorporated into the city undertaking in 1997. The city routes use unidirectional cars, whilst the Stubaitalbahn, a single-track route to Fulpmes, uses bi-directional cars. Many existing cars are second-hand ex-Bielefeld or Hagen in Germany, but a new build of 22 bidirectional low-floor cars is set to be ordered shortly, and extensions to the system are planned.

31 SERIES   2-SECTION CARS

These cars are ex-Bielefeld. All cars except 33/39/42 were formerly 3-section cars which have had the centre sections removed.

Built: 1957/62–63.
Builders – Mech. Parts: Duewag.
Builder – Elec. Parts: Kiepe.
Traction motors: 2 Garbe-Lahmeyer BG 75 of 100 kW.
Wheel arrangement: B-2-B.
Accommodation: 37 seats 78 standees.
Weight: tonnes.

Length: 19.30 m.
Width: 2.20 m.
Maximum speed: km/h.

Former Bielefeld numbers in parentheses.

31	(812)	35	(810)	38	(805)	41	(802)
33	(825)	36	(815)	39	(840)	42	(823)
34	(811)	37	(822)	40	(813)		

51 SERIES   3-SECTION CARS

These cars are ex-Bielefeld like the 31 series above, but they retain their centre sections.

Built: 1962–63.
Builders – Mech. Parts: Duewag.
Builder – Elec. Parts: Kiepe.
Traction motors: 2 Garbe-Lahmeyer BG 75 of 100 kW.
Wheel arrangement: B-2-2-B.
Accommodation:
Weight: tonnes.

Length: 25.30 m.
Width: 2.20 m.
Maximum speed: km/h.

* Renumbered from 32 when modified to 3-section car in 1990.

Former Bielefeld numbers in parentheses.

51	(801)	52	(803)	53*	(814 outer 809 centre)

71 SERIES   2-SECTION CARS

These cars were delivered new to Innsbruck.

Built: 1966–67.
Builders – Mech. Parts: Lohner.
Builder – Elec. Parts: Kiepe.
Traction motors: 2 Elin BG 75 of 100 kW.
Wheel arrangement: B-2-B.
Accommodation: 39 seats 72 standees.
Weight: 24.1 tonnes.

Length: 19.40 m.
Width: 2.20 m
Maximum speed: km/h

71	73	74	75	76	77
72					

81 SERIES STUBAITALBAHN 3-SECTION CARS

These cars are ex-Hagen with centre sections which had been removed from the ex-Bielefeld cars of the 31 series. They entered service in Innsbruck between 1976 and 1981.

Built: 1960–61 (1968§).
Builders – Mech. Parts: Duewag.
Builder – Elec. Parts: Kiepe?.
Wheel arrangement: B-2-2-B.
Traction motors: 2 of   kW.
Weight: tonnes.

Length: 26.71 m.
Width: 2.20 m.
Accommodation: 61 seats 93 standees.
Maximum speed: km/h.

* Renumbered from 89 in 1984.

Former Hagen (Bochum§)/Bielefeld numbers in parentheses.

| 81* | (69/805) | 83 | (63/814) | 85 | (65/810) | 87 | (67/812) |
| 82 | (41§/815) | 84 | (64/813) | 86 | (66/811) | 88 | (68/802) |

3.4. LINZ AG LINIEN

Gauge: 900 mm.
System Length: 15.3 km.
Livery: White with orange lower bodyside band. Only 012–021 are in the fleet livery.

Voltage: 600 V DC.
Depot: Kleinmünchen.

The main tramway in Linz has the unusual gauge of 900 mm. A new subway has been built recently to serve the main station. All trams are unidirectional.

3.4.1. MAIN SYSTEM

CITYRUNNER   7-SECTION CARS

These new 100% low floor cars have seen the demise of the older three-section cars.

Built: 2002–05.
Builders – Mech. Parts: Bombardier Wien.
Builder – Elec. Parts: Elin.
Wheel arrangement: 1A+Bo+Bo+A1.
Traction motors: 6 of 100 kW.
Accommodation: 68 (3) seats 156 standees.
Weight: ? tonnes.
Floor height: 320 mm.

Length: 40.00 m.
Width: 2.30 m.
Maximum speed: 70 km/h.

001 **A**	005 **A**	009 **A**	013	016	019
002 **A**	006 **A**	010 **A**	014	017	020
003 **A**	007 **A**	011 **A**	015	018	021
004 **A**	008 **A**	012			

THIRD SERIES   4-SECTION CARS

Four-section cars.

Built: 1985–86.
Builders – Mech. Parts: Rotax.
Builder – Elec. Parts: Siemens.
Wheel arrangement: B-2-2-2-B.
Traction motors: 2 x Duewag of 150 kW.
Accommodation: 54 seats 141 standees.
Weight: ? tonnes.

Length: 31.78 m.
Width: 2.30 m.
Maximum speed: 70 km/h.

All thought to be in advertising livery.

41	44	47	50	53	55
42	45	48	51	54	56
43	46	49	52		

SECOND SERIES   4-SECTION CARS

These four-section cars were converted from three-section cars.

Built: 1977.
Builders – Mech. Parts: Rotax.
Builder – Elec. Parts: Siemens.
Wheel arrangement: B-2-2-2-B.
Traction motors: 2 x Duewag of 150 kW.
Accommodation: 56 seats 121 standees.
Weight: ? tonnes.

Length: 25.30 m.
Width: 2.23 m.
Maximum speed: 70 km/h.

Most cars are in advertising livery, although 69, 73 and 75 are in plain white.

68	70	72	74	76	78
69	71	73	75	77	79

HISTORIC VEHICLES (All bidirectional)

Number	Built	Type	Builder
6	1950	Bo	Simmering
12	1962	Bo	Simmering
23	1902	Bo	Graz
25	1957	Bo	Gräf und Stift
32	1880	2-axle horse car	Graz
45	1920	Bo	Graz
109	1950	2-axle trailer	Simmering
111	1950	2-axle trailer	Simmering
140	1954	2-axle trailer	Gräf und Stift
141	1954	2-axle trailer	Gräf und Stift

3.4.2. POSTLINGBERGBAHN

Gauge: 1000 mm.
System Length: 2.9 km.
Livery: Cream.

Voltage: 600 V DC.
Depot: Urfahr.

This adhesion mountain tramway has the second steepest gradient in the world at 10.6% (1 in 9.5). The cars are numbered using Roman numerals to distinguish them from the city trams. All are 4-wheeled and bi-directional. It is planned to completely renovate this line and regauge it to 900 mm so that trams will be able to run into the main square in Linz. New modern cars will replace the current museum pieces.

I–III

Built: 1898. Original crossbench cars.
Builder: Graz.
Accommodation:

Length: 6.86 m.

I | II | III

VI/VIII

Built: 1898, rebuilt 1959/1950.
Builder: Graz, rebuilt ESG.
Accommodation: 22 seats 7 standees.

Length: 6.86 m.

VI | VIII

X

Built: 1912, rebuilt 1960.
Builder: Graz, rebuilt ESG.
Accommodation: 22 seats 7 standees.

Length: 8.08 m.

X |

XI/XII

Built: 1948/50.
Builder: ESG.
Accommodation: 22 seats 7 standees.

Length: 9.09 m.

XII

XIV/XVIII

Built: 1954–58.
Builder: ESG.
Accommodation: 22 seats 7 standees.

Length: 9.09 m.

XIV | XV | XVI | XVIII

3.5. WIENER LINIEN GmbH

Gauge: 1435 mm.
System Length: 230 km.
Voltage: 600 V DC.
Livery: Red and white.

Although St. Petersburg used to have the largest tram system in the world, Wien (Vienna) was second, but is now probably the largest since many routes in St. Petersburg have now closed due to them having fallen into disrepair. All Wiener Linien trams are unidirectional, except for those which operate on the former Stadtbahn, now known as U6 which is unidirectional.

DEPOT CODES

BG	Brigittenau	OT	Ottakring
FD	Floridsdorf (Sub-shed: Kagran)	RH	Rudolphsheim
GT	Gürtel	FA	Favoriten (Sub-shed: Simmering)
HN	Hernals	SS	Speising

CLASS A   5-SECTION ULTRA-LOW-FLOOR CARS

Built: 1995–2003.
Builders – Mech. Parts: SGP/Siemens.
Builder– Elec. Parts: Elin.
Wheel arrangement: 1-A-A-A.
Traction motors: 6 of 80 kW.
Weight: 29.30 tonnes.
Accommodation: 42 seats 94 standees.

Length: 24.010 m.
Width: 2.40 m.
Maximum speed: 70 km/h.
Floor height: 197 mm.

1	HN	10	SM	19	OT	27	OT	35	OT	43	HN
2	SM	11	SM	20	OT	28	OT	36	HN	44	HN
3	SM	12	OT	21	OT	29	OT	37	HN	45	HN
4	SM	13	OT	22	OT	30	OT	38	HN	46	HN
5	SM	14	OT	23	OT	31	OT	39	HN	47	HN
6	SM	15	OT	24	OT	32	OT	40	HN	48	HN
7	SM	16	OT	25	OT	33	OT	41	HN	49	HN
8	SM	17	OT	26	OT	34	OT	42	HN	50	HN
9	SM	18	OT						

CLASS B   7-SECTION ULTRA-LOW-FLOOR CARS

Built: 1995–2005.
Builders – Mech. Parts: SGP/Siemens.
Builder – Elec. Parts: Elin.
Wheel arrangement: 1-A-A-A-A-1.
Traction motors: 8 of 80 kW.
Weight: 42.45 tonnes.
Accommodation: 66 seats 141 standees.

Length: 35.470 m.
Width: 2.40 m.
Maximum speed: 70 km/h.
Floor height: 197 mm.

601	SM	618	SM	635	SM	652	FD	669	FD	685	HN
602	SM	619	SM	636	SM	653	FD	670	FD	686	HN
603	SM	620	SM	637	SM	654	FD	671	HN	687	HN
604	SM	621	SM	638	SM	655	FD	672	HN	688	HN
605	SM	622	SM	639	SM	656	FD	673	HN	689	HN
606	SM	623	SM	640	SM	657	FD	674	HN	690	HN
607	SM	624	SM	641	SM	658	FD	675	HN	691	HN
608	SM	625	SM	642	SM	659	FD	676	HN	692	HN
609	SM	626	SM	643	SM	660	FD	677	HN	693	HN
610	SM	627	SM	644	FD	661	FD	678	HN	694	FA
611	SM	628	SM	645	FD	662	FD	679	HN	695	FA
612	SM	629	SM	646	FD	663	FD	680	HN	696	FA
613	SM	630	SM	647	FD	664	FD	681	HN	697	FA
614	SM	631	SM	648	FD	665	FD	682	HN	698	FA
615	SM	632	SM	649	FD	666	FD	683	HN	699	FA
616	SM	633	SM	650	FD	667	FD	684	HN	700	FA
617	SM	634	SM	651	FD	668	FD	685	HN	

CLASS E₂ 2-SECTION CARS

Built: 1977–1990. Based on a design for Mannheim with electronic control.
Builders – Mech. Parts: SGP Simmering, Rotax.
Builder – Elec. Parts: .
Wheel arrangement: B-2-B.
Traction motors: 2 of   kW.
Accommodation: 43 seats 59 standees.

Length: 19.765 m.
Width: m.
Maximum speed: km/h.
Weight: tonnes.

4000 Series (built by SGP)

4001	GT	4018	GT	4034	GT	4050	SS	4066	SS	4082	FA
4002	GT	4019	GT	4035	GT	4051	SS	4067	SS	4083	FA
4003	GT	4020	GT	4036	GT	4052	SS	4068	FA	4084	FA
4004	GT	4021	GT	4037	GT	4053	SS	4069	FA	4085	FA
4005	GT	4022	GT	4038	GT	4054	SS	4070	FA	4086	FA
4006	GT	4023	GT	4039	GT	4055	SS	4071	FA	4088	FA
4007	GT	4024	GT	4040	GT	4056	SS	4072	FA	4089	FA
4008	GT	4025	GT	4041	GT	4057	SS	4073	FA	4090	FA
4009	GT	4026	GT	4042	GT	4058	SS	4074	FA	4091	FA
4010	GT	4027	GT	4043	GT	4059	SS	4075	FA	4092	FA
4011	GT	4028	GT	4044	GT	4060	SS	4076	FA	4093	FA
4012	GT	4029	GT	4045	GT	4061	SS	4077	FA	4094	FA
4013	GT	4030	GT	4046	GT	4062	SS	4078	FA	4095	FA
4014	GT	4031	GT	4047	GT	4063	SS	4079	FA	4096	FA
4015	GT	4032	GT	4048	GT	4064	SS	4080	FA	4097	FA
4016	GT	4033	GT	4049	SS	4065	SS	4081	FA	4098	FA
4017	GT										

4300 Series (built by Rotax)

4301	FA	4305	FA	4309	FA	4313	FA	4317	FA	4321	FA
4302	FA	4306	FA	4310	FA	4314	FA	4318	FA	4322	FA
4303	FA	4307	FA	4311	FA	4315	FA	4319	FA	4323	FA
4304	FA	4308	FA	4312	FA	4316	FA	4320	FA	4324	FA

CLASS E 2-SECTION CARS

Built: 1959–1966.
Builders – Mech. Parts: Lohner.
Builder– Elec. Parts: .
Wheel arrangement: B-2-B.
Traction motors: 2 of 95 or 110 kW.
Accommodation: 39 seats 66 standees.

Length: 20.335 m.
Width: m.
Maximum speed: km/h.
Weight: tonnes.

4402	SS	4423	SS	4425	SS	4433	SS	4439	SS	4441	SS
4422	SS	4424	SS	4432	SS	4434	SS	4440	SS		

CLASS E₁ 2-SECTION CARS

Built: 1967–1976.
Builders – Mech. Parts: Lohner/Rotax or SGP.
Builder – Elec. Parts: .
Wheel arrangement: B-2-B.
Traction motors: 2 of 150 kW.
Accommodation: 39 seats 66 standees.
Weight: tonnes.

Length: 20.335 m.
Width: m.
Maximum speed: km/h.

4400 Series (built by Lohner/Rotax)

4464	GT	4469	GT	4474	OT	4479	OT	4485	RH	4496	RH
4465	GT	4471	OT	4476	OT	4480	OT	4486	RH	4497	RH
4466	GT	4472	OT	4477	OT	4482	OT	4487	RH	4499	RH
4468	GT	4473	OT	4478	OT	4484	OT	4491	RH	4500	SM

4501 SM	4511 SM	4521 SM	4531 OT	4541 OT	4551 OT
4502 SM	4512 SM	4522 SM	4532 OT	4542 OT	4552 OT
4503 SM	4513 SM	4523 SM	4533 OT	4543 OT	4553 OT
4504 SM	4514 SM	4524 SM	4534 OT	4544 OT	4554 OT
4505 SM	4515 SM	4525 SM	4535 OT	4545 OT	4555 OT
4506 SM	4516 SM	4526 SM	4536 OT	4546 OT	4556 OT
4507 SM	4517 SM	4527 SM	4537 OT	4547 OT	4558 OT
4508 SM	4518 SM	4528 SM	4538 OT	4548 OT	4559 OT
4509 SM	4519 SM	4529 SM	4539 OT	4549 OT	4560 OT
4510 SM	4520 SM	4530 SM	4540 OT	4550 OT	

4600 Series (built by SGP)

4631 SS	4674 RH	4732 BG	4774 FD	4806 FD	4837 GT
4632 SS	4675 RH	4733 BG	4775 FD	4807 FD	4838 HN
4633 SS	4677 RH	4734 BG	4776 FD	4808 FD	4839 HN
4634 SS	4680 RH	4735 BG	4777 FD	4809 FD	4840 HN
4635 SS	4682 RH	4736 BG	4778 FD	4810 FD	4841 HN
4636 SS	4683 RH	4737 BG	4779 FD	4811 FD	4842 HN
4637 SS	4685 RH	4738 BG	4780 FD	4812 FD	4843 HN
4638 SS	4686 RH	4739 BG	4781 FD	4813 FD	4844 HN
4639 SS	4687 RH	4740 BG	4782 FD	4814 FD	4845 HN
4640 SS	4688 RH	4741 BG	4783 FD	4815 FD	4846 HN
4641 SS	4689 RH	4742 BG	4784 FD	4816 FD	4847 HN
4642 SS	4691 RH	4743 BG	4785 FD	4817 FD	4848 HN
4647 BG	4692 RH	4744 BG	4786 FD	4818 FD	4849 HN
4647 BG	4694 RH	4745 BG	4787 FD	4819 FD	4850 HN
4649 BG	4695 RH	4746 BG	4788 FD	4820 FD	4851 HN
4650 BG	4697 RH	4747 BG	4789 FD	4821 FD	4852 HN
4653 BG	4698 RH	4748 BG	4790 FD	4822 FD	4853 HN
4654 BG	4699 RH	4749 BG	4791 FD	4823 FD	4854 HN
4659 BG	4704 RH	4750 BG	4792 FD	4824 FD	4855 HN
4660 BG	4706 RH	4752 BG	4793 FD	4825 FD	4856 HN
4661 BG	4710 RH	4755 BG	4794 FD	4826 FD	4857 HN
4662 BG	4711 RH	4756 BG	4795 FD	4827 GT	4858 HN
4663 BG	4713 RH	4757 BG	4796 FD	4828 GT	4859 HN
4664 BG	4715 RH	4761 BG	4797 FD	4829 GT	4861 HN
4665 BG	4719 RH	4762 BG	4798 FD	4830 GT	4862 HN
4666 BG	4725 RH	4763 BG	4799 FD	4831 GT	4863 HN
4667 BG	4726 RH	4768 BG	4800 FD	4832 GT	4864 HN
4668 BG	4727 RH	4769 FD	4801 FD	4833 GT	4865 HN
4670 RH	4728 RH	4770 FD	4802 FD	4834 GT	4866 HN
4671 RH	4729 RH	4771 FD	4803 FD	4835 GT	4867 HN
4672 RH	4730 RH	4772 FD	4804 FD	4836 GT	4868 HN
4673 RH	4731 BG	4773 FD	4805 FD		

CLASS c₃ {#class-c3}

CLASS c$_3$ — TRAILER CARS

Built: 1959–1962.
Length: m.
Weight: tonnes.
Accommodation: 32 seats 43 standees.
Builder: Lohner.
Width: m.
Maximum speed: km/h.

1104 OT	1127 OT	1144 OT	1168 RH	1191 RH	1205 SM
1106 OT	1130 OT	1146 OT	1170 RH	1192 RH	1207 SM
1108 OT	1132 OT	1148 OT	1171 RH	1193 RH	1209 SM
1109 OT	1134 OT	1150 RH	1174 RH	1194 RH	1210 SM
1114 OT	1135 OT	1156 RH	1177 RH	1196 RH	1211 SM
1115 OT	1136 OT	1157 RH	1179 RH	1197 RH	1212 SM
1117 OT	1137 OT	1158 RH	1180 RH	1198 RH	1213 SM
1118 OT	1138 OT	1159 RH	1181 RH	1199 RH	1214 SM
1119 OT	1139 OT	1162 RH	1182 RH	1200 RH	1215 SM
1123 OT	1141 OT	1163 RH	1183 RH	1201 SM	1216 SM
1124 OT	1142 OT	1164 RH	1187 RH	1202 SM	1217 SM
1126 OT	1143 OT	1166 RH	1190 RH	1203 SM	1218 SM

1219	SM	1232	BG	1243	BG	1260	BG	1271	BG	1281	FD
1222	SM	1233	BG	1244	BG	1261	BG	1272	BG	1282	FD
1224	SM	1234	BG	1245	BG	1262	BG	1273	BG	1283	FD
1225	BG	1235	BG	1247	BG	1264	BG	1274	BG	1284	FD
1226	BG	1236	BG	1249	BG	1265	BG	1275	FD	1285	FD
1227	BG	1237	BG	1250	BG	1266	BG	1276	FD	1286	FD
1228	BG	1238	BG	1251	BG	1267	BG	1277	FD	1287	FD
1229	BG	1239	BG	1252	BG	1268	BG	1278	FD	1288	FD
1230	BG	1240	BG	1257	BG	1269	BG	1279	FD	1289	FD
1231	BG	1242	BG	1259	BG	1270	BG	1280	FD	1290	FD

CLASS c_4 TRAILER CARS

This class has three doors and wider windows than Class c_3

Built: 1974–1977.
Length: m.
Weight: tonnes.
Accommodation: .

Builder: Rotax.
Width: m.
Maximum speed: km/h.

1301	FD	1314	FD	1326	FD	1338	FD	1350	HN	1362	HN
1302	FD	1315	FD	1327	FD	1339	FD	1351	HN	1363	HN
1303	FD	1316	FD	1328	FD	1340	FD	1352	HN	1364	HN
1304	FD	1317	FD	1329	FD	1341	FD	1353	HN	1365	HN
1305	FD	1318	FD	1330	FD	1342	HN	1354	HN	1366	HN
1306	FD	1319	FD	1331	FD	1343	HN	1355	HN	1367	HN
1307	FD	1320	FD	1332	FD	1344	HN	1356	HN	1368	RH
1308	FD	1321	FD	1333	FD	1345	HN	1357	HN	1369	RH
1309	FD	1322	FD	1334	FD	1346	HN	1358	HN	1370	RH
1310	FD	1323	FD	1335	FD	1347	HN	1359	HN	1371	RH
1311	FD	1324	FD	1336	FD	1348	HN	1360	HN	1372	RH
1312	FD	1325	FD	1337	FD	1349	HN	1361	HN	1373	RH
1313	FD										

CLASS c_5 TRAILER CARS

These trailers work with Class E_2 motors.

Built: 1977–1980/1985–90.
Length: m.
Weight: tonnes.
Accommodation: 32 seats 59 standees.

Builder: Rotax.
Width: m.
Maximum speed: km/h.

1401	GT	1421	GT	1441	GT	1461	SS	1480	SM	1499	SM
1402	GT	1422	GT	1442	GT	1462	SS	1481	SM	1500	SM
1403	GT	1423	GT	1443	GT	1463	SS	1482	SM	1501	SM
1404	GT	1424	GT	1444	GT	1464	SS	1483	SM	1502	SM
1405	GT	1425	GT	1445	GT	1465	SS	1484	SM	1503	SM
1406	GT	1426	GT	1446	GT	1466	SM	1485	SM	1504	SM
1407	GT	1427	GT	1447	GT	1467	SM	1486	SM	1505	SM
1408	GT	1428	GT	1448	SS	1468	SM	1487	SM	1506	SM
1409	GT	1429	GT	1449	SS	1469	SM	1488	SM	1507	SM
1410	GT	1430	GT	1450	SS	1470	SM	1489	SM	1508	SM
1411	GT	1431	GT	1451	SS	1471	SM	1490	SM	1509	SM
1412	GT	1432	GT	1452	SS	1472	SM	1491	SM	1510	SM
1413	GT	1433	GT	1453	SS	1473	SM	1492	SM	1511	SM
1414	GT	1434	GT	1454	SS	1474	SM	1493	SM	1512	SM
1415	GT	1435	GT	1455	SS	1475	SM	1494	SM	1513	SM
1416	GT	1436	GT	1456	SS	1476	SM	1495	SM	1514	SM
1417	GT	1437	GT	1457	SS	1477	SM	1496	SM	1515	SM
1418	GT	1438	GT	1458	SS	1478	SM	1497	SM	1516	SM
1419	GT	1439	GT	1459	SS	1479	SM	1498	SM	1517	SM
1420	GT	1440	GT	1460	SS						

▲ LTE 2170 001 at Salzburg Itzling on 22 September 2004. This is the same design as the ÖBB Class 2070. **Ray Smith**

▼ This Salzburger Lokalbahn sets ET 57 "Ober Innviertel" and ET 49 "Stonnes Gorgen"pass Salzburg Itzling depot with the 12.40 Lamprechtshausen–Salzburg on 1 April 2005. **David Haydock**

▲ **Feldbach–Bad Gleichenberg**. ET2 at Bad Gleichenberg on 9 February 2005 having just arrived with the 14.27 from Feldbach.

▼ **Gleisdorf–Weiz**. B-B diesel hydraulic loco D4 on ÖBB metals at Gleisdorf on 21 July 2005. Note the full UIC number on the front. **Peter Fox (2)**

▲ **Peggau–Übelbach.** 2-car ex-swiss EMU ET14+ES22 at Übelbach with the 12.13 to Peggau on 09 February 2005.

▼ **Mixnitz–St. Erhard.** A special mixed train from St. Erhard to Mixnitz operated for participants of the IGE Bahntouristik railtour on 09 February 2005, headed by steeple cab Bo-Bo E3. This line is normally freight-only. **Peter Fox (2)**

▲ **Unzmarkt–Tamsweg (Murtalbahn).** Normal services on this narrow gauge StLB branch are operated by railcars. VS42+VT31 are seen at Tamsweg on 19 July 2005.

▼ The StLB runs steam trains for tourists on the Murtalbahn in summer using its own locos, but they do not see much use in winter. 0-6-2Ts U11 and Bh1 (ex-ÖBB 398.01) are seen between Unzmarkt and Murau on 7 February 2005 with a IGE Bahntouristik special to Tamsweg.   **Peter Fox (2)**

⟨LILO⟩

▲ **Linzer Lokalbahn (LILO).** The main services on this line have now been taken over entirely by new Stadler GTW 2/6 units. The new units are being delivered as dual voltage for when the LILO runs into Linz Hbf from 11 November with the existing ones being fitted retrospectively. 22 159 is seen at Niederspaching on 22 July 2005.

▶ On the same day, the former NWP line from Neumarkt-Kalham to Payerbach was still being worked by this ancient 1952-built unit 22 108, seen here at Neumarkt-Kalham.

▶ The LILO posesses a number of steeple-cab electric locos including 22 005, photographed on the same day at Linz Lokalbahnhof. **Peter Fox (3)**

▲ **Lambach–Haag.** This line is now normally operated with modern dual-voltage units built in 1989. 25 103 is seen at Lambach on the 10.52 Haag am Hausruck–Wels on 3 June 2005.

▼ B-B DH loco 20 012 was obtained second-hand from the GKB and is seen at Vorchdorf depot on the same day after having had an overhaul.   **Peter Fox (2)**

▲ **Lambach–Vorchdorf.** Modernised single unit 20 111 arrives at Vorchdorf on 27 April 2004 with the 13.03 ex-Lambach. **W.J. Freebury**

▼ Ex-KFBE twin unit 22 133 + 22 233 at Vorchdorf on 3 June 2005. This is one of two units of this type now transferred to the GV from the LILO. The other three units are now out of service at Waizenkirchen depot. **Peter Fox**

▲ The Wiener Lokalbahn is a railway which runs from Wien Oper to Baden. Although a proper segregated railway, the passenger services use the tram lines of Wiener Linien to operate to their Viennese terminus. Thus trams are used. Car 122 is seen near Meidling on 7 June 2005.

▼ The WLB has taken delivery of six new Bombardier City Trams and a further four are on order. 401 is seen near Meidling on the same day.   **Peter Fox (2)**

▲ Zillertalbahn 0-8-2T No. 4 (ex-JZ 83.076) is on a 10-year lease from Club 760 and is seen at Jenbach on 12 June 2003.

▼ One of the Zillertalbahn's two new Gmeinder diesel locos, No. D13 at Jenbach on 24 May 2005.

Ray Smith (2)

▲ **Gmunden Tramway.** This metre gauge line is claimed to be the world's smallest tramway. Operated by Stern & Hafferl, it joins the town of Gmunden to the station. Car No. 8 is seen leaving the town terminus of Franz-Josefs-Platz for the station on 3 June 2005.   **Peter Fox**

◄ **Innsbruck Tramway.** Car 75 built by Lohner in 1966–67 on a line 2 working to Amras on Innsbruck's metre gauge tramway on 18 September 2001.
                        Ian G. Feather

◄ **Innsbruck Tramway.** Car 52 is a Duewag 3-section car which is second-hand from Bielefeld and is seen on a line 6 working to Bergisel at Mühlsee on 30 April 2005.   **W.J. Freebury**

▲ Although the Graz tramway is standard gauge, it has very narrow trams as exemplified by the new Bombardier Cityrunner trams which are only 2.2 m wide. Car 658 is seen on 10 February 2005 at St. Peter Schulzentrum.

▶ SGP car Car 510 of 1978 in the standard fleet livery on a line 7 working at Jakominiplatz on the same day.

▼ The 600 series cars were rebuilt from 2-section cars and now have low-floor centre sections. An unidentified example is seen outside the Hbf in July 2005. **Peter Fox (3)**

▲ The Linz tramway has an
unusual gauge of 900 mm. New
Bombardier Cityrunner tram 020
is seen at WiFi on a line 2
working to Universität on the
evening of 3 June 2005.

◄ No. 49 is an example of a third
series car built by Rotax in 1985–
86. It is seen on an Urfahr–
Hauptbahnhof line 3 working on
23 July 2005 in the main square
on the occasion of the annual
"Pflaster Spektakel" (Pavement
Festival).   **Peter Fox (2)**

▶ No. 74 is an example of a second series car built Rotax in 1977. It is seen on a line 1 working to Universität on 3 June 2005 at "Wi-Fi".

▶ Unlike the ordinary city tramway, the steeply graded Pöstlingbergbahn is metre gauge. It is claimed to be the steepest adhesion tramway in the world. Cars are numbered with Roman numerals to distinguish them from the city trams. Car VI approaches the bottom terminus at Urfahr on 23 July 2005. **Peter Fox (2)**

▼ A Wiener U-Bahn set on line 3 near the Schönbrunn Palace on 22 August 2003.
Dr. Iain C. Scotchman

▲ The traditional Wiener tram is typified by this photograph of 2-section Class E_2 car 4078 with c_5 trailer 1478 at Wien Oper on 7 June 2005 operating on line 65.

▼ In the last ten years Wiener Linien has introduced a revolutionary ultra-low-floor tram designed by Siemens which comes in both 5- and 7-section versions. A 7-section car, No. 630 is seen at Burggasse on a line 6 working on 4 June 2005.   **Peter Fox (2)**

▲ The line now known as U6 is what is left of the old Wiener Stadtbahn segregated light rail system. Bi-directionaal tram-type vehicles have traditionally operated the line as shown by this view of 4913 with trailer 1903 at Tschertlegasse on 7 June 2005.

▼ Further down the same train is a new Bombardier low floor City Tram No. 2655.   **Peter Fox (2)**

▲ The Class 52 2-10-0s were a numerous class in Austria in the age of steam. Preserved example 52.1227, owned by Brenner & Brenner makes a fine sight as it makes a runpast at Lassnitzhöhe between Graz and Gleisdorf on 6 February 2005 with the IGE Bahntouristik special.

▼ Club U44 operate steam specials on the 760 mm gauge Feistritztalbahn between Weiz and Birkfeld. They lease the line from the StLB north of Oberfeistritz and operate over StLB metals south of there. 0-10-0T Kh.101 (owned by the StLB) double-heads with ex-JZ 0-8-2 83 180 on the IGE special on the above date.   **Peter Fox (2)**

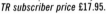

4. WIENER U-BAHN

The Wiener U-bahn is operated by Wiener Linien who operate the trams. Lines U1, U2, U3 and U4 are traditional third-rail Metro lines. Depots are at Erdberg, Hütteldorf and Wasserleitungswiese.

CLASS U/U$_2$ 2-CAR UNITS

Original monomotor design. Used on lines U1, U3 and U4.

Built: 1972–1982.   **System:** 750 V DC bottom contact third rail.
Builders – Mech. Parts: SGP Wien.   **Wheel arrangement:** B-B + B-B.
Builder – Elec. Parts: AEG/Elin/AEG/Siemens.
Traction motors: 2 BBC type GM200 of 200 kW per car (r 4 Elin MCF-031 M06 Z9Z-9 of 75 kW per car).
Length: 18.40 + 18.40 m.   **Width:** 2.80 m.
Weight: 52.60 tonnes.   **Maximum speed:** 80 km/h.
Accommodation: 49 seats 91 standees each car.

r Rebuilt with AC asynchronous traction motors (Class U$_2$).

```
2001 3001 | 2024 3024 | 2047 3047   | 2071 3071 r | 2093 3093   | 2115 3115
2002 3002 | 2025 3025 | 2048 3048   | 2072 3072 r | 2094 3094 r | 2116 3116
2003 3003 | 2026 3026 | 2049 3049   | 2073 3073 r | 2095 3095 r | 2117 3117
2004 3004 | 2027 3027 | 2050 3050   | 2074 3074 r | 2096 3096   | 2118 3118
2005 3005 | 2028 3028 | 2051 3051   | 2075 3075 r | 2097 3097 r | 2119 3119
2006 3006 | 2029 3029 | 2052 3052   | 2076 3076 r | 2098 3098   | 2120 3120
2007 3007 | 2030 3030 | 2053 3053   | 2077 3077 r | 2099 3099   | 2121 3121
2008 3008 | 2031 3031 | 2054 3054   | 2078 3078 r | 2100 3100   | 2122 3122
2009 3009 | 2032 3032 | 2055 3055   | 2079 3079   | 2101 3101   | 2123 3123
2010 3010 | 2033 3033 | 2056 3056   | 2080 3080 r | 2102 3102   | 2124 3124
2011 3011 | 2034 3034 | 2057 3057   | 2081 3081   | 2103 3103 r | 2125 3125
2012 3012 | 2035 3035 | 2058 3058   | 2082 3082   | 2104 3104   | 2126 3126
2013 3013 | 2036 3036 | 2059 3059   | 2083 3083   | 2105 3105   | 2127 3127
2014 3014 | 2037 3037 | 2060 3060   | 2084 3084   | 2106 3106   | 2128 3128
2015 3015 | 2038 3038 | 2061 3061   | 2085 3085 r | 2107 3107   | 2129 3129
2016 3016 | 2039 3039 | 2062 3062   | 2086 3086   | 2108 3108   | 2130 3130
2017 3017 | 2040 3040 | 2063 3063 r | 2087 3087 r | 2109 3109   | 2131 3131
2018 3018 | 2041 3041 | 2064 3064 r | 2088 3088   | 2110 3110 r | 2132 3132
2019 3019 | 2042 3042 | 2065 3065 r | 2089 3089   | 2111 3111   | 2133 3133
2020 3020 | 2043 3043 | 2066 3066 r | 2090 3090 r | 2112 3112 r | 2134 3134
2021 3021 | 2044 3044 | 2067 3067 r | 2091 3091 r | 2113 3113   | 2135 3135
2022 3022 | 2045 3045 | 2068 3068 r | 2092 3092   | 2114 3114   | 2136 3136
2023 3023 | 2046 3046 | 2069 3069 r |
                        2070 3070 r |
```

CLASS U$_1$/U$_{11}$ 2-CAR UNITS

Development of Class U with three-phase drive. Used on lines U1, U2, U3 and U4.

Built: 1986–1997.   **System:** 750 V DC bottom contact third rail.
Builders – Mech. Parts: SGP/Siemens.   **Wheel arrangement:** Bo-Bo + Bo-Bo.
Builder – Elec. Parts: AEG/Elin/ABB/Siemens.
Traction motors: Four Elin MCF-425 V06 Z9Z of 125 kW per car.
Length: 18.48 + 18.48 m.   **Width:** 2.80 m.
Weight: 56.00 tonnes.   **Maximum speed:** 80 km/h.
Accommodation: 49 seats 91 standees each car.

```
2201 3201 | 2211 3211 | 2221 3221 | 2231 3231 | 2241 3241 | 2251 3251
2202 3202 | 2212 3212 | 2222 3222 | 2232 3232 | 2242 3242 | 2252 3252
2203 3203 | 2213 3213 | 2223 3223 | 2233 3233 | 2243 3243 | 2253 3253
2204 3204 | 2214 3214 | 2224 3224 | 2234 3234 | 2244 3244 | 2254 3254
2205 3205 | 2215 3215 | 2225 3225 | 2235 3235 | 2245 3245 | 2255 3255
2206 3206 | 2216 3216 | 2226 3226 | 2236 3236 | 2246 3246 | 2256 3256
2207 3207 | 2217 3217 | 2227 3227 | 2237 3237 | 2247 3247 | 2257 3257
2208 3208 | 2218 3218 | 2228 3228 | 2238 3238 | 2248 3248 | 2258 3258
2209 3209 | 2219 3219 | 2229 3229 | 2239 3239 | 2249 3249 | 2259 3259
2210 3210 | 2220 3220 | 2230 3230 | 2240 3240 | 2250 3250 | 2260 3260
2261 3261 | 2271 3271 | 2281 3281 | 2291 3291 | 2300 3300 | 2309 3309
```

2262 3262	2272 3272	2282 3282	2292 3292	2301 3301	2310 3310
2263 3263	2273 3273	2283 3283	2293 3293	2302 3302	2311 3311
2264 3264	2274 3274	2284 3284	2294 3294	2303 3303	2312 3312
2265 3265	2275 3275	2285 3285	2295 3295	2304 3304	2313 3313
2266 3266	2276 3276	2286 3286	2296 3296	2305 3305	2314 3314
2267 3267	2277 3277	2287 3287	2297 3297	2306 3306	2315 3315
2268 3268	2278 3278	2288 3288	2298 3298	2307 3307	2316 3316
2269 3269	2279 3279	2289 3289	2299 3299	2308 3308	2317 3317
2270 3270	2280 3280	2290 3290			

CLASS V   6-CAR UNITS

New 6-car units featuring through gangways and air conditioning. The end cars are classified v (lower case), this being normal Wiener Linien practice for unpowered vehicles. Used on lines U2 and U3. Note: The 24xx and 28xx cars may be in the opposite order to shown.

Built: 2000–.   **System:** 750 V DC bottom contact third rail.
Builders – Mech. Parts: Siemens.
Builder – Elec. Parts: Siemens.
Wheel arrangement: 2-2 + Bo-Bo + Bo-Bo + Bo-Bo + Bo-Bo + 2-2.
Traction motors: 4 Elin MCF-725 W04 Z9Z of 160 kW per car.
Length: 19.11 + 18.25 + 18.25 + 18.25 + 18.25 + 19.11 m.
Accommodation: 38 (4) + 44 + 44 + 44 + 44 + 38 (4). 1100 standees per train.
Width: 2.85 m.
Weight: 162.60 tonnes.   **Maximum speed:** 80 km/h.

3801	2401	2801	2802	2402	3802	3861	2461	2861	2862	2462	3862
3803	2403	2803	2804	2404	3804	3863	2463	2863	2864	2464	3864
3805	2405	2805	2806	2406	3806	3865	2465	2865	2866	2466	3866
3807	2407	2807	2808	2408	3808	3867	2467	2867	2868	2468	3868
3809	2409	2809	2810	2410	3810	3869	2469	2869	2870	2470	3870
3811	2411	2811	2812	2412	3812	3871	2471	2871	2872	2472	3872
3813	2413	2813	2814	2414	3814	3873	2473	2873	2874	2474	3874
3815	2415	2815	2816	2416	3816	3875	2475	2875	2876	2476	3876
3817	2417	2817	2818	2418	3818	3877	2477	2877	2878	2478	3878
3819	2419	2819	2810	2410	3810	3879	2479	2879	2880	2480	3880
3821	2421	2821	2822	2422	3822	3881	2481	2881	2882	2482	3882
3823	2423	2823	2824	2424	3824	3883	2483	2883	2884	2484	3884
3825	2425	2825	2826	2426	3826	3885	2485	2885	2886	2486	3886
3827	2427	2827	2828	2428	3828	3887	2487	2887	2888	2488	3888
3829	2429	2829	2820	2420	3820	3889	2489	2889	2890	2490	3890
3831	2431	2831	2832	2432	3832	3891	2491	2891	2892	2492	3892
3833	2433	2833	2834	2434	3834	3893	2493	2893	2894	2494	3894
3835	2435	2835	2836	2436	3836	3895	2495	2895	2896	2496	3896
3837	2437	2837	2838	2438	3838	3897	2497	2897	2898	2498	3898
3839	2439	2839	2840	2440	3840	3899	2499	2899	2900	2500	3900
3841	2441	2841	2842	2442	3842	3901	2501	2901	2902	2502	3902
3843	2443	2843	2844	2444	3844	3903	2503	2903	2904	2504	3904
3845	2445	2845	2846	2446	3846	3905	2505	2905	2906	2506	3906
3847	2447	2847	2848	2448	3848	3907	2507	2907	2908	2508	3908
3849	2449	2849	2850	2450	3850	3909	2509	2909	2910	2510	3910
3851	2451	2851	2852	2452	3852	3911	2511	2911	2912	2512	3912
3853	2453	2853	2854	2454	3854	3913	2513	2913	2914	2514	3914
3855	2455	2855	2856	2456	3856	3915	2515	2915	2916	2516	3916
3857	2457	2857	2858	2458	3858	3917	2517	2917	2918	2518	3918
3859	2459	2859	2860	2460	3860	3919	2519	2919	2920	2520	3920

STADTBAHN (LINE U6)

The Wiener Stadtbahn is a segregated light rail system with low platforms which uses bi-directional cars. It is now classified as "U-Bahn" and is known as line U6. Trains are formed $E_6 + c_6 + T + c_6 + E_6$ or T+T+T+T.

System: 750 V DC overhead.
Depots: Michelbeuern, Rösslergasse.

CLASS T   3-SECTION CARS

These bi-directional low-floor cars have a cab at one end only and can therefore only operate in pairs, or in multiple with a Class E$_6$.

Built: 1993–1995, 1999–2000, 38 on order.
Builders – Mech. Parts: Bombardier, Wien.
Builder – Elec. Parts:
Traction motors: 4 of 100 kW.
Accommodation: 58 seats 136 standees..
Floor height: 440/525 m.

Wheel arrangement: Bo-2-2-Bo.
Length: 26.800 m.
Width: 2.65 m.
Weight: 34.7 tonnes.
Maximum speed: 80 km/h

2601	2621	2641	2660	2679	2698
2602	2622	2642	2661	2680	2699
2603	2623	2643	2662	2681	2700
2604	2624	2644	2663	2682	2701
2605	2625	2645	2664	2683	2702
2606	2626	2646	2665	2684	2703
2607	2627	2647	2666	2685	2704
2608	2628	2648	2667	2686	2705
2609	2629	2649	2668	2687	2706
2610	2630	2650	2669	2688	2707
2611	2631	2651	2670	2689	2708
2612	2632	2652	2671	2690	2709
2613	2633	2653	2672	2691	2710
2614	2634	2654	2673	2692	2711
2615	2635	2655	2674	2693	2712
2616	2636	2656	2675	2694	2713
2617	2637	2657	2676	2695	2714
2618	2638	2658	2677	2696	2715
2619	2639	2659	2678	2697	2716
2620	2640				

CLASS E$_6$ 2-SECTION CARS

Built: 1979–1991.
Builders – Mech. Parts: Rotax
Builder – Elec. Parts: .
Traction motors: 4 of 95 or 110 kW.
Weight: tonnes.

Wheel arrangement: B-2-B
Length: 20.10 m.
Width: 2.31 m..
Accommodation: 31 seats 72 standees.
Maximum speed: 80 km/h.

4901	4909	4917	4925	4933	4941
4902	4910	4918	4926	4934	4942
4903	4911	4919	4927	4935	4943
4904	4912	4920	4928	4936	4944
4905	4913	4921	4929	4937	4945
4906	4914	4922	4930	4938	4946
4907	4915	4923	4931	4939	4947
4908	4916	4924	4932	4940	4948

CLASS c$_6$ TRAILER CARS

Built: 1979–1990.
Length: 18.98 m.
Accommodation: 36 seats 75 standees.
Weight: tonnes.

Builder: Rotax.
Width: 2.31 m.

Maximum speed: km/h.

1901	1909	1917	1925	1933	1940
1902	1910	1918	1926	1934	1941
1903	1911	1919	1927	1935	1942
1904	1912	1920	1928	1936	1943
1905	1913	1921	1929	1937	1944
1906	1914	1922	1930	1938	1945
1907	1915	1923	1931	1939	1946
1908	1916	1924	1932		

5. MUSEUMS AND MUSEUM LINES

Preservation in Austria has expanded in the last ten years with the two main factors being the availability of steam locomotives from Romania and the former East Germany with both standard and narrow gauge types imported from the former. The re-equipment of the ÖBB traction fleet has also allowed many of the post-war electric and diesel locmotives to pass into preservation.

Two major collections have continued to expand and now ÖGEG has 104 standard gauge items and EM Strasshof 83!

As always there are regular steam operations on the rack railways and private lines with the Zillertalbahn now offering three return steam trips on some days.

The lists of museums and museum lines is grouped into provinces and arranged in alphabetical order and also includes steam operations on the ÖBB and private lines as a convenient way of giving the reader as much detail as possible. The numbers in brackets are post codes.

The website www.erlebnisbahn.at has useful links to most Austrian museum lines.

KÄRNTEN.

Bad Bleiberg (9530).

The former Bleiberger Bergswerk Union mine has an 800 metre tourist railway of 600mm gauge.

3 Battery Electric locomotives

Treibach Althofen (9330). Kärntner Museumsbahnen (KMB). Gurkthalbahn. Treibach Althofen – Pöckstein. 3 km.

The KMB saved part of the Gurkthalbahn after its closure in 1969 and this became the first Austrian museum line. The main depot is at Pöckstein but some locos are often found stored at Treibach-Althofen station. The line operates Saturdays and Sundays in July – September.

8 steam, 2 diesel locomotives

Web address: www.gurkthalbahn.at

Klagenfurt (9020).

The Bergbau Museum Klagenfurt (Kinkstrasse 6) includes a diesel and an electric loco from industrial concerns.

Nostalgiebahnen in Kärnten (NBiK).

This organisation is responsible for five operations:
- Museum trains are operated over the Weizelsdorf–Ferlach line on summer Saturdays and Sundays (6 km).
- Kärntner Museum for Technik und Verkehr – Historama. This is located in a former factory in Ferlach.
- HISTO-Tram, a line to be built from Ferlach station to the Historama museum (2 km).
- Nostalgic ship on the Wörthersee (MV LORETTO , 1924).
- Workshop in the old ÖBB depot at St. Veit an der Glan (West).

Most of the railway items are at St. Veit and most of the trams are at Ferlach. The St. Veit site is considered a workshop and is not normally open to the public but there is usually one open day a year whilst responsible enthusiasts are not likely to be turned away on a working day.

5 steam, 2 electric, 17 diesels, 5 electric railcars, 1 diesel railcar and 23 trams.

Web address: www.erlebnisbahn.at/nbik

NIEDERÖSTERREICH.

Freiland (3183). Feld und Industriemuseum.

This museum is now well established at its site at Freiland station. It is open on Sundays, May – October, but with very limited operating days.

Gauges: 600, 700, 760 mm. 4 steam, 38 diesel, 3 electric and 3 battery electric locomotives.

Web address: www.erlebnisbahn.at/feldbahn

Gmünd (3950). Gmünd–Gross Gerungs, 760 mm gauge, 44 km. ÖBB Kursbuch Table 801.

ÖBB Nostalgia operates frequent excursions on this otherwise closed line. Services usually alternate between diesel and steam traction. ÖBB also operate a train on the closed line to Litschau on a limited number of summer weekends.

Hadersdorf am Kamp (3943). Österreichische Club für Diesellokgeschichte. (ÖCD).

The ÖCD is a rather new organisation interested in preserving diesel traction. Hadersdorf is the reported headquarters of the group but locomotives and rolling stock are at several locations including Hainfeld.

Heidenreichstein (3860). Waldviertler Schmalspurverein. 760 mm gauge. ÖBB Kursbuch Table 802.

This group operates between Heidenreichstein and Alt Nagelberg. Operations are Saturday and Sundays in the peak tourist season plus a few other dates.

4 steam and 5 diesel locomotives

www.erlebnisbahn.at/wsv

Hirschwang (2651). Museumsbahn Payerbach–Hirschwang (Höllentalbahn). 760 mm gauge, 5.3 km.

This line was known as the Lokalbahn Payerbach – Hirschwang (LBPH) and was electrified from opening in 1918. It is now operated by the Österreichische Gesellschaft für Lokalbahnen (ÖGLB). When the line at Kienberg Gaming was acquired as a museum line most of the former steam fans here decamped to Kienberg and the present day group concentrates on the electric traction which is what the line was all about. One of the original railcar trailers has been converted to a power car and is in effect a true version of the original rolling stock.

3 steam, 3 electric and 9 diesel locomotives, 1 electric railcar.

Website: www.erlebnisbahn.at/hoellentalbahn www erlebnisbahn.at/oeglb

Kienberg Gaming. (3291) Ybbstalbahn Bergstrecke (YB) Kienberg Gaming–Lunz am See. 760 mm gauge, 17.6 km.

In 1988 ÖBB closed the eastern section of the Ybbstalbahn which was subsequently taken over by Österreichische Gesellschaft für Lokalbahnen (ÖGLB). The previous facilities at Kienberg Gaming had to be enlarged to take in the new museum stock which came from other parts of Austria. Trains operate Saturdays and Sundays June to October

4 steam and 6 diesel locomotives.

Website: www.erlebnisbahn.at/oeglb also www.erlebnisbahn.at/bergstrecke

Nasswald (2661). Waldbahnmuseum.

A short 600mm gauge railway has been created to recall the days of the Austrian forest railways.

4 diesels and 2 battery locomotives.

Obergrafendorf (3200). ÖBB Nostalgia & Club Mh6

Part of the locomotive depot at Obergrafendorf has been handed over to a preservation group. Some of ÖBB Nostalgia's narrow gauge steam and diesel locomotives are kept here for use on the Mariazell and Mank lines.

3 steam and 4 diesel locomotives.

Puchberg (2734). Puchberg am Schneeberg–Hochschneeberg. 1000 mm gauge, 9 km. Kursbuch Table 523.

This rack railway was privatised some years ago but is still part owned by ÖBB. Most trains are now worked by diesels with steam in use at peak times or as nostalgia trains at weekends. Operates May to November.

Web: www.schneebergbahn.at

St. Pölten (3100). Brenner und Brenner.

B&B steam locomotives operate on special trains all over Austria but especially in the greater Wien area. Besides enthusiast tours many private charters are run for weddings or firm's outings.

10 steam locomotives

Web Address: www.bb-bluetrain.com

Sigmundsherberg. (3751) Waldviertler Eisenbahnmuseum.

This museum is located in the old ÖBB depot close to Sigmundsherberg station. Open daily May to October.

1 steam, 5 diesels and 1 diesel railcar.

Waidhofen an der Ybbs (3340). Ybbstalbahn.

ÖBB and Club 598 cooperate on running excursion trains to Ybbsitz and Lunz am See.

2 steam and 1 diesel.

Zwettl (3910) Martinsberger Lokalbahnverein (MLV).

This group has been established to operate trains over the freight only line from Zwettl to Martinsberg and has set up shop in the old loco depot at Zwettl. Early days yet but a steam loco may be ready in 2005.

2 steam, 1 diesel.

Web: www.lokalbahnverein.at

OBERÖSTERREICH.

Ampflwang (4843). Österreichische Gesellschaft für Eisenbahn Geschichte – ÖGEG.
Ampflwang–Timelkam 11 km.

ÖGEG has grown considerably in the last ten years and seems to have enormous financial resources judging by the number of additional locomotives that have been purchased. It had to move out of the old premises in the main ÖBB works at Linz when that site was redeveloped and so moved to Ampflwang taking over the site of an old colliery and the branch serving it. Now a replica Austrian roundhouse and workshop is being built on the site to house the most important items. The collection has grown fast in the last few years as ÖBB disposed of old locomotives and opportunities arose to purchase locomotives abroad – especially from Romania. ÖGEG now has a good relationship with the Romanians and is now sending locomotives to Cluj works for overhaul.

In 2005 the Ampflwang – Timelkam line is not operating as all work is being concentrated on preparing Ampflwang for the 2006 Landesaustellung. However main line excursions still operate about ten time a year over ÖBB whilst Santa Specials run on the Salzburger Lokalbahn.

39 steam, 24 diesels, 33 electric, 8 diesel railcars (104 items!)

Web: www.oegeg.at

Bad Ischl (4820). Museumverkehr in Salzkammergut.

A small private museum

2 steam 1 diesel.

Grünberg (9620). Styrtal Museumsbahn. Steyr Lokalbahnhof – Grünberg, 760 mm gauge, 17 km.

When ÖBB closed the Garsten – Grünberg line ÖGEG was quick to step in and by 1985 was already operating trains on this well loved line. Several former ÖBB narrow gauge locomotives have been restored with others being imported from Romania after lines closed there.

10 steam, 5 diesels.

Web: www.oegeg.at

Linz (4020). Dora – Club für Industriebahngeschichte.

This club was formed to restore the preserved Linz steelworks loco DORA (0-4-0T, Jung 3237/1922). Trips around the steelworks with this locomotive are operated several times a year with diesel railcars also being used from time to time.

1 steam, 2 railcars.

Mondsee (5310) Salzkammergut Lokalbahn Museum

The old SKGLB depot in Mondsee has been restored as a museum. The line closed in 1957 but some original locomotives were located and saved with one coming back from Jugoslavia. The museum is open Saturdays and Sundays June–September.

4 steam.

St. Florian. (4490). Club Floriana. St. Florian–Pichling Ort, 900mm.

Stern & Hafferl used to operate this line which closed down in 1974. ÖGEG then took it over but as their main line operations grew a separate group formed Club Floriana and took over the line.

12 trams, 4 electric locos, 1 diesel.

OST TIROL

Lienz (9900). Verein der Eisenbahnfreunde.

This group is housed in the old ÖBB depot at Lienz which dates from 1871. Local excursions operate a few times each year.

2 steam, 4 electric and 2 diesels.

SALZBURGERLAND

Böckstein (5645). Gasteiner Heilstollenbahn. 600mm 2.4 km

Tourist trains operate into this former gold mine.
4 battery electric locomotives

Mauterndorf (5570). Club 760, Taurachbahn. Mauterndorf - St. Andrä. 760mm, 10 km.

This line is the western end of the Murtalbahn which was closed by StLB in 1980 and later taken over by Club 760. After a period of restoration of the track and structures tourist train operations started in 1988. The line normally operates at weekends June – September.

4 steam and 4 diesels.

Web: www.club760.at

St. Wolfgang (5360). St. Wolfgang – Schafbergspitze. 1000mm, 6 km, Kursbuch table 173.

This line is now hived off but is still ÖBB Personenverkehr but Geschaftseinheit St. Wolfgang. This rack railway climbs from 540 metres to 1734 metres above seas level and operates May to October. Normally the new oil-fired rack locomotives are in use with the railcars as back up. The coal fired steam locos operate limited services which are now marketed as nostalgia trains!

Web: www.schafbergbahn.at

Schwarzach St. Veit. (5620). Tauernbahn Museum

This new museum located at the station is scheduled to open in 2005.

1 steam, 1 electric.

Zell am See (5700). ÖBB Pinzgaubahn, 760mm. 54 km.

This line is still operated by ÖBB but the local tourist boards in association with ÖBB Nostalgia operate steam trains every Sunday July – September departing at 09.30 and getting back at 18.32. 399.01 is the regular locomotive but this is getting a new boiler so 699.103 is helping out.

www.pinzgaubahn.at

STEIERMARK.

Eisenerz (8790). Schaubergwerk. 900 mm gauge, 14 km.

The "Iron Mountain" is well known but less known is that tourist trains operate over part of the old mining network and there is a museum.

2 steam, 1 diesel and 20 electric locomotives

Web: www.abenteuer-erzberg.at

Frojach (8841). Club 760 Museum.

Club 760 has a museum at Frojach which is located on the Murtalbahn. The museum is not normally open except for a couple of weeks in the summer. However special arrangements can be made for groups.

7 steam, 2 diesel

Web: www.club760.at

Graz. (8010). Tramway Museum.

This museum is open Friday, Saturday and Sunday afternoons June–September.

16 trams.

Graz (8010). Montan und Werksbahnmuseum, Grazer Schlossberg.

Little is known about this museum located in or under the local castle but it has a large number of locomotives!

2 steam, 54 diesels, 10 electrics, 23 battery electrics and 1 compressed air locomotives.

Knittelfeld (8720). Eisenbahnmuseum.

Some of the old buildings no longer needed for ÖBB use have been converted into a railway museum for the area. One building houses what is reputed to be the largest collection in the world of railway caps! The locomotives and rolling stock are mostly displayed in the open and subject to winter weather conditions. The museum is open Tuesdays, Thursdays and weekends May to October. The locomotives can be seen at any time with the permission of depot staff.

4 electric and 4 diesel locomotives.

Mariazell (8630). Museumstramway Mariazell–Erlaufsee. 2.5 km.

A purpose built standard gauge tramway open at weekends July – September.

3 steam, 4 diesel, 3 electric, 24 trams and 3 electric railcars

Murau (8850). StLB Unzmarkt –Tamsweg "Murtalbahn" 760 mm gauge, Kursbuch table 630.

The Murtalbahn is 65 km long and has its operating base at Murau (km 27). On Tuesdays and Wednesdays June to September steam train excursions run on the Murau to Tamsweg section. This is not a museum railway but a very active narrow gauge railway running passenger and freight trains.

5 steam.

Mürzzuschlag (8680). Südbahn Kulturbahnhof

In connection with the 150th anniversary of the Semmering line (a UNESCO World Heritage site) the depot at Mürzzuschlag has been converted into a museum. The site is still being developed and thus more rolling stock may arrive.

2 steam, 1 diesel.

Stainz (8510). Stainzerlokalbahn, Stainz – Preding Wieselsdorf, 760 mm gauge, 11.4 km.

This line lost its passenger traffic as long ago as 1951 and freight finished in 1980. The line was saved and today the "Flascherlzug" runs once again albeit with a Romanian Resita 0-8-0T providing power!

7 steam, 4 diesels.

Vordernberg (8794). Verein Erzbergbahn. Vordernberg Markt–Eisenerz. 18.5 km.

The famous "Iron Mountain" rack railway must be known to many enthusiasts. It closed in 1988 but the rack rail had been removed earlier as diesel traction was used latterly. The Verein Erzbergbahn runs tourist trains over the route on Sundays July–September using some of the diesel railcars that were once in normal service on the route.

2 diesels and 4 diesel railcars.

Weiz (8160). StLB Feistritztalbahn Weiz–Birkfeld, 760 mm gauge, 24 km.

This StLB line once ran through from Weiz to Ratten but was cut back to Birkfeld in 1980 and the track lifted. In 1993 StLB cut back its operation to Anger but this time no tracks were lifted and the Anger to Birkfeld section became a museum line. Club U44 is the supporting organisation but as elsewhere a company was set up to run the museum operation – the Freistritztalbahn. StLB still operate freight trains from Weiz to the talc mines at Anger but steam hauled tourist trains operate Weiz to Birkfeld on Thursday and Sundays in the main tourist season June–September but there are some additional Saturday workings in September and October. Club U44 now has the old locomotive depot at Birkfeld but also rents space in the StLB depot at Weiz.

5 steam, 4 diesels.

TIROL

Innsbruck (6020). Tiroler Museumsbahn (TMB) 1000 mm gauge.

The old Stubaitalbahn depot is now home to this society and its collection. There are three old Stubaitalbahn cars as well as some Innsbruck trams in the collection.

Jenbach (6200). Achenseebahn, Jenbach – Achensee. 1000 mm gauge, 7 km. Kursbuch Table 311.

This line has a surprise for visitors in 2005 – a brand new steam loco! Many years ago the AB had four steam locomotives but No. 4 was scrapped. Over the years new parts have been provided for the other three locomotives including new frames etc. AB decided they needed a fourth steam loco again and so began searching through their stores and recovered a set of frames and wheels. A boiler has been obtained from a narrow gauge locomotive in Poland. The whole lot has now been assembled and a new No. 4 will enter service in 2005! A "phoenix" arises from the back of the depot! Operates daily May to October.

4 steam and 1 diesel.

Jenbach. (6200). Zillertalbahn, Jenbach to Mayrhofen, 760 mm gauge, 32 km. Kursbuch table 310.

This narrow gauge line continues to thrive and steam tourist trains are a feature of its operations. Now there are three return trips with steam in the peak season otherwise just two returns May to October.

Jochberg. (6373). Schaubergwerke Kupferplatte. 600 mm gauge.

This copper mine near Kitzbühel runs tourist trains into the mine daily May to October with departures on the hour 09.00–16.00 except at 12.00.

Web: www.schaubergwerke.at/kupferplatte

VORARLBERG

Bezau. (6870). Bregenzerwald Museumsbahn, Bezau–Bersbuch. 760 mm gauge, 6 km.

This former ÖBB line closed in 1980 after a severe rockfall damaged and blocked the line. A preservation group was formed and reopened part of the line in 1987. In 1999 another storm caused a bridge to be washed away. The preservation group raised funds and got the military involved and the bridge was reconstructed in time for trains to operate again in 2000. The line now operates at weekends plus other odd days June–October with steam traction alternating with diesel.

2 steam, 4 diesel

Lustenau. (6893). International Rhein Regulierrung – IRR. 750 mm gauge.

The IRR is an industrial railway used to transport materials to strengthen and maintain the banks of the Rhein. Verein Rheinschauen operate steam trains most weekends May to September with some Friday operations as well.

2 steam, 1 diesel.

WIEN AREA.

Gross Schwechat. (2320) Eisenbahn Museum, Verein Eisenbahn Freunde VEF.

The VEF is a well established society having been founded in 1950. Their base at Gross Schwechat is in the old Pressburgerbahn depot where they have preserved an interesting selection of rolling stock. Open Sundays May to October.

6 steam, 6 electrics, 1 battery electric, 25 diesels, 2 diesel railcars.

www.sabor.co.at/vef

Gross Schwechat. (2320). Klein und Lokalbahnverein.

This group shares premises with the VEF and has a large collection of 600 mm gauge items.

5 steam, 45 diesels, 5 electrics, 1 battery electric and 1 compressed air.

Mödling. (2340). Mödlinger Stadtverkehrs Museum. MStM.

A small museum is being established here.

8 trams.

Strasshof. (2231). Das Heizhaus. 1. Österreichische Strassenbahn und Eisenbahn Klub (1ÖSEK) and Österreichisches Eisenbahnmmuseum.

This is the former ÖBB locomotive depot at Strasshof but note that the nearest station is Silberwald and not Strasshof! The 1ÖSEK saved the depot when ÖBB closed it in 1978 and opened it as a museum six years later. In recent years, cooperation with the Technische Museum, Wien, has seen most of the locomotives from that museum moved to Strasshof. Also here now are some of the ÖBB Nostalgia locomotives.

52 steam, 17 diesels, 12 electrics, 3 electric railcars and 4 diesel railcars.

Wien – Prater. Lilliputbahn im Prater. 381 mm gauge, 2.5 km

The Wien Prater park and its big wheel are world famous and the same probably applies to its miniature railway. The railway operates April to October but steam is only used at weekends.

2 steam and 5 diesels.

Wien-Erdberg (1030). Strassenbahn Museum. Ludwig Kössler Platz, Wien 3.

The former Wien tramway depot is now the Wiener Strassenbahn Museum and involves not only the operator, Wien Verkehrsbetriebe (WVB) but also the VEF society and Wien Tramway Museum.

1 steam, 43 trams.

Wiener Lokalbahn

The Wiener Lokalbahn has restored four of its old cars with the Hofsalonwagen dating back to 1900. They are normally kept at the depot at Inzersdorf.

PLATFORM 5 MAIL ORDER

THE ELECTRONIC TIMETABLE
CD-ROM Verlag

The electronic timetable contains full railway timetable information* for most European countries including Great Britain, France, Germany, Belgium, The Netherlands, Luxembourg, Italy, Switzerland, Austra etc. It can produce complete travel itineraries for both international and domestic journeys, plus diagrammatic journey maps and full arrival/departure listings for any station in any country. Capable of running in English, French, German or Italian languages. Minimum system requirements: Windows 98 or later,486/33 MHz, 8MB RAM. UK/Europe **£9.95** (post free), Rest of World **£10.95** (including postage).

*In some countries where a timetable change occurs during the period of validity, information is included only up to the date of timetable change. Regular updates can be downloaded over the internet free of charge by choosing 'file', 'update' and following the instructions given.

Special note: New versions of the timetable are issued in June and December every year. We can accept advance orders for new versions from the beginning of May and November respectively. Alternatively, if you would like to be notified when new editions become available, please contact our mail order department.

GLACIER EXPRESS DVD
DAMPFBAHN FURKA-BERGSTRECKE DVD
GOTTHARDBAHN DVD
Eisenbahn Kurier

Three high quality DVDs from German publisher, Eisenbahn Kurier, now available with English commentary. The first follows the route of the Glacier Express through spectacular alpine scenery in all weathers, looking at the trains, the landscape and places of interest along the way. The second looks at the operations of the Furka-Bergstrecke, a revived steam operation high in the Alps over the route formerly used by the Glacier Express before construction of the Furka base tunnel. The third takes a journey along Switzerland's Gotthardbahn, taking in outstanding scenery, items of railway interest and other interesting features along the way. Includes a mixture of archive and present-day material, including a range of vintage and modern locomotives & rolling stock. Running time 68 minutes, 55 minutes and 110 minutes respectively. **£17.50, £14.95 and £17.50 respectively.**

ALSO AVAILABLE:
Die Centovallibahn (English/German) £17.50

Special note: All the above films are also available on video at the same prices, but commentary on video is in GERMAN ONLY.

Please note: Postage and packing on DVDs should be calculated at £1.00 (UK), £2.00 (overseas) per DVD, irrespective of retail price.

HOW TO ORDER

Telephone your order and credit/debit card details to our 24-hour sales hotline:
0114 255 8000 (UK) + 44 114-255-8000 (from overseas) or Fax: +44(0)114-255-2471.
An answerphone is attached for calls made outside of normal UK office hours.

Please state type of card, card number, issue no./date (maestro cards only), expiry date and full name & address of cardholder.
Or send your credit/debit card details, sterling cheque or British Postal order payable to Platform 5 Publishing Ltd. to:

Mail Order Department (EHA), Platform 5 Publishing Ltd.,
3 Wyvern House, Sark Road, SHEFFIELD, S2 4HG, ENGLAND

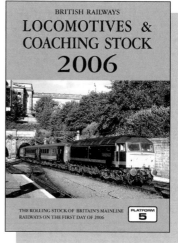

6. PRESERVED LOCOMOTIVES & RAILCARS

STATUS CODES

A	Active (location could vary).	M	Museum or Museum line loco.
P	Plinthed ('Denkmal').	R	Under restoration (perhaps at another place).
K	Retained for special excursions.	S	Stored or for spares.

6.1. ÖBB STEAM LOCOMOTIVES

Standard gauge

Number	Type	Built	Status	Location.
12.10	2-8-4	1936	M	EM Strasshof.
15.13	2-6-2	1910	M	EM Strasshof.
16.08	2-6-4	1911	MA	EM Strasshof. Preserved as KKStB 310.23.
30.33	2-6-2T	1897	MA	EM Strasshof.
30.109	2-6-2T	1900	MR	Brenner & Brenner, St. Pölten.
33.102	4-8-0	1923	M	EM Strasshof.
"33.132"	4-8-0	1925	MA	Brenner & Brenner, St. Pölten (Ex JZ 10-005)
35.233	2-6-2	1916	M	EM Strasshof.
38.4101	4-6-0	1912	MA	EM Strasshof.
42.2708	2-10-0	1946	M	EM Strasshof.
42.2721	2-10-0	1947	MA	Luxembourg.
50.685	2-10-0	1940	M	ATM Sinsheim, Germany.
50.1171	2-10-0	1942	MA	Brenner & Brenner, St. Pölten.
52.100	2-10-0	194	M	EM Strasshof ex JZ 33-044.
52.221	2-10-0	1943	MR	St. Sulpice, Switzerland.
52.855	2-10-0	1944	M	Sigmundsherberg.
52.1198	2-10-0	1943	MA	ÖGEG, Ampflwang.
52.1227	2-10-0	1944	MA	Brenner & Brenner, St. Pölten.
52.2436	2-10-0	1943	P	Kyoto, Japan.
52.3314	2-10-0	1944	MR	CFV3V Mariembourg, Belgium
52.3316	2-10-0	1944	M	ÖGEG, Ampflwang.
52.3504	2-10-0	1943	MR	Luxembourg.
52.3517	2-10-0	1943	MA	ÖGEG, Ampflwang.
52.3816	2-10-0	1944	MA	Lienz.
52.3879	2-10-0	1944	MA	VSM, Beekbergen, Netherlands.
52.5804	2-10-0	1943	M	Neuenmarkt Wirsberg, Germany.
52.7046	2-10-0	1943	P	Selzthal.
52.7102	2-10-0	1943	P	Wien Briggettenau.
52.7409	2-10-0	1943	MA	Würzburg Zell, Germany.
52.7593	2-10-0	1944	P	Strasshof (Bundestrasse 205).
52.7594	2-10-0	1944	MA	EM Strasshof.
52.7596	2-10-0	1944	MR	EFZ Tübingen. Germany.
52.7612	2-10-0	1944	MA	Brenner & Brenner, St. Pölten.
152.3109	2-10-0	1942	M	TM Speyer, Germany.
152.4552	2-10-0	1944	MS	ÖGEG, Ampflwang.
152.4867	2-10-0	1942	MA	H.E. Frankfurt/M, Germany.
53.7101	0-6-0	1868	MR	EM Strasshof (as KEB 106 *FUSCH*).
153.7114	0-6-0	1869	MR	EM Strasshof (as Südbahn 852).
54.14	2-6-0	1899	M	EM Strasshof.
55.5708	0-8-0	1887	M	EM Strasshof.
56.3115	2-8-0	1913	M	GKB Lieboch.
56.3255	2-8-0	1919	MS	Benešov, Czech Republic.
156.3423	2-8-0	1920	M	EM Strasshof.
57.223	0-10-0	1916	M	EM Strasshof.
257.601	0-10-0	1921	M	EM Strasshof.
257.605	0-10-0	1921	MS	EM Strasshof.
58.744	2-10-0	1923	M	EM Strasshof.
258.902	2-10-0	1912	M	EM Strasshof.

69.02	2-2-2T	1898	M	EM Strasshof.
770.86	2-4-0T	1913	MA	Brener & Brenner, Salzburg.
175.817	2-6-2T	1912	M	EM Strasshof.
77.28	4-6-2T	1920	MS	ÖGEG, Ampflwang.
77.66	4-6-2T	1913	M	EM Strasshof.
77.244	4-6-2T	1927	MA	Brenner & Brenner, St. Pölten. (restored as 77.250).
77.250	4-6-2T	1927	MR	Schaan Vaduz, Lichtenstein, (exhibited as 77.244).
78.606	4-6-4T	1931	P	Amstetten Eggersdorferstrasse.
78.618	4-6-4T	1938	MR	ÖGEG, Ampflwang.
86.476	2-8-2T	1943	MR	ÖGEG, Ampflwang.
088.01	0-4-0T	1906	M	EM Strasshof.
789.837	0-6-0T	1921	M	BEM Nördlingen, Germany.
989.01	0-6-0T	1944	MS	Probstdorf.
91.32	2-6-0T	1900	M	Mürzzuschlag. (Kulturbahnhof).
91.107	2-6-0T	1908	MA	Gross Schwechat.
92.2220	0-8-0T	1898	P	Puchberg (near station).
92.2231	0-8-0T	1909	MS	EM Strasshof
92.2234	0-8-0T	1910	S	EM Strasshof.
"92.2271"	0-8-0T	1919	MR	Zwettl.
392.2510	0-8-0T	1927	MS	ÖGEG, Ampflwang.
392.2530	0-8-0T	1927	MR	ÖGEG, Ampflwang.
93.1326	2-8-2T	1927	MR	ÖGEG, Ampflwang.
93.1332	2-8-2T	1927	MA	Weizelsdorf.
93.1335	2-8-2T	1927	M	Sigmundsherberg.
93.1360	2-8-2T	1927	MA	Eurovapor – Fützen, Germany
93.1364	2-8-2T	1927	MS	Brenner & Brenner, St. Pölten.
93.1378	2-8-2T	1927	MA	Eurovapor – Kandern,Germany
93.1379	2-8-2T	1927	P	Bhf Schwarzach St. Veit.
93.1394	2-8-2T	1927	M	ÖGEG, Ampflwang.
93.1403	2-8-2T	1927	M	EM Strasshof.
93.1410	2-8-2T	1928	MS	Exertalbahn, Rinteln, Germany.
93.1420	2-8-2T	1928	MA	Brenner & Brenner, St. Pölten.
93.1421	2-8-2T	1928	MR	Brenner & Brenner, St. Pölten.
93.1422	2-8-2T	1928	MA	Grosspetersdorf.
93.1434	2-8-2T	1928	MR	Zwettl.
93.1455	2-8-2T	1931	MA	ÖGEG, Ampflwang.
694.503	0-10-0T	1913	MS	ÖGEG, Ampflwang.
95.112	2-10-2T	1922	P	Bhf Payerbach.
97.201	0-6-2T	1890	M	TM Wien (Dismantled and sectioned).
97.203	0-6-2T	1890	P	Grosspetersdorf.
97.208	0-6-2T	1892	MA	EM Strasshof.
97.210	0-6-2T	1893	M	Darmstadt Kranichstein, Germany.
97.217	0-6-2T	1908	P	Vordernberg Markt Hauptplatz.
197.301	0-12-0T	1912	MA	EM Strasshof.
297.401	2-12-2T	1941	P	Bhf Vordernberg Markt.
3071.07	2-4-2T	1935	MA	EM Strasshof (restored as DT 7).

760 mm gauge

Number	Type	Built	Status	Location.
298.05	0-6-2T	1898	P	ÖBB TS Werke Knittelfeld.
298.14	0-6-2T	1898	MR	Bieringen. Germany.
298.24	0-6-2T	1902	MR	Bezau.
298.25	0-6-2T	1902	MA	Mauterndorf.
298.51	0-6-2T	1898	MA	ÖGLB Kienberg Gaming.
298.52	0-6-2T	1898	MA	Grünburg.
298.53	0-6-2T	1898	MA	Grünburg.
298.54	0-6-2T	1898	MR	Obergrafendorf.
298.55	0-6-2T	1898	P	Bhf Mittersill.
298.56	0-6-2T	1899	MA	Mauterndorf.
298.102	0-6-2T	1888	MA	Grünburg.
298.104	0-6-2T	1890	MA	ÖGLB Kienberg Gaming.
298.106	0-6-2T	1914	MR	Grünburg.
298.205	0-6-2T	1902	MR	ÖGLB Kienberg Gaming.
298.206	0-6-2T	1902	P	Langschlag Bhf.

398.01	0-6-2T	1905	A	Murau (as StLB Bh1).
498.03	0-6-2T	1929	P	Bhf Bezau.
498.04	0-6-2T	1929	MR	ÖGLB Grunburg.
498.06	0-6-2T	1930	P	St. Veit a.d. Glan (as 498.04).
498.07	0-6-2T	1931	P	Obergrafendorf, ESV Sportplatz.
498.08	0-6-2T	1931	MA	Bezau.
598.01	0-6-4T	1896	P	Eichgraben.
598.02	0-6-4T	1896	MR	Club 598, Waidhofen a.d. Ybbs (as Yv2).
598.03	0-6-4T	1896	MS	Club 598, Waidhofen a.d. Ybbs.
698.01	0-4-0T	1941	M	Bad Ischl.
798.101	0-6-0TT	1941	MA	Putbus, Germany.
898.01	0-6-0T	1941	MR	KMB, Treibach Althofen.
199.02	0-8-2T	1926	M	KMB, Treibach Althofen.
199.03	0-8-2T	1926	P	Izola, Slovenia.
299.02	0-8-4T	1907	S	ÖBB TS Werke Knittelfeld.
499.01	0-10-0T	1924	M	KMB, Treibach Althofen.
699.01	0-8-0	1944	MA	Mauterndorf.
699.02	0-8-0	1944	M	TM Berlin, Germany.
699.101	0-8-0T	1944	MA	KMB. Treibach Althofen.
699.103	0-8-0T	1944	MA	Grünburg.

1000 mm gauge

Number	Type	Built	Status	Location.
999.105	0-4-2RT	1894	M	EM Strasshof.

6.2. ÖBB ELECTRIC LOCOMOTIVES

Number	Type	Built	Status	Location.
1010 002	Co-Co	1955	MS	Wien West
1010 003	Co-Co	1955	MA	Wien Nord (ÖBB Nostalgie).
1010 004	Co-Co	1955	MS	ÖGEG, Timelkam.
1010 005	Co-Co	1955	MS	ÖGEG, Timelkam.
1010 009	Co-Co	1956	MS	ÖGEG, Ampflwang.
1010 010	Co-Co	1956	MS	Wien Nord (ÖBB Nostalgie).
1010 011	Co-Co	1956	MS	EM Strasshof.
1010 013	Co-Co	1956	MS	ÖGEG, Ampflwang.
1010 014	Co-Co	1956	MS	ÖGEG, Ampflwang.
1010 015	Co-Co	1956	MS	ÖGEG, Ampflwang.
1110 008	Co-Co	1958	MS	ÖGEG, Ampflwang.
1110 015	Co-Co	1958	MS	Knittelfeld (ÖBB Nostalgie).
1110 020	Co-Co	1960	MS	ÖGEG, Ampflwang.
1110 023	Co-Co	1960	MS	Wien West.
1110 025	Co-Co	1960	MS	ÖGEG, Ampflwang.
1110 505	Co-Co	1957	MA	Innsbruck (ÖBB Nostalgie).
1110 522	Co-Co	1960	MS	ÖGEG, Timelkam.
1110 524	Co-Co	1960	M	Graz.
1110 526	Co-Co	1960	MS	ÖGEG, Ampflwang.
1110 528	Co-Co	1960	MS	ÖGEG, Ampflwang.
1110 529	Co-Co	1961	MS	ÖGEG, Timelkam.
1110 530	Co-Co	1961	MS	Bludenz (ÖBB Nostalgie).
1018 002	1Do1	1940	MS	ÖGEG, Ampflwang.
1018 004	1Do1	1940	M	Prora, Germany.
1018 005	1Do1	1940	MS	Wien Nord (ÖBB Nostalgie).
1018 007	1Do1	1940	MS	ÖGEG, Ampflwang.
1018 008	1Do1	1940	MS	ÖGEG, Ampflwang.
1020 003	Co-Co	1941	MS	ÖGEG, Ampflwang.
1020 010	Co-Co	1943	MS	Kornwestheim, Germany.
1020 012	Co-Co	1943	MS	ÖGEG, Timelkam.
1020 014	Co-Co	1944	MS	ÖGEG, Ampflwang.
1020 017	Co-Co	1944	M	Nördlingen, Germany.
1020 018	Co-Co	1940	A	EC Lienz.
1020 022	Co-Co	1940	MS	ÖGEG, Ampflwang.
1020 023	Co-Co	1940	MS	Lienz.
1020 024	Co-Co	1941	MS	ÖGEG, Timelkam.
1020 037	Co-Co	1943	MS	ÖGEG, Ampflwang.
1020 038	Co-Co	1943	MS	ÖGEG, Ampflwang.
1020.042	Co-Co	1943	MA	Bludenz, (owned by Roco models).
1020 044	Co-Co	1945	MA	Innsbruck (ÖBB Nostalgie).
1020 047	Co-Co	1954	MA	Wien Nord (ÖBB Nostalgie).
1040 001	Bo-Bo	1950	MA	Selzthal (ÖBB Nostalgie).
1040 008	Bo-Bo	1951	M	EM Strasshof.
1040 009	Bo-Bo	1951	M	Sigmundsherberg (ÖBB Nostalgie).
1040 013	Bo-Bo	1953	MS	Selzthal.
1040 015	Bo-Bo	1953	MS	ÖGEG, Ampflwang.
1041 001	Bo-Bo	1952	MA	Selzthal.
1041 005	Bo-Bo	1952	MS	ÖGEG, Ampflwang.
1041 006	Bo-Bo	1952	MS	ÖGEG, Ampflwang.
1041 015	Bo-Bo	1953	MS	Strasshof.
1041 202	Bo-Bo	1952	MA	Selzthal (ÖBB Nostalgie).
1141 003	Bo-Bo	1956	S	Linz (for private purchaser?).
1141 007	Bo-Bo	1956	MS	Gross Schwechat.
1141 016	Bo-Bo	1956	MS	Knittelfeld.
1141 020	Bo-Bo	1957	MS	ÖGEG, Ampflwang.
1141 021	Bo-Bo	1957	MS	Wien Nord (ÖBB Nostalgie).
1141 022	Bo-Bo	1957	MS	Wien Nord (ÖBB Nostalgie).
1141 024	Bo-Bo	1957	MS	Wien Nord.
1141 028	Bo-Bo	1957	S	Wien West.
1042 021	Bo-Bo	1964	MS	Wien Nord.

1042 046	Bo-Bo	1966	MS	Wien Nord.
1044 501	Bo-Bo	1974	S	Wien West.
1045 009	Bo-Bo	1928	MA	Attnang Puchheim (ÖBB Nostalgie).
1045.012	Bo-Bo	1927	P	Attnang Puchheim.
1045 014	Bo-Bo	1928	MS	Strasshof.
1145 002	Bo-Bo	1929	MA	Wien Süd (ÖBB Nostalgie).
1145 009	Bo-Bo	1931	MS	Wien Nord.
1245 001	Bo-Bo	1934	MS	EM Strasshof.
1245 002	Bo-Bo	1934	MS	ÖGEG, Ampflwang.
1245 004	Bo-Bo	1934	MA	Saalfelden (ÖBB Nostalgie).
1245 005	Bo-Bo	1934	MA	Selzthal (ÖBB Nostalgie).
1245 514	Bo-Bo	1938	M	Schwarzach St. Veit.
1245 516	Bo-Bo	1938	MS	ÖGEG, Ampflwang.
1245 518	Bo-Bo	1938	MS	ÖGEG, Timelkam.
1245 522	Bo-Bo	1938	MA	Lienz.
1245 525	Bo-Bo	1938	MA	Knittelfeld (ÖBB Nostalgie).
1245 530	Bo-Bo	1938	MS	Knittelfeld.
1245 533	Bo-Bo	1938	MS	Saalfelden.
1046 001	Bo-Bo	1956	MS	ÖGEG, Ampflwang.
1046 005	Bo-Bo	1956	MS	Wien West.
1046 007	Bo-Bo	1956	MS	ÖGEG, Ampflwang.
1046 016	Bo-Bo	1959	MR	ÖBB Nostalgie.
1046 019	Bo-Bo	1959	MR	Wien Nord (ÖBB Nostalgie).
1046 020	Bo-Bo	1959	MR	Wien Nord.
1046 024	Bo-Bo	1959	MS	? (for Private purchaser).
1146 001	Bo-Bo	1986	MS	Wien
1060.01	1C	1911	M	EM Strasshof.
1061.02	D	1926	MS	ÖGEG, Ampflwang.
1161 012	D	1932	MR	St. Veit a. d. Glan.
1161 017	D	1932	P	Bischofshofen.
1161 019	D	1940	MS	ÖGEG, Ampflwang.
1161 020	D	1940	MR	Lienz.
1062 007	C	1954	MS	Wien Nord (ÖBB Nostalgie).
1062 012	C	1955	MS	ÖGEG, Ampflwang.
1067 003	C	1963	M	Knittelfeld.
1067 004	C	1964	M	ÖGEG, Ampflwang.
1570.01	1A-Bo-A1	1926	M	EM Strasshof.
1670.09	1A-Bo-A1	1928	MA	Saalfelden (ÖBB Nostalgie).
1670.24	1A-Bo-A1	1929	MA	Bludenz.
1670.25	1A-Bo-A1	1929	MA	Wien Nord (ÖBB Nostalgie).
1670.102	1A-Bo-A1	1932	MS	ÖGEG, Ampflwang.
1670.104	1A-Bo-A1	1932	MS	Bludenz (ÖBB Nostalgie).
1072.01	1B1	1913	MS	Wien Nord (ÖBB Nostalgie).
1072.05	1B1	1913	MS	Gross Schwechat.
1073.03	1C1	1923	MS	ÖGEG, Ampflwang.
1073.20	1C1	1925	MS	ÖGEG, Ampflwang.
1080 001	E	1924	MA	Selzthal (ÖBB Nostalgie).
1080 007	E	1924	MS	Selzthal.
1080 011	E	1924	MS	ÖGEG, Ampflwang.
1180 004	E	1926	MS	ÖGEG, Ampflwang.
1180 009	E	1927	MA	Bludenz (ÖBB Nostalgie).
1280.14	E	1929	MS	ÖGEG, Ampflwang.
1985.02	Bo	1913	MA	Wien Gross Schwechat.
1089.06	1C-C1	1924	M	ATM Sinsheim, Germany.
1189.02	1C-C1	1926	MA	Wien West (ÖBB Nostalgie).
1189.05	1C-C1	1927	MS	EM Strasshof.
1189.09	1C-C1	1927	P	ÖBB Wolfurt.

6.3. ÖBB DIESEL LOCOMOTIVES

Number	Type	Built	Status	Location.
2020.01	B-B dh	1959	MS	ÖCD Hadersdorf.
2043.01	B-B dh	1964	MA	Knittelfeld.
2143 003	B-B dh	1965	MS	ÖCD Hadersdorf.
2045.01	Bo-Bo de	1952	MS	ÖCD Hadersdorf.
2045 009	Bo-Bo de	1953	MS	ÖCD Hadersdorf (Stored ÖBB TS Werke St. Pölten).
2045 012	Bo-Bo de	1954	MS	ÖGEG, Ampflwang.
2045 013	Bo-Bo de	1954	P	ÖBB TS Werke St. Pölten (missing 07/05).
2045.15	Bo-Bo de	1954	M	Lienz.
2045 017	Bo-Bo de	1954	M	Sigmundsherberg.
2045 019	Bo-Bo de	1954	MS	ÖGEG, Ampflwang.
2045 020	Bo-Bo de	1954	MA	Krems (ÖBB Nostalgie).
2050 002	Bo-Bo de	1958	MA	Wien Ost (ÖBB Nostalgie).
2050 003	Bo-Bo de	1958	MS	Wien Ost.
2050 004	Bo-Bo de	1958	M	Sigmundsherberg (ÖBB Nostalgie).
2050 005	Bo-Bo de	1958	MA	ÖGEG, Ampflwang.
2050 008	Bo-Bo de	1959	MS	ÖGEG, Timelkam.
2050 009	Bo-Bo de	1959	MA	Wien Ost (ÖBB Nostalgie).
2050 011	Bo-Bo de	1961	MS	ÖGEG, Timelkam.
2050 012	Bo-Bo de	1961	MS	ÖGEG, Timelkam.
2050 015	Bo-Bo de	1962	MS	ÖGEG, Timelkam.
2050 016	Bo-Bo de	1962	MS	ÖGEG, Timelkam.
2050 017	Bo-Bo de	1962	MS	ÖGEG, Timelkam.
2050 018	Bo-Bo de	1962	M	Mürzzuschlag, Kultur Bahnhof.
2060 003	B dh	1954	M	Bad Ischl.
2060 004	B dh	1954	MA	EM Strasshof.
2060 011	B dh	1955	M	Sigmundsherberg.
2060 012	B dh	1955	MS	St. Veit an der Glan.
2060 055	B dh	1956	MS	St. Veit an der Glan.
2060 057	B dh	1956	M	Knittelfeld.
2060 058	B dh	1956	MS	ÖGEG, Ampflwang.
2060 064	B dh	1956	MS	St. Veit an der Glan.
2060 074	B dh	1956	MS	EM Strasshof.
2060 092	B dh	1962	MS	ÖGEG, Ampflwang.
2060 099	B dh	1962	MS	ÖGEG, Ampflwang.
2061.01	B dh	1940	MS	ÖCD Hadersdorf (Elsdorf Stras?).
2062 003	B dh	1958	MR	ÖCD Amstetten.
2062 029	B dh	1960	MS	ÖCD Wien Nord.
2062 034	B dh	1961	MS	ÖGEG, Ampflwang.
2062 038	B dh	1961	MS	ÖGEG, Ampflwang.
2065.01	C dh	1940	MS	ÖCD Hadersdorf.
2066.01	C dh	1940	MA	Saalfelden (ÖBB Nostalgie).
2090 001	Bo de	1930	MR	Obergrafendorf.
2190.01	Bo de	1934	MS	ÖGLB Kienberg Gaming.
2190.02	Bo de	1934	MS	ÖGLB Hirschwang.
2190 003	Bo de	1936	MR	Obergrafendorf.
2091.01	1Bo1 de	1936	MR	Hirschwang.
2091.02	1Bo1 de	1936	MR	Obergrafendorf.
2091.03	1Bo1 de	1936	MR	Mauterndorf.
2091 004	1Bo1 de	1936	MS	Bezau.
2091 007	1Bo1 de	1936	MR	Gmünd, ÖBB Nostalgie.
2091 008	1Bo1 de	1940	MR	Bezau.
2091 009	1Bo1 de	1940	MR	Waidhofen, ÖBB Nostalgie.
2091 011	1Bo1 de	1940	MR	Obergrafendorf, ÖBB Nostalgie.
2092 001	C dh	1944	P	Puchstaben.
2092 003	C dh	1943	MR	Obergrafendorf, Club Mh6.
2092 004	C dh	1943	MR	Obergrafendorf, ÖBB Nostalgie.
2093.01	Bo-Bo de	1930	MA	Kienberg Gaming.
X110.02	B dm	1935	MA	Ebermannstadt, Germany.
X111.04	B dm	1944	M	EM Strasshof.
X111.06	B dm	1944	MS	St. Veit a.d. Glan. (Missing).

```
X112.001   B dh    1934  MS   St. Veit a.d. Glan. (missing).
X112.02    B dh    1934  M    TM Berlin, Germany.
X112.06    B dh    1935  MR   EM Strasshof.
X112.07    B dh    1935  M    Knittelfeld.
X130.01    Bo de   1934  MR   EM Strasshof.
X130.02    Bo de   1935  M    Ferlach.
X130.03    Bo de   1935  M    Ferlach.
X150.01    B dh    1943  MR   ÖCD Hainfeld.
X150.03    B dh    1943  M    Vordernberg.
X150.04    B dh    1943  M    Vordernberg.
X150.05    B dh    1943  M    Sigmundsherberg.
X150.08    B dh    1943  M    Knittelfeld.
X150.09    B dh    1944  MS   ÖGEG Ampflwang.
```

6.4. ÖBB ELECTRIC RAILCARS

Number	Type	Built	Status	Location.
4030 210	Bo-Bo	1962	MA	EM Strasshof
4041.01	Bo-2	1929	MS	EM Strasshof
4041.03	Bo-2	1929	MS	Floridsdorf (ÖBB Nostalgie)
4041.05	Bo-2	1929	MS	EM Strasshof
4042.01	Bo-2	1936	MS	ÖBB, ex StLB ET 11
4042.02	Bo-2	1936	MR	ÖBB, ex StLB ET 12
4060.02	Bo-Bo	1936	MA	Strasshof (recently MBS ET 10.106).
4061.13	Bo-Bo	1958	MA	Wien Nord (ÖBB Nostalgie)

6.5. ÖBB DIESEL RAILCARS

Number	Type	Built	Status	Location.
5029.01	A-1 dm	1927	M	Gross Schwechat.
5041.03	Bo-2 de	1933	M	Gross Schwechat.
5042.14	1A-A1 de	1937	MA	Wien Nord (ÖBB Nostalgie)
5044.06	B-2 dh	1938	MR	ÖCD Hainfeld
5144 001	B-2 dh	1951	P	Semmering
5144 003	B-2 dh	1951	MS	ÖCD Hainfeld
5144 004	B-2 dh	1951	MS	ÖCD Hainfeld
5145 001	B-2 dh	1952	MR	Wien Ost (ÖBB Nostalgie)
5145 009	B-2 dh	1954	MR	ÖGEG Ampflwang
5145 011	B-2 dh	1954	MA	Wien Ost (ÖBB Nostalgie)
5145 013	B-2 dh	1956	MR	Wien Ost
5145 014	B-2 dh	1956	MA	Wien Ost (ÖBB Nostalgie)
5046 201	B-2 dh	1954	MS	EM Strasshof
5046 204	B-2 dh	1955	MS	ÖGEG Ampflwang
5046 206	B-2 dh	1955	MS	EM Strasshof
5046 214	B-2 dh	1955	MS	ÖGEG Ampflwang
5046 215	B-2 dh	1955	MS	ÖGEG Ampflwang
5046 216	B-2 dh	1955	MS	Linz Steelworks
5146 201	B-2 dh	1959	MS	ÖGEG Ampflwang
5146 206	B-2 dh	1961	M	Budapest, Hungary, (as GySEV 5146 02)
5146 207	B-2 dh	1961	MS	ÖGEG Ampflwang
5146 208	B-2 dh	1961	MS	ÖGEG Ampflwang
5081 002	A-A dh	1964	MS	ÖGEG Ampflwang
5081 003	A-A dh	1964	MS	Aachen, Germany
5081 013	A-A dh	1965	P	Bhf Eisenerz.
5081 014	A-A dh	1965	MS	EM Strasshof
5081 019	A-A dh	1965	MS	Linz Steelworks
5081 054	A-A dh	1965	M	BEM Nördlingen, Germany
5081 561	A-A dh	1965	MS	Augsburg, Germany
5081 562	A-A dh	1965	MA	Vordernberg.
5081 563	A-A dh	1967	MA	Vordernberg.
5081 564	A-A dh	1967	MA	Vordernberg.
5081 565	A-A dh	1967	MA	Vordernberg.

6.6. ÖBB DEPARTMENTAL STOCK

Number	Type	Gauge	Built	Status	Location.
X512.08	B dm		1963	MR	EM Strasshof.
X534.60	1A de		19xx	M	Sigmundsherberg.
X610.913	B dm	760 mm	1925	MR	Hirschwang.
X614.10	B dm		1954	MR	Ferlach.
X614.16	B dm		1955	MR	Ferlach.
X614.30	B dm		1955	MR	Ferlach.
X614.80	B dm		1955	MR	Lambach.
X614.902	B dm	760 mm	1952	MR	Kienberg Gaming or Heidenreichstein.
X614.909	B dm	760 mm	1955	MR	Kienberg Gaming.
X616 003	B dm		19xx	M	Vordernberg.
X616 010	B dm		19xx	M	Unter Retzbach.
X616 084	B dm		19xx	M	Vordernberg.
X616 901	B dm	760 mm	19xx	M	Grünberg.
X616 903	B dm	760 mm	19xx	M	Grünberg.
X616 910	B dm	760 mm	19xx	M	Maunterndorf.
X616 912	B dm	760 mm	19xx	M	Birkfeld.
X626 102	B dm		19xx	M	Knittelfeld.

6.7. OTHER RAILWAYS' STEAM LOCOMOTIVES

Note: Standard gauge unless shown otherwise.

Number	Rly	Gauge	Type	Built	Status	Location
1.20	BBÖ		4-4-0	1883	MS	EM Strasshof (Partially sectioned)
494.62	BBÖ		0-6-0T	1887	P	Rohrbach-Berg
827	BBÖ		4-4-0	1848	MS	EM Strasshof
465[60]	BDZ	600 mm	0-8-0T	1917	MR	Gross Schwechat
16.18	BDZ		2-10-0	1949	MS	ÖGEG Ampflwang
16.19	BDZ		2-10-0	1949	MS	ÖGEG Ampflwang
764.219	CFF	760 mm	0-8-0T	1917	MR	Club 760 Frojach
764.222	CFF	760 mm	0-8-0T	1910	MR	FIM Freiland.
764.224	CFF	760 mm	0-8-0T	1910	MR	FIM Freiland.
764.243	CFF	760 mm	0-8-0T	1911	MR	Graz.
764.403R	CFF	760 mm	0-8-0T	1984	MR	Heidenreichstein
764.404R	CFF	760 mm	0-8-0T	1984	MR	Stainz
764.411R	CFF	760 mm	0-8-0T	1986	MA	Stainz
764.434	CFF	760 mm	0-8-0T	1954	MS	Tschagguns
764.435	CFF	760 mm	0-8-0T	1954	MS	Tschagguns
764.480	CFF	760 mm	0-8-0T	1957	MR	Grünberg
764.007	CFI	760 mm	0-8-0T	1953	MA	Grünberg
142.063	CFR		2-8-4	1939	MA	ÖGEG Ampflwang (as "12.14").
230.174	CFR		4-6-0	1933	MS	ÖGEG Ampflwang (as "638.2174")
230.301	CFR		4-6-0	1935	MA	ÖGEG Ampflwang (as "638.1301")
50.459	CFR		0-10-0	1930	MS	ÖGEG Ampflwang (as "657.3459")
50.519	CFR		0-10-0	1931	MS	ÖGEG Ampflwang (as "657.2519")
50.770	CFR		0-10-0	1938	MA	ÖGEG Ampflwang (as "657.2770")
01 533	DR		4-6-2	1934	MA	ÖGEG Ampflwang
44 661	DR		2-10-0	1941	MA	ÖGEG Ampflwang
44 1595	DR		2-10-0	1943	MS	ÖGEG Ampflwang
44 1614	DR		2-10-0	1943	MS	ÖGEG Ampflwang
50 1002	DR		2-10-0	1940	MS	ÖGEG Ampflwang
50 3506	DR		2-10-0	1940	MS	ÖGEG Ampflwang
50 3519	DR		2-10-0	1940	MA	ÖGEG Ampflwang
50 3670	DR		2-10-0	1941	MS	Gross Schwechat
50 3689	DR		2-10-0	1940	MS	ÖGEG Ampflwang
52 8003	DR		2-10-0	1944	MS	ÖGEG Ampflwang
52 8096	DR		2-10-0	1943	MS	ÖGEG Ampflwang
52 8124	DR		2-10-0	1943	MS	ÖGEG Ampflwang
52 8186	DR		2-10-0	1944	MS	ÖGEG Ampflwang
52 8196	DR		2-10-0	1944	MS	ÖGEG Ampflwang
86 056	DR		2-8-2T	1932	MS	ÖGEG Ampflwang.
86 501	DR		2-8-2T	1942	MA	ÖGEG Ampflwang.
1	GB	1000 mm	0-4-0RT	1886	M	EM Strasshof GB = Gaisbergbahn
372	GKB		4-4-0	1891	MR	EM Strasshof.
406	GKB		4-4-0	1896	MS	Ljubljana, Slovenia.
415	GKB		4-4-0	1897	MA	Brenner & Brenner, St. Pölten
674	GKB		0-6-0	1860	M	TM Budapest, Hungary.
680	GKB		0-6-0	1860	MS	TM Berlin.
1851	GKB		0-6-0T	1898	M	EM Strasshof.
17	GySEV		0-6-0	1885	M	Budapest, Hungary.
121	GySEV		2-6-2T	1914	P	Neufeld/Leitha.
122	GySEV		2-6-2T	1916	P	Bad Neusiedl.
123	GySEV		2-6-2T	1925	P	Marz Rohrbach.
124	GySEV		2-6-2T	1950	MA	Gross Schwechat
324,1518	GySEV		2-6-2	1910	P	Sopron, Hungary.
424,140	GySEV		4-8-0	1941	MS	Fertöboz, Hungary.
520,030	GySEV		2-10-0	1943	MS	Fertöboz, Hungary.
1932	JZ	760 mm	0-10-0	1945	MR	Club 760 Frojach.
28-053	JZ		0-10-0	1914	P	Knittelfeld
33-032	JZ		2-10-0	1944	MS	EM Strasshof (HDZ 30 017)
33-240	JZ		2-10-0	1943	MS	EM Strasshof (DRB 52 460)

33-329	JZ		2-10-0	1943	MS	Mürzzuschlag, Kultur Bahnhof (DRB 52 5422)
73-019	JZ	760 mm	2-6-2	1913	M	Club 760, Frojach.
83-159	JZ	760 mm	0-8-2	1948	M	Club 760, Frojach.
83-180	JZ	760 mm	0-8-2	1949	MA	Club U44, Weiz.
97-029	JZ	760 mm	0-6-4RT	1914	M	Club 760, Frojach.
37 AJAX	KFN		0-4-2	1841	MR	EM Strasshof
94 LICAON	KFN		2-4-0ST	1851	MA	EM Strasshof
97.73	KKStB		0-6-0T	1894	MR	EM Strasshof
180.1	KKStB		0-10-0	1900	MS	EM Strasshof
229.222	KKStB		2-6-2T	1918	M	EM Strasshof.
4	LG	1106 mm	4-4-0T	1854	M	TM Wien (LG = Lambach–Gemunden)
377,247	MAV		0-6-0T	1895	P	Wulkersprodersdorf
377,262	MAV		0-6-0T	1895	M	Historama, Ferlach
1	NÖLB		0-4-0T	1905	M	Mariazell.
Pt47-138	PKP		2-8-2	1949	MA	Brenner & Brenner, St. Pölten (as "919.138")
S 4	SKGLB	760 mm	0-6-2T	1890	M	Mondsee.
S 5	SKGLB	760 mm	0-6-2T	1890	M	Mondsee.
S 9	SKGLB	760 mm	0-6-2T	1893	M	Mondsee.
S 12	SKGLB	760 mm	0-6-2T	1906	MA	Mauterndorf.
Kh 111	StLB	760 mm	0-10-0T	1930	M	Club 760, Frojach.
S 7	StLB	760 mm	0-6-2T	1893	M	Club 760, Frojach.
S 11	StLB	760 mm	0-6-2T	1894	MA	Stainz.
U 7	StLB	760 mm	0-6-2T	1894	P	Birkfeld.
U 8	StLB	760 mm	0-6-2T	1894	M	Birkfeld.
U 9	StLB	760 mm	0-6-2T	1894	P	St. Pölten Hbf (as "298.09").
U 11	StLB	760 mm	0-6-2T	1894	M	Club 760, Frojach.
Z 6	StLB	760 mm	0-6-0T	1893	MA	Mauterndorf.
699.01	StLB	760 mm	0-8-0T	1944	MA	Llanfair, United Kingdom.
11810	StLB	760 mm	0-6-0	1944	MA	Abreschwiller, France.
1665	Sudb		0-6-0	1895	M	EM Strasshof (MAV 333,002).
290c	Sulm		0-6-0T	1907	MS	Lienz.
1	ZB	760 mm	0-6-2T	1900	P	Jenbach.

6.8. OTHER RAILWAYS' DIESEL & ELECTRIC

Note: Standard gauge unless shown otherwise.

Number	Rly	Gauge	Type	Built	Status	Location
VT 10.01	GKB		A-1 dm	1953	MA	Ferlach.
VT 10.02	GKB		A-1 dm	1953	MR	Graz.
VT 10.05	GKB		A-1 dm	1955	M	Bayerische Eisenstein, Germany.
VT 10.08	GKB		A-1 dm	1962	M	Nördlingen, Germany.
VT 10.09	GKB		A-1 dm	1962	M	GKB Museum, Lieboch.
D 1	LBPH	760 mm	0-6-0 dh	1943	MS	Bezau.
E I	LBPH	760 mm	Bo E	1903	MA	Hirschwang.
E II	LBPH	760 mm	Bo E	1903	MA	Hirschwang.
E III	LBPH		Bo E	1903	P	Reichenau.
V 10.015	MBS		B dh	1942	MS	ÖCD Hadersdorf.
L 4	RB	1000 mm	Bo RE	1909	M	Innsbruck.
13257	SBB		1C-C1 E	1919	M	EM Strasshof.
ET 11	StLB		Bo-2 er	1936	MS	St. Veit an der Glan (ÖBB 4041.01).
ET 12	StLB		Bo-2 er	1936	MS	St. Veit an der Glan (ÖBB 4041.02).
RT 2	StLB	760 mm	B dm	1941	A	KMB Treibach Althofen.
Te 2	StLB		Bo-Bo er	1928	MR	Mariazell.
VL 01	StLB	760 mm	D dh	1942	MA	Mauterndorf (restored as SKGLB D40).
VL 3	StLB	760 mm	C dh	1943	MA	Stainz.
VL 5	StLB	760 mm	B dm	1938	MS	Frojach.
ET 4	SVB		Bo er	1908	MA	Mariazell.
ET 5	SVB		Bo er	1908	M	Bayerische Eisenstein, Germany.
ET 16	SVB		Bo er	1911	MR	Mariazell.
1	STB	1000 mm	Bo-Bo er	1904	MR	Innsbruck.
2	STB	1000 mm	Bo-Bo er	1904	MR	Innsbruck.
4	STB	1000 mm	Bo-Bo er	1905	MR	Innsbruck.
E 20.001	StH		Bo-Bo E	1915	R	Gross Schwechat.
E 22.003	StH		Bo-Bo E	1916	MR	Mariazell.
ET 22.105	StH	1000 mm	Bo er	1921	MR	Vorchdorf.
ET 23.101	StH	1000 mm	Bo er	1912	R	Historama, Ferlach.
ET 25.105	StH		Bo er	1921	MR	Mariazell.
ET 26.101	StH	1000 mm	Bo er	1912	R	Historama, Ferlach.
ET 26.106	StH	1000 mm	Bo-Bo er	1936	MR	Hilden, Germany.
ET 26.107	StH	1000 mm	Bo-Bo er	1936	M	Ferlach.
ABmot 12	GySEV	760 mm	A-1 dm	1926	S	Fertöboz, Hungary.
D 7[I]	ZB	760 mm	Bo-Bo de	1940	MR	Kienberg Gaming.
D 7[II]	ZB	760 mm	B-B dh	1961	MR	Stainz, (ex MAV Mk48 2019).

APPENDIX 1. BUILDERS

ABB	Asea Brown Boveri
ACMV	Ateliers de Constructions Méchaniques SA, Vevey, Switzerland
Adtranz	ABB Daimler Benz Transportation – various plants
AEG	Allgemeine Elektrizitätsgesellschaft, Berlin or Wien
ASEA	Allmänna Svenska Elekriska AB, Västerås, Sweden
BBC	Brown Boveri et Cie, Baden, Switzerland and Mannheim, Germany
Beilhack	Martin Beilhack, Rosenheim, Germany
BMAG	Berliner Maschinenenfabrik A.G. vormals L. Schwartzkopff, Berlin-Wildau
Bombardier	Bombardier Transportation (Various plants e.g. Bombardier Aachen
Büssing	Büssing Fahrzeug- und Motorenbau, Braunschweig, Germany
CAT/Caterpillar	Caterpillar Inc. Illinois USA but plants worldwide.
Demag	Demag AG, Duisburg, Germany
DD/Djuo Djakavic	Djuro Djakovic Industrija Lokomotive, Strjeva I Mostova, Slavonski Brod, Yugoslavia
Deutz	See KHD
Duewag	Düsseldorfer Waggonfabrik AG, Düsseldorf, Germany
Elin	Elecktrische Industrie A.G. Weiz, Austria
ESG	Elektrizitats und Strassenbahngesellschaft, Linz, Austria
Falun	AB Svenska Järnvägsverkstäderna, Falun, Sweden
FFA	Flug und Fahrzeugewerke AG, Altenrhein Switzerland
Floridsdorf	Wienerlokomotivfabrik, Wien Floridsdorf
Ganz	Ganz Waggon und Machinenfabrik, Budapest, Hungary
Ganz Mavag	Ganz Mavag Mozdony-, Vagon, és Gépgyár, Budapest, Hungary
Ganz Hunslet	Ganz Hunslet, Budapest, Hungary
Gebus	Gelinck und Judtmann, Wien
GM	General Motors, La Grange, Illinois, USA
Gmeinder	Gmeinder & Co. Gmbh, Mosbach, Baden, Germany
Graff	Niedersachsisches Waggonfabrik, Josef Graff, Elze, Germany
Graz	Johann Weitzer, Waggonfabrik, Graz
Györ	Waggon és Gépgyár, Budapest, Hungary
Hagglund	Hagglund & Söner, Örnsköldsvik, Werk Falun, Sweden
Henschel	Henschel & Sohn, Kassel, Germany
Hunslet Barclay	Hunslet Barclay Ltd, Kilmarnock, Scotland
Jung	Arn.Jung Lokomotivfabrik GmbH, Jungenthal bei Kirchberg an der Sieg, Germany
JW/Jenbach	Jenbacher Werke, Jenbach, Tirol, Austria
Kable Gmeinder	see Gmeinder
KHD	Klöckner Humboldt Deutz AG, Köln, Germany
Knotz	Franz Knotz KG, Stahl & Kesselbau, Wien (now Bombardier-Rotax)
Krauss, Linz (KrL)	Lokomotivfabrik Krauss & Co., Linz
Krauss-Maffei	Krauss-Maffei AG, München Allach, Germany
Krauss, München (KrM)	Lokomotivfabrik Krauss & Co. Werk München, Germany
Kiepe	Th. Kiepe, Düsseldorf, Germany
Layritz	Elisabeth Layritz GmbH, Penzberg, Bayern, Germany
LEW	VEB Lokomotivbau Elektrotechnische Werke "Hans Beimler", Berlin-Hennigsdorf, East Germany
LKM	VEB Lokomotivebau und bahnbedarf "Karl Marx", Potsdam-Babelsberg, East Germany
Lindner	Gottfried Lindner AG, Ammendorf, Halle, Germany
Linz	Elektrobau, Linz
Lohner	Karosseriewerk Lohner, Wien, Austria
Lugansk	Lugansker Lokomotivfabrik, Oktoberrevolution, Lugansk, USSR (Ukraine)
Maffei	J.A. Maffei AG, München, Germany
MaK	Maschinenbau Kiel, Germany
MAN	Maschinenfabrik Augsburg-Nürnberg, Nürnberg, Germany
MFO	Maschinenfabrik Oerlikon, Zürich Oerlikon, Switzerland
Mavag	Mávag Mozdony és Gépgyár, Budapest, Hungary
MTU	Motoren und Turbinen Union, Friendrichshafen, Germany
Nohab	Nydqvist & Holm, AB, Trollhättan, Sweden
ÖAM	Österreichische Alpin Montageselleschaft, Zeltweg

OK	Orenstein & Koppel, Berlin Drewitz, Germany (Steam)
	Orenstein-Koppel und Lübecker Maschinenbau AG, Dortmund Dorstfeld, Germany (Diesels)
Plasser	Plasser und Theurer, Bahnbaumaschinen, Purkersdorf and Linz, Austria
Rotax	Rotax, Wien, Austria
RTM	Rotterdamsche Tramweg Maatschappij
Schöma	Christoph Schöttler Maschinenfabrik GmbH, Diepholz, Germany
SGP G (or W or F)	Simmering Graz Pauker, Graz (or Wien Simmering or Wien Floridsdorf)
SIG	Schweizerische Industrie Gesellschaft, Neuhausen am Rheinfall, Switzerland
Siemens	Siemens Transportation Systems, various works in Austria and Germany
Simmering	Maschinen und Waggonbau AG Wien Simmering
Skoda	Skoda Werke, Plzen, Czechoslovakia (now Czech Republic)
SLM	Schweizerische Lokomotive und Maschinenfabrik, Winterthur, Switzerland
SSW	Siemens Schuckertwerke, Wien + elsewhere
Stadler	Stadler Rail AG. Bussnang and Altenrhein Switzerland; Berlin-Pankow, Germany
SWS	Schweizerische Waggons und Aufzugefabrik AG, Schlieren, Switzerland
SWP	Schindler Waggon AG, Pratteln, Switzerland
StEG	Maschinenfabrik der Staatseisenbahngesellschaft, Wien, Austria
Tobisch	Franz Tobisch, Wien, Austria
U23A	Uzinele 23 August, Bucuresti, Romania
Uerdingen	Waggonfabrik Uerdingen AG, Krefeld-Uerdingen Germany
VOEST	Voest Alpine, various plants, Austria
VSFT	Vossloh Schienenfahrzeugetechnik GmbH, Kiel, Germany
Westwaggon	Vereinigte Westdeutsche Waggonfabrik AG, Köln, Germany
Windhoff	Rheiner Maschinenfabrik Windhoff AG, Rheine, Westfalen, Germany
WrN	AG der Lokomotivfabrik, formerly G. Sigl, Wiener Neustadt
WMD	Waggon und Machinenbau Gmbh, Donauworth, Germany
Voith	J.M. Voith Gmbh, Heidenheim (Brenz), Germany, and St. Pölten, Austria

PLATFORM 5 MAIL ORDER

CALENDARS from EISENBAHN KURIER

A range of high quality calendars from German publisher Eisenbahn Kurier are available annually from the Platform 5 Mail Order Department. Each calendar is produced on high quality art board and presented in one month per page format with German public holidays highlighted. Spiral bound.

Prices of 2006 calendars are shown. For future years, the new EK calendars are usually available from mid-September. Please enquire for details of price and availability.

The following calendars are produced annually:

GLACIER EXPRESS KALENDAR
Following the route of the world's slowest express train in colour.

ALPENBAHNEN KALENDAR
Mountain railways of Germany, Austria, Switzerland and France in colour.

STADTVERKEHR IN ALLER WELT KALENDAR
The best colour tramway and light railway photography from around the world.

GROSSE DAMPFLOK KALENDER
Archive black & white photography of German steam locomotives in action.

MODELLBAHNEN KALENDAR
Scenes from the highest quality continental model railway layouts in colour.

NORDAMERIKA KALENDAR
Modern trains in North America in colour.

DEUTSCHLANDREISE KALENDAR
Colour railway photography from all over Germany

GLOBETROTTER KALENDAR
Steam, diesel and electric traction from around the world in colour.

	TR Subs Price	
Deutschlandreise 2006	£9.95	£7.95
Alpenbahnen 2006	£14.95	£12.95
Glacier Express 2006	£12.95	£10.95
Grosse Dampflok Kalender 2006	£9.95	£7.95
Stadtverkehr In Aller Welt 2006	£14.95	£12.95
Nordamerika 2006	£9.95	£7.95
Globetrotter 2006	£14.95	£12.95
Modellbahnen 2006	£9.95	£7.95

Postage & Packing per EK calendar: £1.00 (UK); £2.00 Europe; £3.00 Rest of World.

HOW TO ORDER

Telephone your order and credit/debit card details to our 24-hour sales hotline:

0114 255 8000 (UK) + 44 114-255-8000 (from overseas) or Fax: +44(0)114-255-2471.

An answerphone is attached for calls made outside of normal UK office hours.

Please state type of card, card number, issue no./date (maestro cards only), expiry date and full name & address of cardholder.

Or send your credit/debit card details, sterling cheque or British Postal order payable to Platform 5 Publishing Ltd. to:

**Mail Order Department (EHA), Platform 5 Publishing Ltd.,
3 Wyvern House, Sark Road, SHEFFIELD, S2 4HG, ENGLAND**

APPENDIX 2. VEHICLE TYPE CODES FOR RAILCARS & MULTIPLE UNITS

The abbreviations in common use in Austria are used, with the normal British codes in brackets. The Austrian codes are:

ET	Electric power car	A	First Class
ES	Driving trailer for above	B	Second Class
VT	Diesel power car	AB	Composite
VS	Driving trailer for above	D	Vehicle with luggage compartment
T	Trailer	4	Vehicle with 4 axles (instead of 2)
h	Electric heating	BR	Buffet Car
I	Control wired	WR	Restaurant Car

Note: The continental system does not differentiate between open and compartment stock nor indicate toilet facilities.

British codes are also shown in brackets as follows:

D	Driving	F	First	O	Open
M	Motor	S	Second	K	Side Corridor
T	Trailer	C	Composite	B	Brake
L	Lavatory	RB	Buffet		

Under 'accommodation' are shown the number of first and second class seats with tip-up seats in saloons in parentheses, followed by the number of toilets, e.g. 24/49(3) 1T indicates 24 first class seats, 49 second class seats, three additional tip-up seats and one toilet. TD indicates a toilet suitable for disabled people, W indicates a wheelchair space.

APPENDIX 3. COMMON TERMS IN GERMAN AND ENGLISH

die Lokomotive (Lok) – locomotive (loco).
der Reisezugwagen – passenger coach.
das Gleis – track.
die Fahrkarte – ticket.
das Ausbesserungswerk (abbreviated to AW) – works.
das Reichsbahnausbesserungswerk (abbreviated to RAW) – works (former DR).
das Bahnbetriebswerk (abbreviated to Bw) – depot.
die Direktion (abbreviated in Austria to Dion) – division.
die Baureihe – Class (as in *Baureihe 2016* – Class 2016).
der Speisewagen – restaurant car.
die Klasse – Class (as in *Erste Klasse* – First Class).
das Abteil – compartment.
der Schlafwagen – sleeping car.
das Bier – Beer.
der Liegewagen – couchette car.
der Fahrplan – timetable.
fahrplanmässig – scheduled, timetabled.
die Verspätung – lateness.
die Dampflok – steam loco.
der Lokführer* – driver.
die Ellok – electric loco.
der Zugführer* – guard.
die Diesellok – diesel loco.
der Bahnsteig – platform.
der Schienenbus – railbus.
der Bahnhof (abbreviated to Bhf) – station.
der Hauptbahnhof (abbreviated to Hbf) – main station.
der Hauptgüterbahnhof (abbreviated to Hgbf) – main goods depot.
der Verschiebebahnhof (abbreviated to Vbf) – marshalling yard.

(*Note: these terms also have feminine forms, i.e. die Lokführerin, die Zugführerin)

APPENDIX 4. DEPOT & LIVERY CODES
ÖBB DEPOT CODES

P5 Code	ÖBB Code	Servicestelle (depot)
AM	Ams	Amstetten
AT	At	Attnang-Puchheim
BM	Bm	Bruck an der Mur
BL	Bl	Bludenz
FK	Fk	Feldkirch
GM	Gm	Gmünd
GZ	Gz	Graz
IN	In	Innsbrück
KD	Kd	Knittelfeld
KL	Zv	Kledering
KR	Bk	Krems
LE	Lie	Lienz
LZ	Lz	Linz
NS	Nb	Wiener Neustadt
OG	Og	Obergrafendorf
SB	Sb	Salzburg.
SL	Sl	Selzthal.
SP	Pb	St. Pölten.
ST	St	Spittal Millstattersee
VH	Vt	Villach.
WE	We	Wels.
WF	Wf	Wien FJB.
WH	Wh	Waidhofen a.d. Ybbs.
WL	W	Wörgl.
WO	Of	Wien Ost.
WT	Wol	Wolfurt
WS	Wb	Wien Sud.
WW	Ws	Wien West.
ZS	Z	Zell am See.

ÖBB LIVERY CODES

Since the founding of ÖBB there have only been a few livery schemes. The immediate post WWII period saw all electric and diesel locomotives painted dark green with railcars in blue and cream. A change took place in the late 1960s when the 1042s were being delivered and these locos, having started off in green, changed over to blood-orange with yellow lining whilst the railcar livery remained the same.

The 1990s saw the blood orange replaced by red (verkehrsrot) with a wide cream band at the base of the body side which continued around the cab. This was later changed to a white band. At the same time white replaced cream on the railcars. Classes 1014, 1822 had a variant on this livery in that the two prime colours were reversed over the cabs.

For the 21st century ÖBB now has the red as a standard livery on locomotives but with no lining whilst railcars are starting to appear in red, grey and white (the white being the sliding doors). Like many other countries departmental stock is in yellow but some Klima snowploughs having started off in green and changed to red are now appearing in orange!

ÖBB locos are assumed to be the new red (verkehrsrot) livery unless otherwise noted. Livery codes used are as follows:

A   Advertising livery.
C   DMU livery (white/blue/red).
G   Green.
I   InterCity livery (white/grey/red).
O   Blood orange.
M   Mariazellerbahn loco. livery (red/cream).
N   Non standard livery – see note.
R   New DMU/EMU livery (grey with red areas at ends and white doors).
RB   Red and beige.
S   S-bahn livery (cream/blue).
V   Valousek design (red, white and blue).
Y   Yellow.
YR   Yellow/red.

INTRODUCING......
TODAY'S RAILWAYS UK

From the January 2006 issue, entrain - the UK railway magazine from Platform 5 Publishing, will be revamped and restyled, including a change of name. The Platform 5 UK railway magazine will in future be known as Today's Railways UK, whilst Today's Railways will in future be known as TODAY'S RAILWAYS EUROPE.

Today's Railways UK will still contain the very latest news from Britain and Ireland and unrivalled coverage of rolling stock news, plus all our regular features, interesting articles and much, much more. But it will also feature a fresh new look and clearer presentational style, combined with objective reporting and considered opinion of the current UK railway scene.

If you haven't seen a copy of **entrain** recently, why not take a fresh look at Today's Railways UK?

Consequently, the European railway magazine from Platform 5 Publishing which until now has been called Today's Railways, will in future be known as Today's Railways Europe. There will be minor changes to the style and presentation of Today's Railways Europe, but the content will be largely unaltered. Today's Railways Europe will continue to be the only English language railway magazine exclusively devoted to events on all Europe's railways.

For the latest news that matters at home and abroad, only Today's Railways gives you the complete news service every month.

Today's Railways UK: on sale second Monday of every month.
Today's Railways Europe: on sale fourth Monday of every month.

Guarantee your copies every month with post-free subscriptions direct from Platform 5.

Subscription orderline: (+44) 0114 255 8000
An answerphone is attached for calls made outside normal UK office hours. Fax: (+44) 0114 255 2471

Special note: The decision to change the name of entrain to Today's Railways UK was taken after the covers of this book had been printed, hence the name entrain appears in the adjacent advertisement. Please remember to ask for Today's Railways UK instead of entrain. The date of publication remains the 2nd Monday of every month.